JUST ADD WRITER

JUST ADD *writer*

WRITING MEDIA TIE-IN FICTION

Tim Waggoner

GUIDE DOG BOOKS

RAW DOG SCREAMING PRESS

www.rawdogscreaming.com

Cover Design © 2024 by C.V. Hunt
www.cv-hunt.com

Interior Layout by D. Harlan Wilson
www.dharlanwilson.com

Guide Dog Books
Bowie, MD

DEDICATION

This one's for Michael A. Stackpole, who wrote in my copy of his *Star Wars* novel *X-Wing: Rogue Squadron* in 1996: "Good luck on getting gigs in the subsidiary book market."

ACKNOWLEDGEMENTS

Thanks to John Edward Lawson for suggesting I write this book, Jennifer Barnes for publishing it, and D. Harlan Wilson for editing it. Also thanks to all the writers who were kind enough to do mini-interviews for the book, and thanks to all the editors I've worked with over the years in my tie-in career. And, as always, thanks to super agent Cherry Weiner for her guidance, support, and friendship.

CONTENTS

Media Tie-In Bibliography **9**
Introduction **12**

CHAPTER ONE Overview of Media Tie-In Fiction **15**
CHPATER TWO My Pulse-Pounding Adventures in Tie-In Land (2004-2005) **28**
CHPATER THREE My Pulse-Pounding Adventures in Tie-In Land (2006-2010) **45**
CHAPTER FOUR My Pulse-Pounding Adventures in Tie-In Land (2013-2019) **60**
CHAPTER FIVE My Pulse-Pounding Adventures in Tie-In Land (2017-2019) **74**
CHAPTER SIX My Pulse-Pounding Adventures in Tie-In Land (2021-2024) **88**
CHAPTER SEVEN How to Get Tie-In Writing Experience **107**
CHAPTER EIGHT The Business of Tie-Ins **123**
CHAPTER NINE Writing Tie-Ins: Short Stories, Novels, and Novellas **134**
CHAPTER TEN Writing Tie-Ins: Novelizations **153**
Outro **162**
Resources **163**
Biography **166**

APPENDIX ONE Sample Story **167**
APPENDIX TWO Sample Pitches **181**
APPENDIX THREE Tie-In Proposal **184**
APPENDIX FOUR Tie-In Outline **187**
APPENDIX FIVE Sample Chapters **195**

MEDIA TIE-IN BIBLIOGRAPHY

I've listed the IP when it's not obvious in the title of the work.

NOVELS

Conan: Spawn of the Serpent God. Titan Books, 2025.

MaXXXine: The Official Novelization. A24 Books, 2025.

Pearl: The Official Novelization. A24 Books, 2025.

X: The Official Novelization. A24 Books, 2024.

Terrifier 3: The Official Novelization. Titan Books, 2025.

Terrifier 2: The Official Novelization. Titan Books, 2024.

Planet Havoc: A Zombicide Invader Novel. Aconyte Books, 2022.

Halloween Kills: The Official Novelization. Titan Books, 2021.

Alien: Prototype. Titan Books, 2019.

Supernatural: Children of Anubis. Titan Books, 2019.

Kingsman: The Golden Circle: The Official Novelization. Titan Books, 2017.

xXx: The Return of Xander Cage: The Official Novelization. Titan Books, 2017.

Resident Evil: The Final Chapter: The Official Novelization. Titan Books, 2017.

Supernatural: Mythmaker. Titan Books, 2016.

Supernatural: The Roads Not Taken. Insight Editions, 2013.

Supernatural: Carved in Flesh. Titan Books, 2013.

Lady Ruin. Wizards of the Coast, 2010.

Stargate SG-1: Valhalla. Fandemonium Books, 2009.

Blade of the Flame 3: Sea of Death. Wizards of the Coast, 2008.

Blade of the Flame 2: Forge of the Mindslayers. Wizards of the Coast, 2007.

Blade of the Flame 1: Thieves of Blood. Wizards of the Coast, 2006.

A Nightmare on Elm Street: Protégé. Black Flame, 2005.

A Shadow Over Heaven's Eye. White Wolf Publishing, 2005.
Dragonlance, the New Adventures: Return of the Sorceress. Wizards of the Coast, 2004.
Defender: Hyperswarm. I-Books, 2004.
Dragonlance, the New Adventures: Temple of the Dragonslayer. Wizards of the Coast, 2004.
Dark Ages: Gangrel. White Wolf Publishing, 2004.

NONFICTION

The Men of Letters Bestiary: Winchester Family Edition. Insight Editions, 2017.

COMIC BOOK SCRIPTS

"The Nest." *Kolchak the Nightstalker 50th Anniversary Graphic Novel*. Moonstone Books, 2022.

SHORT STORIES

"A Deeper Song." *Tales of the Reconvergence*. Hex Publishers, 2023.
"Raiders of the Poisoned Plains." *Wendigo Tales*. Pinnacle, 2020.
"Skin Man." *Anathemas*. Black Library, 2020.
"The Way to a Man's Heart." *C.H.U.D. Lives!* Crystal Lake Publishing, 2018.
"Foundling." *X-Files: The Truth Is Out There*. IDW, 2016.
"Her Corner of the Sky." *V-Wars: Night Terrors*. IDW, 2015.
"Across Silent Seas." *Doctor Who: Destination Prague*. Big Finish, 2007.
"The Blade of the Flame." *Tales of the Last War*. Wizards of the Coast, 2006.
"Collect and Save." *The Transformers Legends*. I-Books, 2005.
"Weapon of Flesh and Bone." In collaboration with R. Davis. *The Further Adventures of Xena*. Ace, 2001.
"Seeker." *Dark Tyrants*. White Wolf Publishing, 1997.

ORIGINAL WORK

The Desolation War. Aethon Books, 2024.
Lord of the Feast. Flame Tree Press, 2024.
The Book of Madness. Aethon Books, 2024.
The Atrocity Engine. Aethon Books, 2024.
A Hunter Called Night. Flame Tree Press, 2023.
We Will Rise. Flame Tree Press, 2022.
Your Turn to Suffer. Flame Tree Press, 2021.
The Forever House. Flame Tree Press, 2020.

They Kill. Flame Tree Press, 2019.

Blood Island. Severed Press, 2019.

The Mouth of the Dark. Flame Tree Press, 2018.

The Teeth of the Sea. Severed Press, 2017.

Eat the Night. DarkFuse, 2016.

Dream Stalkers. Angry Robot, 2016.

Dark Art. Past Curfew Press, 2014.

Night Terrors. Angry Robot, 2014.

The Way of All Flesh. Samhain Books, 2014.

Ghost Town. Pocket Books, 2012.

Ghost Trackers. Pocket Books, 2011.

Nekropolis: Dark War. Angry Robot, 2011.

Nekropolis: Dead Streets. Angry Robot, 2010.

Nekropolis. Angry Robot, 2010.

Last of the Lycans: Monarch of the Moon. Actionopolis, 2010.

Cross County. Wizards of the Coast, 2008.

Darkness Wakes. Leisure Books, 2006.

Godfire 2: Heart's Wound. Five Star/Thorndike Books, 2006.

Godfire 1: The Orchard of Dreams. Five Star/Thorndike Books, 2006.

Pandora Drive. Leisure Books, 2006.

Like Death. Leisure Books, 2005. Reprinted by Apex Publications, 2011.

Necropolis. Five Star/Thorndike Books, 2004.

The Harmony Society. Prime Books, 2003. Reprinted by Dark Regions Press, 2012.

Dying for It. Foggy Windows Books, 2001.

INTRODUCTION

When I was young, sometime in the late 1960s or early 1970s, I wrote my first book.

Sort of.

Back then, I was a monster kid. Movies, comics, magazines, toys—I loved everything horror, and my bible was *Famous Monsters of Filmland*. There were no streaming services back then, no cable TV, no videos that could be rented, no Internet to look up information. If a movie didn't come on the weekly local horror show—*Shock Theater* with Dr. Creep—I didn't get to see it. I was a huge fan of all the classic movie monsters: Dracula, Frankenstein, the Wolf-Man and the rest, but I especially loved kaiju. (We just thought of them as giant monsters back then.) King Kong and Godzilla were my favorites, and when I read an article in *FMOF* about a movie in which those two titans of terror met and fought (appropriately titled *King Kong vs Godzilla*), I wanted to see it more than anything. I kept waiting for it to show up on *Shock Theater*, but it never did, so I decided to make my own version.

I got a stenographer's pad, turned it sideways so it kind of looked like a book, and then I drew my version of the behemoths' battle with written text beneath the pictures. One of the images from the film that I'd seen showed King Kong and Godzilla fighting with a building between them, one designed in traditional Japanese style, with slightly curving eaves extending from a large roof. I'd seen Godzilla destroy such buildings in any number of films, so I recognized them as belonging to Japanese culture. I had no idea what this type of building was called, so when I drew this scene, I was stuck on how to describe it. I'd heard the word *geisha* somewhere, and I knew they were woman who wore white makeup and dressed in fancy old-fashioned Japanese clothes, but that was all. I decided to call the building Kong and Godzilla were about to demolish the Geisha House. I felt weird about the name (and if I'd know what geishas were, I'd have felt even more awkward about it!). I knew it couldn't be the real name, but I had no idea how to go about finding out what such a building was really called. So I stuck with Geisha House and felt like a bad writer for not doing my research. I don't remember much more about the book. I think at one point, firefighters showed up to battle a blaze Godzilla created, but that's all. When I was finished, I showed the book to my parents. They flipped through a couple pages, said "This is nice, dear," and handed it back to me. My first reader reviews were positive, but less than stellar. Good preparation for the writer's life.

So my first "book" was a media tie-in.

A few years later, when I hit sixth grade, I decided I wanted to be a comic book artist. I needed characters and stories to draw, though, so I created a team of superheroes based on my friends and myself (I figured if I put my friends in the comic, they'd read it—which turned out to be sound marketing strategy.) *The Six Million Dollar Man* was one of my favorite TV shows at the time, so I made my friends and myself into a group of cyborg superheroes called *The Bionic Team.* My friends loved the comic (which I drew on notebook paper), but they thought my stories were far better than my art. This bugged me at the time because I didn't care about the stories. They were just a vehicle for me to practice drawing. Turned out my friends knew what they were talking about. My art was nothing special, but my stories showed promise, and I began to invest more time and effort into writing them. The comic—which was also a media tie-in of sorts—lasted until my junior year of high school, when I shifted over to writing stories using only words full-time.

Fast forward four decades, and I've traditionally published over fifty novels and seven collections of short stories. And around half of those novels have been media tie-ins.

Remember those primitive times I grew up in? Tie-in fiction was a way to relive a movie you enjoyed or experience new adventures of characters from shows that were cancelled. I loved reading novelizations because they contained extra scenes that weren't in the film, and—best of all—they could delve into characters' internal worlds, letting readers know what their thoughts and feelings were during scenes. *Star Trek* novels let me continue traveling through the galaxy with Kirk and crew before *Trek* movies and new series began appearing. And Margaret Weis and Tracy Hickman's first *Dragonlance* trilogy introduced me to game-based tie-ins. I read tons of original fiction during my formative years as well, but tie-ins offered distinct pleasures of their own.

In a very real sense, tie-ins are a modern version of the oldest storytelling tradition of our species. Tales of the gods and great heroes and leaders were passed down from generation to generation, embellished, altered, becoming new stories about long-established "characters." Legends were told and retold. How many versions are there of King Arthur's story? Of Robin Hood's? In the modern day, we have multiple versions of James Bond, Superman, Batman, Spider-Man, Wonder Woman, Sherlock Holmes … Humans have been telling stories about shared characters for thousands of years. These stories fulfill a deep need in humans for community and connection. That's where fandoms come from, but people who don't consider themselves fans of any particular character or story setting are still familiar with Dorothy and her three friends, Snow White, Frankenstein … Shared characters like these are an integral part of worldwide culture.

Those of us who write tie-in fiction are part of a long and noble tradition, and if you'd like to join us, I'm glad you're here because I wrote this book for you. And if you're primarily interested in gaining a behind-the-scenes glimpse into the wild and wooly world of tie-in writing, you're welcome here, too.

A word of caution before we proceed. Writing tie-ins is a difficult field to break into, and it requires a specific skillset *in addition* to being an experienced pro-level fiction writer. And even when you've written a few tie-ins for publishers, gigs can still be hard to come by.

EXERCISES

At the end of each chapter are a couple exercises. Feel free to engage with them however you wish. You can do every single one of them, do only the ones that appeal to you, do them as you read the book or after you've finished, read and ponder them instead of writing anything down, or ignore them entirely. Do whatever works best for you.

VOICES FROM THE TRENCHES

Before I began drafting this book, I reached out to a number of my tie-in-writing colleagues and asked them to respond to the following questions:

- How did you get into writing tie-ins?
- What do you like about writing tie-ins? What are the rewards for you?
- What challenges have you faced in your career as a tie-in writer?
- Does writing tie-ins require a different skill set than other types of writing? If so what are these skills?
- Do you think it's possible to be pigeonholed as a tie-in writer, making it more difficult to publish your own work? If so, how do you deal with this?
- What advice do you have for writers who want to break into the media tie-in field?

I did this because I didn't want my voice to be the only one you heard in this book. No one writer knows everything about their field—I sure as hell don't—so I wanted to offer you as many different perspectives on tie-in writing as I could. I received many wonderful responses, and I've spread them throughout the book at the end of each chapter (after the exercises). As you might expect, there's some commonality in the responses, which I think reinforces the points these writers make, but there are a lot of differences, too. I hope you find these short interviews interesting and useful, and I also hope you'll hunt down and read the work of these writers so you can learn even more from them.

CHAPTER ONE
OVERVIEW OF MEDIA TIE-IN FICTION

What is media tie-in fiction? A media tie-in is an officially licensed work of prose fiction based on characters/settings/scenarios created and owned by someone else. And these IPs—intellectual properties—originally appeared in different forms of media: a movie, a TV show, a videogame, a board game, a comic, etc. A writer is hired specifically by the license holder—often via a publisher—to produce this work. The license holder is boss, and the writer is a hired hand. You create what the license holder wants and the final product must meet the license holder's approval. Your name will be on the book, but the license holder owns everything in it—every character, event, and setting, even the ones you've created whole cloth. While you have restrictions regarding what you can and can't do with the IP, there is room for individual creativity and style, just not as much as when you write your own original fiction.

Why would anyone want to write under these conditions?

Writing tie-in fiction is fun. Like any other writing, it's work, but it's *fun* work. I published my first tie-in story in 1997, and in the decades since, I've gotten to write fiction based on *Supernatural, The X-Files, Alien, Doctor Who, A Nightmare on Elm Street, Transformers, Halloween* and more. My imagination was shaped by pop culture as I grew up, and it's been wonderful to make a contribution, however small, to so many media properties I've loved.

It's challenging. We'll go over specific techniques for writing tie-in fiction in later chapters, but tie-ins require you to understand the media property—the milieu, the characters, their voices—and bring it to life in prose form while adding much more depth. You need to collaborate closely with the license holder and please them, while also writing a book you're proud of. It's a complex balancing act, and I find it stretches me in different ways than writing my original fiction does.

You may write in different genres, so there's variety. One time you write a kids' novel based on a space adventure property, the next you write a novelization of a fantasy film, after that you write a military adventure based on a videogame, and then you write a short story about an iconic horror villain for an anthology. Sure, some tie-in writers find a niche—such as writing *Star Trek* novels—and stick with it throughout their careers, but others enjoy the freedom that comes from not knowing what their next gig will be.

You develop different writing skills. I already mentioned several such skills when I discussed challenges above. In addition, you have to learn how to take something that's primarily experienced by the senses and communicate it in words. Food critics, sports writers, nature writers, travel writers all do the same thing. With media tie-in fiction, you're usually taking visual media of some sort (often with sound effects and special effects) and translating it into prose. You also may broaden your research skills because you'll need to find information on some specialized topics, like what an elephant smells like, how high satellites orbit the Earth, or how fast Sonic the Hedgehog can run.

You have a knack for it (not every writer does). Some writers can move between genres and styles easier than others. Same for those writers whose imaginations can slip inside characters and worlds they didn't create. Some writers can work within the collaborative dynamic of tie-in writing, some prefer not to, and some would rather die than not have total control over their fiction. If you do have the knack and the right temperament, tie-in writing might be for you.

You get paid. You're not going to get rich writing tie-ins. For that matter, you're not going to get rich writing *any* kind of fiction. Yeah, there are authors who are exceptions to this rule, but not many. If you want to make money writing, write nonfiction or get into ghostwriting. I write fiction because I love it, and it's the truest, deepest expression of who I am. The type of fiction I love to write best is horror and dark fantasy, the weirder, the better. Because of this, most of my novels have been published by medium to small presses, and the advances range from okay to laughably small (or nonexistent). I tend to get higher advances for tie-in novels than for my original fiction (but not always). I might get ten times the advance from a tie-in publisher than I would from a small-press one. I have a day job as a college English professor, so I don't have to live off my writing, but my bank account always welcomes money from tie-in advances. And there's been more than one time when that money has made a big difference during unforeseen disasters, such as suddenly needing to buy a new car or replace the roof on my house. If someone were able to write several tie-in novels a year and could count on the income being steady year in and year out (which is a mighty big *if*), they could conceivably support themselves entirely from their writing.

TYPES OF TIE-IN FICTION

Novelizations: A film script turned into a novel.

Novels, Novellas, Short Stories: New fiction using characters or a setting owned by a license holder.

Comics: New stories or a film adaptation featuring characters or a setting owned by a license holder.

Fictional Nonfiction: A nonfiction form such as a journal, memoir, autobiography, or guidebook that is written as if a character owned by a license holder composed it.

Material for Young Readers: Writing for young adult, middle-grade, and child audiences in any of the above categories.

How is tie-in fiction different than fan fiction? The key difference appears in the first sentence of this chapter: *officially licensed.*

Just like a scriptwriter is hired to write an episode of your favorite TV series or a sequel to a movie you love, tie-in writers are professionals hired to write fiction based on a media property that you love. We might be fans of the property too, or we might not. (If we aren't, we might become fans during the process of writing about a property.) Fan fiction is written by enthusiasts who want to interact with a media property they love in a creative way. I'm by no means knocking fan fiction. My version of *King Kong vs Godzilla* was fan fiction, and so were my *Bionic Team* comics (especially since I would sometimes have media characters like Spider-Man, Darth Vader, or Kermit the Frog show up in stories. Did I mention the comics were comedy as much as adventure?).

Fan fiction writers are amateurs, maybe only in the sense that they aren't being paid for their work, but also because they may be new at the craft of fiction writing and are still learning. Since they aren't writing at the direction of a license holder, they can do whatever they want in their stories with no restrictions. They can even have characters from one franchise interact with characters from another, something the individual license holders might never permit. People read, write, and share fan fiction for fun, and there's not a damn thing wrong with that. And some people use it as a training ground before going on to write original fiction of their own.

License holders, including creators of original work, are officially supposed to disapprove of fan fiction because if they don't, they're giving others tacit permission to use their IP, and they might end up losing the copyright to it. My guess is that most writers don't care if fan fiction based on their characters exists or they're actually flattered by it, but they have to *pretend* they don't approve of it in order to maintain copyright to their work. So don't use any of my original characters or settings in your fan fiction. I do not approve (wink, wink).

Later on in the book, I'll talk more about writing fan fiction as a way to prepare yourself to write tie-in fiction.

HOW TIE-IN FICTION *DOESN'T* WORK

You can't decide to write a piece of tie-in fiction on your own and then publish it. I once received an email from a gentleman who'd finished an *Alien* novel and wanted to know who at Titan Books he should contact about getting it published. I felt terrible for this guy, but I had to explain to him how the tie-in process works. Book editors obtain a license to publish a certain amount of tie-in novels about a specific IP, like *Alien*, they seek out established authors and contract them to write the books. The editor and the license holder shape the idea for the book along with the writer, and once they approve a final outline for a novel, then the writer can begin writing it. I advised the man to make enough changes to his book so that it no longer was a strict tie-in to *Alien* but a piece of fiction that was clearly inspired by *Alien* while still being original. Pro writers refer to this as *filing off the serial numbers*. I don't know what the guy did, but I hope he started writing original fiction.

You can't begin your writing career by writing tie-in fiction. There are exceptions. For example, if you work for a game company that wants to start producing tie-in fiction based on their properties, and they intend to publish it themselves, they might hire someone from within the company to write it. But this is rare. Editors and license holders want to hire established writers to produce tie-in fiction.

You won't land a tie-in writing gig just because you're a huge fan of a media property. Editors and license holders like it if you're a fan of an IP, but it isn't necessary. They want to know that you're a professional writer with a good track record of producing publishable fiction. They know such writers can learn about the IP quickly enough to get up to speed.

MYTHS ABOUT WRITING TIE-IN FICTION

Tie-in fiction is inferior hack work. Back in the 1950s and 1960s, it wasn't uncommon for some publishers to bring out quickly written tie-in novels that had simplistic plots written in equally simple prose. But those days were over a long time ago. Tie-in fiction writers today work as hard at their craft as any other writer. Since tie-in fiction is written to entertain, you're not going to see experimental narrative techniques or in-depth character studies more common to literary writers, but you will get a damn good book to read.

Tie-in fiction is easier to write than original fiction. It's no easier or harder to write than original fiction. It's just different, and it's not even all that different. All the same basic skills of writing good fiction apply—characterization, plot, setting, description, dialogue, use of language, pace … The collaborative nature of writing tie-in fiction might make it harder for some writers, though, along with adapting their voice and style to that of the IP property.

Tie-in writers only care about money. Hell, who doesn't care about money? Writers have to eat just like everyone else. But money isn't the sole motivation for writers. If all we wanted was to make money, we would've become doctors or lawyers. But tie-in fiction writers consider themselves professionals, so of course they wish to be paid for their labor. Beyond this, since the license holder will own all the rights to any work tie-in writers produce, writers can never make any additional profit off it. If they aren't paid for writing a book or story, they won't receive any money for their time, effort, and creativity.

Writing about public domain characters is tie-in fiction, too. Tie-in fiction is officially licensed by a license holder, remember? Public domain characters and settings are no longer owned by individual people or companies. They're owned by the world. That's why people can write books, produce comics, and make films based on Dracula and Frankenstein. Beyond the legal reason, there's an artistic reason such works aren't tie-ins. You have the freedom to do whatever you want with these characters. Want to make Baron Frankenstein into Baroness Frankenstein? Go for it. Want to make King Arthur an android sent from the future to be King of Britain? Write that story! Want to make Winnie-the-Pooh into a horror movie villain? Too late—someone's already beat you to it. There's no one to tell you what you can and can't do with these characters, and you can follow your creative impulses wherever they take you. Later, we'll talk about how you can use writing about public domain characters as preparation for writing *officially licensed* tie-in fiction.

You could make the argument that fiction genres like science fiction, fantasy, romance, horror, mystery, western, etc. are actually tie-ins, in the sense that they're based on successful stories that were once original and considered Literature with a capital L. These stories influenced publishers and writers to imitate them, and readers loved them and wanted more. Over time, the tropes in these genres became so codified that writers could consciously follow them. Writers have lots of freedom when employing these tropes, but they have restrictions, too. Murders must be solved by the end of mystery novels, romance novels need to have a happily ever after ending, etc. Writers of literary fiction tend to view writers of genre fiction as producing formulaic fiction (which is why I think it's hysterical when some genre writers look down on tie-in writers.)

OTHER TYPES OF TIE-IN FICTION

Fiction written under house names. A house name is when a publisher creates a book series where each volume may be written by different authors, but for marketing purposes, is credited to a single, shared pseudonym. Sometimes this name is an author who started the series, and the publisher buys the right to use their name as the author on future editions. For example, Don Pendleton, creator of the Men's Adventure hero *The Executioner,* wrote thirty-seven novels featuring his character. The rest of the books in the series—all 416 of them—bore his name but were written by other writers. When writing under a house name, the true author may or may not be credited in some small way. *The Executioner* books would include a statement inside the book, practically hidden among the publishing information, which went something like this: "Gold Eagle acknowledges REAL AUTHOR's contribution to this book." House names were much more common in the past, but they're still used for children's book series, with Erin Evans of *Warriors* fame being a notable example.

Are these books tie-ins? It depends on who you ask. A lot of publishing professionals regard tie-ins as works of fiction based on other media properties, such as movies, videogames, etc., but not based on other people's literary creations. On the other hand, as long as someone else owns the IP, some do consider books written under a house name to be tie-ins. They're basically the same in terms of both craft and business concerns, so I tend to think of them as tie-ins. And if they aren't exactly the same thing, they're closely related.

Ghostwriting. Ghostwriting is when an author is hired to write a book that will be published under someone else's name (often a famous someone), and that person gets all the credit for the writer's work. That person will also see all the profits from the book. Writing under a house name is a form of ghostwriting, except the publisher is the one who gets the lion's share of the money. Ghostwriting is far more prevalent in nonfiction than fiction, and often the "author" is kind enough to mention the real writer's "assistance" in the acknowledgements. (This is called a semi-visible ghost because the author's name does appear in the book, even if the full extent of their contribution isn't spelled out.) William Shatner did this with his *Tek War* series, always making sure to credit Ron Goulart as a co-author.

Some years back, fantasy author Dennis L. McKiernan—my friend and mentor—was offered a gig to write a tie-in based on a fantasy computer game (I don't recall which one.) Dennis told the publisher he wasn't interested, and they asked if they could use his name as the author and have someone else ghostwrite the book (paying Dennis a fee for using his name, of course). Dennis politely declined.

Gothic thriller writer V.C. Andrews wrote seven books before she died. Her family hired Andrew Neiderman to produce more books under her name, and they kept his identity a secret for many years before finally allowing him to tell the public. Neiderman has been writing as "V. C. Andrews" longer than the actual V.C. Andrews did, and he's produced almost 200 books under her name.

There are also famous writers who eventually tire of producing new books on the schedule that readers and publishers demand (or who burn out entirely), and sometimes they or their publisher hire ghostwriters to continue producing books under their name. I have no idea how prevalent this practice is, but I've been told that it happens a lot more than you'd think. So if you read the next novel by one of your favorite authors and it sounds like it wasn't written by them, maybe it wasn't.

Is ghostwriting a form of tie-in writing? It depends on the type you do. If a business person hires you to write a book for them so they can put their name on it and bolster their credentials as an "expert," then it's not tie-in writing. Neither is penning the autobiography for a famous movie star, pop singer, or athlete. But if you ghostwrite a novel based on an IP someone else owns, then it does count. And, of course, the demarcation can be fuzzy at times.

There's a moral question at the heart of ghostwriting. Is it fraud? Publishers sell a book as written by a specific person, and when readers purchase that book, they expect it to actually be written by the credited author. If it isn't, they're purchasing a product that's been falsely advertised. The V. C. Andrews estate included a note with each of the novels ghostwritten by Neiderman, saying the family selected a writer to write novels based on notes and outlines left behind after the real V.C. Andrews died. This was true for a few books, but Neiderman soon started writing Andrews books on his own, and the note never changed. So not exactly total truth in advertising, but a hell of a lot better than most ghostwritten books. Ghostwriting has been around for ages, and publishers don't consider it fraud, but I'm not so sure they're right. I'd rather know who wrote the book I'm buying.

Why would anyone ghostwrite? Some people love to write but they don't care whether they receive credit or not. Plus, ghostwriting can pay well, sometimes *really* well. But unless you get permission, as Neiderman eventually did, you can never tell anyone that you ghostwrote that wildly popular novel currently sitting atop the bestseller lists. (Your eternal silence is part of the deal.)

I've never ghostwritten a book, but I was a semi-visible ghost for two books written with Jason Hawes and Grant Wilson of SyFy's *Ghost Hunters* fame. It was a good experience, the guys were great, and I got my name on the cover (even if my name was smaller than Jason and Grant's). I don't count these books as tie-ins, though, since they contained original characters and storylines.

CURRENT ATTITUDES TOWARD TIE-IN FICTION

In the past, many people wrote tie-in fiction under a pseudonym, as if they didn't want people to know they'd done something so shameful. But attitudes toward tie-in fiction have changed dramatically over the years, especially among younger readers and writers. Writing tie-in fiction is seen as cool and something to aspire to. Maybe these younger folks grew up even more saturated in popular culture than my generation did. And maybe the mainstream success of properties like *Doctor Who* and Marvel superheroes have helped to change attitudes toward tie-fiction. It's not uncommon these days for people to ask me about my tie-in novels more than my original ones, and they often seem impressed by the fact that I write tie-in fiction. Do I resent people not caring as much about my original fiction? No. I'm just glad people care about my work at all.

Now that you have a solid foundation in the basics of writing tie-in fiction, starting in the next chapter, I'm going to tell you what it's *really* like to be a tie-in author. Buckle up! But first …

EXERCISES

1. Are there any tie-in novels that you've read that you especially enjoyed, even loved? Make a list of them. Then go through the list and write down the specific qualities each book had that made it so enjoyable for you. When you're finished, look over the list and see if you can find any common elements that stick out. Did the characters affect you the most? The setting? The action? Getting a sense of what narrative elements you respond to most strongly can give you some insight into how you might write your own tie-in fiction. More character-oriented, more setting-oriented, etc.

2. Are there any specific IPs that you'd love to write for? Make a list, and for each item write a reason why this IP is so attractive to you as a writer. Doing this can give you insight into what kind of IPs you might like to write for someday—specific ones, of course, such as *Star Wars* or *The Fast and the Furious*, but also different genres, like action-adventure, science fiction, or romance.

3. Do you think you'd prefer to write tie-in fiction for adults or for young people? Why does writing for one audience interest you more than writing for the other? Do you think you might like to focus your efforts more toward one audience than another? If so, why?

VOICES FROM THE TRENCHES

MATT FORBECK

How did you get into writing tie-ins? I started out working on tabletop games for Games Workshop and TSR, among many other companies, but those two had divisions that published novels too. Despite the fact I'd written millions of words for them, their editors balked at signing me on to write novels, as I didn't have a book to show them. I was complaining about this situation at a convention when Ed Pugh of Reaper Miniatures overheard me and leaned over to say, "I'll hire you to write a novel, Matt!" I wrote *The Big Dance*, a short novel based on Reaper's game C.A.V., which pitted giant mechs battling against each other. Once that came out, I showed copies to Games Workshop and TSR, and the editors there signed me on to write books for them straight away.

What do you like about writing tie-ins? What are the rewards for you? It's fantastic fun to work in a world that you already love. It's like moving into a fantastic house that you've leased for a few months. You get to enjoy all the amazing bits you've seen from the street, poke around in all the parts you wanted to know more about, and at the end you pack up your laptop and go home to your own place.

What challenges have you faced in your career as a tie-in writer? Mostly it's been great. The biggest challenges, though, have been writing books based on things (usually games) that haven't been finished and released yet. Since they're still in flux, it's hard to pin anything down, and arbitrary changes can surface at any moment.

Does writing tie-ins require a different skill set than other types of writing? If so what are these skills? It's pretty much the same thing as writing for yourself, with the exception being that you don't own the work, since it's based on someone else's stuff. That means you don't have the final say about what happens in it. That's not usually a problem, but if you have a hard time letting go of that control, you might reconsider taking on a tie-in job.

Do you think it's possible to be pigeonholed as a tie-in writer, making it more difficult to publish your own work? If so, how do you deal with this? I haven't found that to be the case, although I'm sure some people have had that happen. It feels like it's easier to get siloed into a particular genre rather than as a tie-in writer.

Sometimes that works in your favor. When Lucasfilm was looking for someone to write the junior novel for *Rogue One*, they went looking for an author who'd written chapter books and military SF. There aren't too many folks who fit that bill, so they contacted me.

What advice do you have for writers who want to break into the media tie-in field? Write your own stuff first. Create something in the same vein of what you want to write tie-ins for, to show that you can handle the genre and fan base, but make it your own. That way you'll have something to show prospective editors, even if it's unpublished at the moment. And you might even get that original work published too.

MATT FORBECK is an award-winning, *New York Times*-bestselling author and game designer of over thirty-five novels and countless games. His projects have won a Peabody Award, a Scribe Award, and several ENnies and Origins Awards. He lives in Beloit, Wisconsin, with his wife and a rotating cast of college-age kids. For more about him and his work, visit forbeck.com.

RAYMOND BENSON

How did you get into writing tie-ins? I suppose my first experience in tie-in writing was when I was working as a designer/writer for computer games in the 1980s. I had already written and published a non-fiction book, *The James Bond Bedside Companion*, and this opened doors for me that didn't exist before. My literary agent at the time had a software developer client that had a license for James Bond titles. They were looking for a writer and my agent thought of me. Just as computer games and PCs were coming into homes, I suddenly found myself on the ground floor of this industry. I did two Bond titles and one Stephen King adaptation. This work continued into the 1990s. All during this time period, John Gardner was the author of continuation James Bond novels for the Ian Fleming Estate (the publishing arm of which was then called Glidrose Publications). I had become acquainted with the folks in charge of Glidrose during the writing of the *Bedside Companion* and we had stayed in touch. When Gardner announced his retirement from the gig in 1995, the chairman of Glidrose called me out of the blue and asked if I'd be interested in "giving it a shot." My first published novel, then, was not only a tie-in, but a James Bond novel! It was truly a fortunate and unorthodox entry into fiction publishing.

What do you like about writing tie-ins? What are the rewards for you? I certainly enjoyed writing Bond novels, which I did for seven years. Of nine books, six were original adventures and three were novelizations of film screenplays. After Bond, I was luckily then on editors' short lists for other types of tie-ins, which I have continued to do sporadically in-between my original works. The financial rewards of doing high-profile tie-ins (Bond, Tom Clancy spin-offs, popular videogame adaptations) are certainly a factor in doing them. I suppose I can say that I enjoy writing my own original books more, but if a tie-in involves penning an original story rather than an adaptation, that is more fun. Then there's the other type of tie-in that is called "ghostwriting." Sometimes that is a full-blown tie-in fiction work and other times it's nonfiction. These jobs can be very lucrative but one often receives no public credit!

What challenges have you faced in your career as a tie-in writer? There have been a few instances in which the time frame involved with the writing of a tie-in was incredibly tight. Sometimes just a few weeks! I'm a fast writer, but when one has to familiarize oneself with a franchise or intellectual property, come up with a storyline, get it approved, and then write the thing, the looming deadline can be nerve-wracking. And while most of my experiences with tie-ins have been good, there was the occasional one or two in which the licensor was difficult to work with.

Does writing tie-ins require a different skill set than other types of writing? If so, what are these skills? I was a theatre major in college and spent many years directing stage works before I turned to writing. There's an old adage that if you major in theatre, you can do anything. Ha! Well, it does teach you how to work collaboratively, and that is probably the main skill needed in writing tie-ins. The writer must be malleable in terms of the IP requirements and be able to work well with the licensor bosses. As mentioned above, time is also a factor. These things often need to be written quickly. The writer who can not only produce a manuscript fast, but also present it clean, error-free, and with little to revise, is ideal to an IP and publisher of tie-ins. Being able to read and understand scripts with the intention of expanding them into prose is also an asset. Again, the theatre training came in handy for me!

Do you think it's possible to be pigeon-holed as a tie-in writer, making it more difficult to publish your own work? If so, how do you deal with this? Yes. After my Bond years, I felt I was considered by publishers as the "Bond guy" and that was all I could do. Luckily, the kinds of tie-in work I was offered were somewhat similar in genre and style. However, my own original works are very different, and there was always some resistance from agents and publishers in that regard. I simply soldiered through, however, and eventually found the right publisher for the novel I was submitting. I have no real complaints.

What advice do you have for writers who want to break into the media tie-in field? It seems to me that the prime trick is to be on an editor's radar that you're capable of doing tie-ins. No one can simply apply for a tie-in job. One is generally asked by the publisher to do it, or, in some cases, by the IP holder. It often depends on the arrangement the licensor has with the publisher. You must become known to editors by publishing your own books or by networking at writers conferences and such. If you meet an editor that you know works on tie-ins, let him or her know that you're interested! I hate to say that luck has a lot to do with it, but it's true.

RAYMOND BENSON is the author of over forty published books. He is most well-known as the third—and first American—writer of continuation James Bond novels for the Ian Fleming Estate (1997-2002). His best-selling and acclaimed five-book serial, *The Black Stiletto*, is in development as a feature film or television series. Recent fiction includes the 2022 IPPY Gold Medal Winner for Mystery, *The Mad, Mad Murders of Marigold Way*, as well as *Blues in the Dark*, *In the Hush of the Night*, and *The Secrets on Chicory Lane*. Benson is also a sought-after tie-in and ghostwriter, a musician/composer, a film historian, and a lecturer. He is based in the Chicago area. Website: raymondbenson.com.

WILL MURRAY

How did you get into writing tie-ins? I discovered an outline to an unused Doc Savage novel written by series originator Lester Dent, and with the permission of his widow, I pitched it to Bantam Books, and wrote it on spec. Eleven years later, they published it and asked for more.

By that time, I had interviewed the creators of the Destroyer paperback series, Warren Murphy and Richard Sapir, and they liked the interview so much they asked me to collaborate with them on a non-fiction book on the series, *The Assassin's Handbook*. This led me to writing my first Destroyer novel, and subsequently forty more in the series. So when opportunities like writing a *Mars Attacks* or *Nick Fury, Agent of S.H.I.E.L.D.* novel came along, I had a solid reputation.

What do you like about writing tie-ins? What are the rewards for you? I love not only playing with characters that I grew up reading, such as Doc Savage, Tarzan and others, but stepping into the shoes of the original writers, and attempting to emulate their styles, specific vocabularies, and creative sensibilities. This way I get to be not just Will Murray, novelist, but multiple authorial personalities as well. Some of my novels are crossovers. *King Kong vs. Tarzan* and *Tarzan, Conqueror of Mars*. I like to say I write the books I wish someone else had written when I first discovered these characters. Consequently, I've become some of my favorite authors by proxy.

What challenges have you faced in your career as a tie-in writer? Very few. Probably because I immerse myself in the assignment. You have to be willing to make changes you might or might not agree with. You can make your case for your point of view, but ultimately you must please the licensor.

Does writing tie-ins require a different skill set than other types of writing? If so what are these skills? Flexibility is key. A tie-in book requires not only a knowledge of the characters and the world in which the series is set, but an ability to adapt your own style and creative point of view towards an honest entry in a pre-existing series. Not every writer can do this. When taking on a pre-existing property, many writers try to bend the characters in a direction more comfortable for them as authors. This I think is wrong. You have to adapt your mindset and skills to the job, not twist the characters to suit your own needs—or limitations.

Do you think it's possible to be pigeonholed as a tie-in writer, making it more difficult to publish your own work? If so, how do you deal with this? While it certainly is, a versatile writer can break out of that imprisoning frame. These days it's probably important to be versatile just for its own sake. If you write fiction, you should be able to write nonfiction, and vice versa. Using pseudonyms of course can help you diversify your professional persona and overcome any attempts to typecast you.

What advice do you have for writers who want to break into the media tie-in field? No one is going to hire an unpublished writer to contribute to an established property, especially when numerous published writers are vying for the same assignment. You have to break in somewhere and I think it doesn't greatly matter where you break in. Sell your first piece of writing. Give it away if you have to. But get published. Then get published again and again. Build up a body of work. Many writers started by contributing to fanzines which paid them nothing. But they developed skills and reputations that carried them into the professional arena. Starting small doesn't matter. You are climbing the ladder and your first step is the most important one.

WILL MURRAY is the author of nearly 75 novels, including some 20 posthumous Doc Savage collaborations with Lester Dent, and 40 books in the long-running Destroyer series. Other Murray novels star the Executioner, Pat Savage and the *Mars Attacks* characters. His year-2000 book, *Nick Fury, Agent of S.H.I.E.L.D.: Empyre*, foreshadowed the 9/11 terrorist attacks.

Murray has penned several milestone crossover novels. He pitted Doc Savage against King Kong in *Skull Island*, and followed up with *King Kong vs. Tarzan*. His 2015 Doc Savage novel, *The Sinister Shadow*, revived the famous radio and pulp mystery man. He reunited them for *Empire of Doom*. His first Spider novel, *The Doom Legion*, revived that famous crime buster, as well as James Christopher (a.k.a. Operator 5) and the renowned G-8. *Fury in Steel* finds the Spider being hunted by the FBI's Suicide Squad. The Spider clashed with the Skull Killer and his Nemesis, the Scorpion, in *Scourge of the Scorpion*. *Tarzan, Conqueror of Mars* is another historic crossover, this time with John Carter of Mars. *Tarzan: Back to Mars* is the sequel.

For anthologies, Murray has written such iconic characters as Superman, Batman, Wonder Woman, Spider-Man, Ant-Man, The Hulk, The Avenger, The Green Hornet, the Grey Seal, Red Finger, John Silence, Honey West, Sherlock Holmes, Cthulhu, Dr. Herbert West, The Secret 6, Zorro, and Lee Falk's immortal Ghost Who Walks, the Phantom. A regular contributor to Belanger Books and MX Publishing Sherlock Holmes anthologies, he has penned more than 30 new tales. Murray's Holmes stories have been collected in *The Wild Adventures of Sherlock Holmes*. *The Wild Adventures of Cthulhu* reprints Murray's Cthulhu Mythos stories. For Marvel Comics, he created the Unbeatable Squirrel Girl with legendary *Spider-Man* artist Steve Ditko. His website is adventuresinbronze.com.

CHAPTER TWO
MY PULSE-POUNDING ADVENTURES IN TIE-IN LAND
2004-2005

I started writing fiction seriously, with the intent of making it my life's work, when I was eighteen (over forty years ago). I tried different genres—fantasy, science fiction, and horror, mostly, but I also tried suspense, thrillers, and mysteries, and I flirted with westerns and romance, too. I suppose it's no surprise so much of my original work is a mix of genres. I was determined to become a professional writer, and I decided one of the best ways to increase my odds of success was to try a lot of different things. In my late twenties, I realized there was a strong market for tie-in novels (alas, the market isn't quite so strong today), so I thought I'd explore that avenue, along with everything else I was trying.

Dennis McKiernan was friends with author Michael A. Stackpole, and he introduced us. Mike wrote both original and tie-in fiction, and he was kind enough to give me advice and even take me around at an Origins convention one year and introduce me to owners of game companies that might be looking to produce novels. Nothing came of that, though, but I still learned a ton about the business from Mike—especially how to network with publishers—and I'm forever grateful for him taking the time to counsel a young writer who'd only published a handful of short stories.

Rather than give you a lot of generic or second-hand information about what the tie-in writing life is like, I've decided to discuss my own experiences as a tie-in writer and share whatever lessons I've learned along the way. A quick note before we start: If you notice sometimes large gaps of time between the tie-in projects I talk about, it's because that's when I was writing and publishing original novels.

Dark Ages: Gangrel
White Wolf Publishing (2004)

In 2004, the two most successful game companies were Wizards of the Coast and White Wolf, and both published tie-in fiction based on their IPs. After years of trying to get original fantasy novels published (with no success), I'd started leaning more toward horror. Horror was my first love, and horror folk felt more like my tribe than fantasy or science fiction writers. Don't get me wrong—I fit with them, too, but they're more like beloved cousins, while horror people are my brothers and sisters.

In the 1990s, I had an account on GEnie, one of the precursors to modern-day social media, and there I had the opportunity to learn from and network with many professional writers of SF/F/H. When Robert Weinberg contracted to write a trilogy for White Wolf set in their *Vampire: The Masquerade* game milieu, he started posting detailed updates on writing the books on GEnie, and he continued to do so for all three volumes—and he was happy to answer any questions people might have. Getting insight into the process of writing tie-in novels as they were being written by a professional author was an invaluable learning experience. It was then that I became determined to write a tie-in novel for White Wolf one day. Later, other horror authors wrote tie-ins for White Wolf—Rick Hautala, James Moore, Nancy Collins, Richard Lee Byers, David Niall Wilson—and I read their books to learn even more. And, of course, I religiously checked White Wolf's website to see if and when they ever had any open calls. Eventually my persistence was rewarded. White Wolf was going to publish an anthology based on their *Vampire: The Dark Ages* game setting, and they were seeking submissions. I wrote a story, they published it, and it got my foot in the door.

I began attending Gencon, the huge annual gaming industry convention, and I was able to speak to fiction editors at both White Wolf and Wizards of the Coast. I asked them what their future publishing plans were, what kind of stuff they were looking for, etc. (These are always good questions to ask editors, whether they publish tie-in or original fiction.) I can't remember if I heard about White Wolf's plan to publish a thirteen-book series in their *Dark Ages* setting at Gencon, or if I read about it on their website, or what, but I got in touch with the editor of the *Dark Ages* anthology and put myself forward as a candidate for one of the slots. I'd only published two small-press novels by this point, but I'd published over fifty short stories (many of them for theme anthologies edited by Martin L. Greenberg), and that was enough to get me a contract to write book number ten in the series. I was, as you might imagine, pretty damn thrilled.

Each book in the series focused on one pre-existing character from each of the different vampire clans, and number ten dealt with the Gangrel—the most bestial of the clans—and one of their most powerful members, the Mongol warrior Qarakh. There were certain canonical events in game lore that I was supposed to cover in my book, and it also had to clearly connect to the volume before it and the one after it. Plus, it had a historical setting. *And* I wasn't allowed to kill off Qarakh since his character still existed in the present day under a different name. These were a lot of special conditions to deal with for my first tie-in novel! It came with a premade title—*Dark Ages Clan Novel 10: Gangrel*—so I didn't have to worry about coming up with one of my own.

I was familiar with the game lore from reading White Wolf's fiction, but I'd never played the game. (I generally don't like games of any kind and rarely play them, although I did play D&D for a while in my twenties and enjoyed it.) White Wolf sent me various source books, and I read everything I could find on the Gangrel and Qarakh, as well as the overall political situation among the vampire clans during that time. I also hit the Internet and researched Mongol culture in the Middle Ages. Up to this point, I'd mostly set my stories in the present day or in an imaginary fantasy land, so I was intimidated by needing to use an actual historical setting. How could I ever know enough information about the game *and* the time period to start outlining and drafting the book?

I came up with several solutions that still serve me in good stead to this day, whether I'm writing tie-in or original fiction.

- **I worked to capture the feel of the game setting.** If you're writing in a shared universe, one that most readers who come to the book are familiar with, it needs to feel *right* to them. Writers and literature teachers talk about verisimilitude, the feeling that fiction seems real to the reader. Tie-in fiction needs to seem like a real story that would take place in the setting you're given. For example, Middle Earth, Narnia, Westeros, Oz, and Conan's Hyborian Age are all fantasy realms, yet the stories that take place in each setting are very different in tone and content. I think this quality—I'll call it IP Verisimilitude for lack of a better term—is perhaps the most important quality to strive for when writing tie-in fiction.
- **I focused on the characters.** Stories are ultimately about people, even if those people happen to be vampires. The more interesting you can make your characters, the more you can get readers to care about them, the more invested readers become in what happens to them. *Vampire: The Dark Ages* is a roleplaying game, and the setting is a place for players to play. It's the *role* that's most important in roleplaying, and that means character. Focusing on character is far more important than cramming every game (or in this case historical) detail into your story. In many ways, the setting is like a stage upon which the characters perform.
- **I focused on action as well.** The Gangrel are animalistic and combative, and Qarakh was a warrior, so of course action was going to be a big part of the story. Action is dramatic and captures readers' attention. They want to know what their favorite character will do next and how they'll triumph, assuming they even manage to survive. When you focus on the *characters* involved in the action, the specifics of the IP setting don't matter as much.
- **The book had a limited, specific setting.** I can't remember if the setting was already indicated in the brief story description given to me by the editor or if I chose it, but much of the novel takes place in a forest. Gangrel are wild, remember? Forests in the Middle Ages aren't that different than forests now, and I didn't have to worry about knowing details of cities that existed at the time. Plus, it was a setting I could *control*. I could do anything I wanted to with the setting, even destroy the whole damn forest if I wanted. If the story had been set in Paris, I wouldn't have had the same freedom. This is a technique that I use a lot when I write tie-in fiction. I try to create a space all my own within the overall IP setting that gives me as much freedom as possible to tell my story.

I had other people helping me get details right, too. I had an editor well versed in the game setting, and I corresponded with the writers whose books came before and after mine—Janet Trautvetter (*Dark Ages: Toreador*) and Sarah Roark (*Dark Ages: Tremere*)—to make sure our three books connected properly.

Dark Ages: Gangrel was one of the most complex tie-in projects I've been involved in, and while it was a *lot* for a beginning tie-in writer to handle, it was excellent experience. The entire *Dark Ages* series was reprinted a few years ago, and it's still available if you'd like to check it out.

Dragonlance, the New Adventures: Temple of the Dragonslayer
Dragonlance, the New Adventures: Return of the Sorceress
Wizards of the Coast (2004)

Around this time, I'd been reading a how-to book called *The Renegade Writer* by Linda Formichelli and Diana Burrell. The authors were nonfiction writers, and the premise of the book was that beginning writers are told "the right way" to approach editors and land gigs, but once you break in, you learn there are a different set of rules for professional writers. I'd started regularly attending the World Fantasy Convention by this time, and I'd learned that this was true in fiction publishing. The authors advised readers to ignore the beginners' rules and go straight to pro tactics. I decided to give it a try and see what happened. I'm not the most assertive person, but I found a phone number for Wizards of the Coast online and gave them a call. I'd sent various writing samples to them over the years (as their website suggested writers do if you wanted to write for them), but I'd never heard back. I told this to whoever answered the phone (I can't remember who it was). She apologized and forwarded me to editor Philip Athans, who also apologized. I was shocked. I couldn't believe that *The Renegade Writer*'s advice had worked. We started talking about what projects I might write for them, and Phil mentioned that WotC had been thinking of doing a YA *Dragonlance* series, but they hadn't gotten around to it yet. Would I be interested in that? Of course, I said yes! After all, the original three Weis and Hickman *Dragonlance* books were the first D&D tie-ins I read. I reread the trilogy, and I picked some *Dragonlance* modules at Half-Price Books for research. I then developed a group of characters with backstories, goals, etc. for the series. I wrote an outline for the first novel and sent it to Phil. I don't recall having to revise it much, and when the final outline was approved, I started writing the book, titled *Temple of the Dragonslayer*.

I had a literary agent at the time, but one of the things professional writers don't talk about much is how often they end up finding their own deals and their agent then negotiates the contract. I guess the expectation is that agents find the deals and negotiate contracts, and of course that happens. But it's not the only thing that happens.

The book was supposed to be 62,000 words, or something like that, but when I'd finished the first draft, Phil told me they'd decided it should be 72,000 words. I looked for places in the story where I could expand without having to gut the manuscript and start over, and this is when I learned another valuable lesson, one that I pass onto students in my novel writing classes. At one point in the story, my heroes reached the valley where the titular temple is located. In the original draft, relieved and exhausted, they head down into the valley. In the revised version, one of the characters is kidnapped by goblins before they can enter the valley and they set out to rescue her. I knew what I was adding wasn't going to significantly impact the overall plot of the story, but I didn't want the new sequence to be meaningless filler, either. I'd played enough D&D to know that goblins seem to pop up randomly during adventures, so I decided to explain why that happened. I also wanted to gently critique this aspect of the game. I often do this kind of thing with both my tie-in and original fiction, playing with and critiquing genre tropes. I also tried to show different sides of my characters during this sequence. My heroes discovered the goblins had an underground city which lay at the center of a network of tunnels with openings all over the land. My heroes fought the goblins, rescued their friend, then returned to the valley. *Then* they went down to the temple. The new sequence—which miraculously was around 10K words—slipped into the story easily, with hardly any revision to the existing draft necessary, and viola! Book finished.

Because of how fast WotC wanted to release volumes in the series, one person couldn't write all the books. (I don't think they realized how fast I can write. I bet I could've done it!) Book 2 was written by Stephen D. Sullivan, and Book 3 was written by Dan Willis. I wrote Book 4, *Return of the Sorceress*. Both of my volumes were published in 2004. I skimmed Stephen and Dan's books to get up to speed on what had happened to my characters since Book 1. I couldn't bring myself to read them in detail because I knew those writers had done things with my characters that I wouldn't. That's as it should be, but I was too close to my characters at the time. Since I knew other writers would contribute future volumes, I included a flash-forward sequence in my story where the characters see a brief scene of their fighting a battle in the future. I threw in different weird details, such as their seeming to be allied with one of their current foes, and I gave one of the characters a magic object to wield (if I remember right). I had no idea what any of these things meant, but I thought other writers might have fun setting up this scene (and explaining what the hell was going on) in their own books later on.

Writing these two books taught me a couple things:

- **It helps to think of novels as made up of modular pieces which can be moved around as needed, or which can be spread apart so that you can drop in a new module.** This isn't always possible, of course. Stories have a beginning, middle, and end, along with a clear chain of causes and effects throughout. But the structure of a novel can be a lot more fluid and malleable than writers might think.
- **When you write tie-ins, your characters aren't really yours.** I had understood this intellectually, but these two books were where I learned it emotionally. I loved my characters, but I knew I had to give them up and let other authors use them too. (And it wasn't as if I had a choice.) I wrote no further volumes in the series, and I've never read any of the ones written after *Return of the Sorceress*. I haven't read any plot summaries posted on the Internet either. I don't want to know what other writers did with my children.

- **But you should still create the best characters you can.** Some writers suggest you should save your best characters and ideas for your original fiction, and I can't really argue with that. But if I take on a job to write a tie-in, I treat it the same as I would my original work. I was on a convention panel with Mike Stackpole once, and speaking of tie-ins, he said, "If my name goes on a novel, it's *my* novel." He busted his ass to make sure all the books he wrote were equally good, and I took that to heart and have strived to do the same throughout my career.

- **I learned I could write YA novels.** I've only written a handful since then, but it's good to know I can, and that I enjoy it, too!

- **I learned that my writing—including tie-in writing—can have a profound impact on readers.** One year, I attended the Ohioana Book Festival as a participating author. At one point, a young woman came to my table and asked if I was the Tim Waggoner who had written *Temple of the Dragonslayer*. I said I was, and she told me she'd read and loved the book when she was a kid, and it was the book that had made her want to be a writer. If I hadn't already believed it was important to write my tie-ins with the same craft and care as my individual work, this experience would've convinced me. Plus, is there any better compliment a writer can ever receive on their work?

- **Royalties are awesome!** I don't recall what the advances for these two books were, but they weren't huge. Most tie-in writing is work-for-hire, meaning that you're paid a flat fee and that's the end of it. But WotC's contracts included royalties, and I've regularly received checks for both books over the last twenty years. The checks are never for large amounts—maybe $20 or so—but they're always welcome, and because of them, these books might well qualify as the most successful I've ever written, at least in terms of money.

- **A final word of caution.** As I mentioned in the previous chapter, when it comes to approaching tie-in editors, you need to be a fairly established author with a fair amount of publishing credits. And despite how things worked out for me with WotC, I do *not* advocate that writers cold call editors and try to snag a tie-in gig over the phone. It was a bold move in 2004, and just as likely to backfire on someone (or even more likely to). Given the rise of social media in the last twenty years, people have become a lot more wary of being contacted out of the blue, and I highly doubt you'd be able to get through to an editor the way I did in 2004. And if by some miracle, you did get them on the phone, I don't think they would be very receptive. These days, people try to contact editors and agents via email or social media, but even then, you're most likely not to get a response. Things have gone back to the way they used to be, with editors and agents expecting you to follow whatever guidelines they have posted on their websites. But if you have a face-to-face conversation with a tie-in editor at a convention, and you sense it's going well, it doesn't hurt to see if they might have any tie-in projects you might be right for.

Defender: Hyperswarm
I-Books (2004)

Now that I've told you not to cold call editors, I did it again with this book, and again it worked. I can't remember the name of the editor I spoke to—it was so long ago—but they had two unassigned tie-projects. One was for a fantasy videogame, and the other was for the Defender videogame. I'd played the original arcade version of Defender in the '80s, so I picked that one. Plus, I'd written fantasy before, but I'd never written science fiction, so I thought this would be a great learning opportunity. I made a huge mistake during the conversation, though. The editor said their advances weren't very high, and I said, "That's okay." Where I grew up, that phrase is a way of saying *I understand*. The editor took it to mean that I would be happy to take whatever advance they offered. When my agent contacted them to negotiate the deal, the editor said, "It's too late! He already accepted!" Sure enough, the advance was small, but my agent said he could've gotten them to double it. I'd known better than to discuss money with an editor (if you have an agent), and I vowed to be extra careful in the future.

By this point, I'd learned that tie-in publishers normally didn't give you any materials to help you write your book, so I knew I was on my own in terms of research. (WotC was an exception. They sent me the annotated omnibus of Weis and Hickman's original *Dragonlance* trilogy when I was writing *Temple of the Dragonslayer*.) I mentioned earlier that I don't like playing games, so I found a cheat guide to Defender (I either bought it from Amazon or found it in a used bookstore) and learned the basic storyline: the solar system has been settled by humanity, who left a polluted, unlivable Earth behind. An alien race called the Manti attack the system, and space pilot Mei Kyoto destroys them by driving the moon into the Earth. (The swarm was on Earth at the time, in case you're wondering.) I decided I'd make my book a sequel to the game, beginning it on the one-year anniversary of Mei's victory, when of course a new Manti swarm attacks. I wanted to recreate the gameplay in my book as much as possible, so I bought the game. I wasn't about to play the damn thing, though, so I took it home, hooked it up to the VCR, and handed the game system control to my oldest daughter Devon (my daughters *loved* playing videogames) and told her to play as long as she could. I taped several sessions of Devon playing the game, and later I played them back, fast-forwarding to the interstitial scenes where characters talked to each other, argued, gave exposition, etc. I wanted to know what they looked like, how they spoke, what their personalities were like, etc. I also wanted to watch how the ships and Manti moved and what their attacks looked and sounded like. I took notes, and when I was ready, I started writing.

A bit of trivia: I wasn't sure what cover image the publisher would use for the book, but my guess was the same artwork that adorned the game would be on the cover. The art shows a fighter ship flying across the surface of a planet, with someone garbed in a spacesuit hanging onto one of the wings for dear life. No one told me that I had had to incorporate the cover scene into my story, but when I was a kid, I always *hated* it when the image on the cover never showed up in the story. Because of this, I wrote the cover scene into the book. (And yes, that image did end up on the cover.)

Trivia Part 2: Since no details were given in the game about the colonies in the solar system, I made up all those details. My favorite thing I created was the Phillip McGraw Wellness Center, located on Jupiter. Philip McGraw is Dr. Phil's real name, and I imagined that in the future, he was revered as a great healer. When you're a writer, sometimes you put certain details into a story for your own amusement.

Trivia 3: I realized early on that I needed to know what would happen to the Earth if the moon really collided with it. I checked with science fiction author—and NASA scientist—Geoffrey A. Landis. Geoff said Earth was too big to be destroyed by the moon striking it, so no Death Star-style explosion. Instead, the planet's surface would become a molten mass and all life would be extinguished. (Isn't that comforting to know?)

Exalted: A Shadow Over Heaven's Eye
White Wolf Publishing (2005)

White Wolf created a new role-playing setting, one unconnected from the horror games they'd become known for. Exalted was a martial arts/fantasy game inspired by anime and classic fantasy novels, and there were five main characters who appeared in the rulebook, each of which had magical abilities and super martial arts powers. White Wolf decided to bring out a novel featuring each character, and I was contracted to write one about a character named Swan. I don't remember if I asked the editor if I could write it or the editor asked me. However it happened, I got the gig. The title *A Shadow Over Heaven's Eye* was inspired by a line from Shakespeare's Sonnet 18—"Sometimes too hot the eye of heaven shines."

Overall, the writing went well, but I had trouble translating some aspects of the game into fiction.

The game describes The Exalted as "channeling Essence" to invoke their powers. The description read as if this was a conscious choice for the characters, like Johnny Storm shouting "Flame on!" to start his fire powers working. (Although I always took his shout to be psyching himself up rather than a magic word like *Shazam*.) There was nothing in the gamebook text to suggest the Exalted's powers were automatic. So I would write sentences like "Swan channeled Essence and PERFORMED A SUPERHUMAN MARTIAL ARTS MOVE." When the editor saw the draft, he asked me to take out the references to channeling Essence, as it was an automatic process. I knew better than to let the reader "hear the dice roll," and I should've asked the editor to clarify the whole channeling Essence thing.

The five Exalted didn't advertise their powers, and while they didn't have secret identities as such, they did have normal jobs. Swan was a freelance diplomat, and some of his Exalted powers related to diplomatic skills. This seemed kind of silly to me, and I couldn't figure out a good way to work any of those abilities into the story, so I decided to ignore them. When the editor read the draft, he told me to revise it to show one of Swan's magic diplomatic powers, specifically his ability to "penetrate the bureaucracy." WTF? How the hell was I supposed to do *that*? I used the same technique I employed in *Temple of the Dragonslayer* and created a new story module that I could slip into the existing narrative without having to revise too much of the original text. The city Swan was in existed in the game already, and it did have an immense bureaucracy, so all I had to do was show him "penetrate" it. I decided to make Swan need a permit of some kind for a reason I can't remember, and which isn't important after all these years. I sent him to a local government office where one department sent him to another, which sent him to another, and so on. As Swan maneuvered his way through this labyrinth of rules and regulations, he moved higher up in the building, one floor at a time, until finally he came to the top. There was a single office there, and inside was a man playing a version of solitaire. This man could issue the permit Swan needed, but no one had ever succeeded in reaching his office before, and he was massively lonely. He asked Swan if he wouldn't mind playing cards with him awhile, and Swan smiled and agreed.

I wrote this scene to show Swan interacting with people in the various departments he visited and to show him using his diplomatic charm. I created the lonely man at the top because I thought the whole idea of magically penetrating the bureaucracy was ridiculous, and I wanted to satirize it (hopefully in a subtle enough way that the editor wouldn't get mad). The editor loved the scene, and all was well.

I did one other thing while writing *Exalted: A Shadow Over Heaven's Eye.* I usually have several novel projects lined up at any given time (I start to get nervous if I don't have at least a couple ahead of me to work on). When I wrote this novel, I knew I was going to write a trilogy for Wizards of the Coast in their new Eberron setting. I'd had to write an outline for the editor to get the contract, so I knew who the main characters were and what the basic story was. Some of Swan's abilities were similar to the skills one of the characters in the trilogy—the preternaturally skilled assassin turned warrior priest Diran Bastain—so I decided to put several action scenes in Swan's book that would allow me to practice the kind of action sequences I would be writing for Diran. I do this now and again, using scenes in one book as practice for similar scenes in an upcoming one, kind of like how an artist will do a study of a subject before starting the actual painting. I don't repeat the scenes exactly, but they do echo each other. I doubt any readers have ever noticed I do this. Why would they? But it's a technique that has worked well for me, and this novel was the first time I used it.

I can write characters interacting all day long, but writing action doesn't come naturally for me, although I've gotten better at it over the years. Writing Swan's fight scenes was the first time I was able to get good experience writing action, and as I said, this book helped prepare me to write action in the *Blade of the Flame* series.

What did I learn from writing this book?

- **Ask your editor.** I still suck at doing this, so I'm not sure I can honestly count this as something I've learned. I don't like asking for help and would rather do things on my own. The more I'm left alone to get on with my work, the happier I am. And while in this case, it only meant some simple and easily handled revision, I can't count on things always working out this way.
- **I got much better at writing action scenes.** They still don't come naturally to me even now, but both editors and readers have praised the action in my books, so I'm doing something right.
- **I can use one book to help me learn to write the next.** This is always true, of course. Each thing

we write helps us write the next thing we'll write. But in this case, I was able to practice the kind of action scenes I would need to write for my Eberron trilogy, and I definitely felt more comfortable about tackling those novels after writing Swan's adventure.

- **I now know how to penetrate the bureaucracy.** So I've got that going for me, which is nice.

A Nightmare on Elm Street: Protégé
Black Flame (2005)

But before I started on the Eberron books, I landed this sweet tie-in gig. Sometimes it works that way with tie-ins. You never know when you'll see an announcement that a publisher is accepting proposals for a new tie-in series, or—as you build your tie-in credits—when editors will seek you out and offer you a gig. It's too good to pass up, and you take the deal and fit it into your writing schedule as best you can. I'm lucky to be a fast writer. I like to take three months to write a book (which feels like a leisurely pace to me), but I can write them much faster if necessary.

I think in this case, Black Flame put out an announcement that they were looking for writers to do books for several horror movie properties: *Friday the 13th, Jason X, Final Destination*, and *A Nightmare on Elm Street*. I believe I sent several short novel pitches for all these properties, the publisher asked me to develop my *Elm Street* one into a full outline, and I got the contract.

To say I was excited to be writing Freddy Krueger is an understatement. I was twenty when the first film in the franchise came out, so I didn't grow up with Freddy as a horror icon. My childhood horror icons were the Universal Monsters, the monsters of Hammer films, and the gothic villains (especially the ones played by Vincent Price) in Roger Corman's Edgar Allan Poe movies. But I loved the character, and by this time I'd developed a surreal, nightmarish style for my original horror fiction, so getting to write about Freddy's dark dreamworld seemed like a perfect fit for me. Plus, this was the first time I got to write about an established movie character, who in this case was also a worldwide pop culture icon.

I couldn't get started right away, though. The publisher had approved my outline, but whoever was in charge of licensing at New Line Cinema still needed to approve it. Without the approval of the license holder, there's nothing you can do. (Novelizations are an exception, since the movie script is like an outline. As soon as you get the script, you can start writing.) My editor and I waited to hear from New Line.

And waited.

And waited.

My editor became worried that if I didn't start writing soon, we wouldn't make the publication deadline. Since tie-in projects are generated by the publisher, they're already on the publisher's schedule, which means tie-in writers get a lot of short deadlines. (Again, I'm lucky to be a fast writer.) Finally, my editor told me to start writing. He thought my story was great and New Line was certain to approve it. I wrote sixty pages when New Line told my editor that they were *not* going to approve my outline. My story was about Freddy accidentally becoming human again. At first, he's upset to be cast out of the dream realm and stuck in a limited mortal body, but he soon adjusts. He's alive and unscarred, and he begins to enjoy the pleasures that physical existence can bring—the taste of ice cream, the feel of a breeze on your skin, killing a victim the old-fashioned way … He sleeps like any other human, and when he visits the dream realm at night, he discovers something has taken his place as King of Nightmares. Freddy is determined to return to the dream realm, unseat this usurper, and get his crown back. But first he has to find a way back. I'd been considering making Freddy's father be the new King of Nightmares, a conglomerate spirit since Freddy was, as the films established "the bastard son of a hundred maniacs." I wasn't sure New Line would let me get away with it, though.

The reason New Line wouldn't approve my story was that they didn't want to bring up Freddy's past as a child molester/child murderer. By this point in the film series, Freddy had turned from a truly frightening monster into a comedic character that figuratively (and sometimes literally) winked at the audience. That was Freddy's current "brand," and New Line preferred no one remember who and what he started out as.

I had anticipated this issue, and I'd planned to show Freddy stopping outside an elementary school playground to watch the kids. He would try to engage a couple in conversation, but in the years since he'd died, children had been taught about stranger danger, and they knew to avoid him. I didn't plan to explicitly state why Freddy had stopped at the playground, but those readers who remembered the first film would understand the dark subtext of the scene. After that, I would never refer to Freddy's past as a child molester again.

But New Line wouldn't budge, and so I had to come up with a new story and outline fast. I did so, and thankfully New Line approved of this one, and I could finally start writing. My original story was titled *Dreamspawn*, and it was scheduled to be the second *Elm Street* book Black Flame would bring out. Because the situation with New Line slowed everything down for me, the publisher decided to make my new book—this one titled *Protégé*—the third in the series, so I would have more time to write it. Black Flame had already produced a cover for *Dreamspawn* with me listed as the author, and when Christa Faust's book got moved to the number two slot, for some reason the publisher released it as *Dreamspawn*. Maybe because they already had that title in their schedule and promotional materials. To this day, you can still find images of the original cover on the Internet of *Dreamspawn* with me listed as the author.

Even though I couldn't use my original idea, I had a blast writing the novel. There were several high school bullies in the book, all of whom eventually die, and I gave them the first names of real bullies I'd known in high school. (Writers always get our revenge in the end!) I decided to portray Freddy as the horror jester he'd become, but throughout the course of the novel, I "devolved" him, portraying him as increasingly dark and evil, toning down and eventually eliminating the humor. I thought of this as removing the various layers of masks that he wore, leaving only the horrible empty Nothing that he truly was. By the end of my book, I'd returned Freddy to the profoundly disturbing evil thing that he was in the first film. A bit of pop culture critique on my part.

Protégé was also the book where one of my favorite lines that I've ever written—whether in my original or tie-in fiction—appeared.

The Firebird picked up speed, baleful flames trailing behind the vehicle as if it were a fiendish comet shot straight out of Satan's sulfurous bunghole.

It's so ridiculous and over-the-top, like Freddy himself, and I laughed as I wrote it.

Over the years, I've had people ask if I still have the pages I wrote for the original version of *Dreamspawn*, so they could read them. I've looked, but I haven't been able to find them. My papers are collected by the University of Pittsburgh's Horror Studies Program—notes, novel and story drafts, editorial comments, correspondence, as well as old flash drives, 3. 5 disks, and floppy disks, and a couple hard drives of old computers. The original *Dreamspawn* pages might well be somewhere in all that stuff, so if you want to find them, you'll need to make a trip to Pittsburgh and be prepared to do some searching.

Lessons learned from writing this novel:

- **Never—and I mean NEVER—start writing a draft without the license holder approving your outline first.**
- **It's better to show the license holder several short pitches for them to pick from and approve before you start writing the outline.** Black Flame didn't do this, but most of my other tie-in editors have. It saves a lot of headaches.
- **I can capture a pre-existing character's voice.** I'd written characters that others had created before this, but they weren't as fully fleshed out as Freddy was. He had a style and tone all his own, thanks to the scriptwriters and the brilliant Robert Englund. I worked hard to replicate Freddy on the page, and readers and reviewers seemed to think I did a good job.
- **It's fun *and* deeply satisfying to kill childhood bullies in your fiction.**

Postscript 1: After I finished Protégé, Black Flame contracted me to write a *Final Destination* novel. In it, the Deathforce would manifest through a group of zombies, and the group of people trying to stay alive included a serial killer who worshipped the Deathforce. I wrote only one chapter before the Black Flame line was canceled, and I never finished the book. The editor wanted to call it *Final Destination: Dead City* because he was a huge fan of Italian zombie movies (*Dead City* was the name of one such film) and that was the title we'd planned to use. I eventually recycled the idea of a serial killer in a zombie apocalypse for my original novel *The Way of All Flesh* which came out from Samhain Books in 2014.

Postscript 2: After I finished *Dead City*, I'd planned to pitch a *Jason X* novel where Jason X is sent back in time by a group of scientists to kill his previous self, thereby saving hundreds of people he'd killed—and their descendants who would now be alive in the galaxy in the future. I planned to have Jason X encounter the Jason from each of the preceding movies until he finally reached the first movie, when his mother was the killer. I wished Black Flame had lasted long enough for me to do that book. It would've been a hell of a lot of fun to write.

EXERCISES

1. Make a list of tie-in properties you'd love to write for. What do you love about these properties? Do you see any commonality in them? (Are they all science fiction or horror or kids' properties, etc.?)
2. Pick one of these properties and come up with an original story idea involving it. Write a short summary of your idea.

VOICES FROM THE TRENCHES

DEBORAH DAUGHETEE

How did you get into writing tie-ins? Before I got my first job as a staff writer on a television show, I worked for Dan Curtis as his Writer's Assistant. Dan was the creator of *Dark Shadows*. Years later, when Jim Pierson discovered I was sick and couldn't write television anymore, he called and asked if I would like to write a *Dark Shadows* Audio Drama for Big Finish. Jim knew I was a huge *Dark Shadows* fan. Of course, I said yes, and I ended up writing three.

What do you like about writing tie-ins? What are the rewards for you? Crafting stories for shows that once captivated my imagination is an exhilarating experience. Imagine being an ardent fan of iconic series like *Dark Shadows* and then, in a twist of fate, finding yourself breathing new life into their narratives. And imagine the original cast from that '60s show actually recording your words. Absolute magic!

Currently, I'm immersed in scripting for *Kolchak: The Night Stalker*, again from the creative minds of Dan Curtis working with Richard Matheson. To write for characters that I once admired from afar, characters that were a part of my formative years, is not just rewarding—it's a dream turned reality, a full-circle moment in my creative journey.

What challenges have you faced in your career as a tie-in writer? My challenges have been my health, which eventually stole my ability to write. But then I had a double lung transplant and only last year recovered my ability to write stories that are worthy of publication. The Night Stalker stories have been an incredible blessing. Nancy Holder introduced me to Moonstone Publications. I have a story coming out in February and am currently working on a Sherlock Holmes/*Night Stalker* novella.

Does writing tie-ins require a different skill set than other types of writing? If so, what are these skills? Writing tie-ins is much like writing for television in that you are navigating an established world with established characters. Personally, I think it's important also to replicate the tone of the original works. The challenge is to find a way into a world that is unique and all your own while respecting the original. For instance, in my *Dark Shadows* audio drama *Echoes of Insanity*, Willy is sent to Windcliff [in the original series], but we are never told what happens to him there. So that was my entry into his story.

Do you think it's possible to be pigeonholed as a tie-in writer, making it more difficult to publish your own work? If so, how do you deal with this? I haven't been pigeonholed and really wouldn't mind it.

What advice do you have for writers who want to break into the media tie-in field? My advice is to keep your eyes open to opportunities. If you know someone who is writing in the field, ask them for introductions. Be sure to do your homework and immerse yourself in the world in which you are writing. Respect that world and its characters.

DEBORAH SMITH DAUGHTEE has spent most of her career writing and producing such television shows as *Murder, She Wrote*; *Dr. Quinn, Medicine Woman*; and *Touched by an Angel*. She has published short stories in magazines and anthologies, and she has written audio dramas set in the world of the 1960s classic television show *Dark Shadows*, including her Scribe Award-nominated *The Lost Girl*. She is currently writing stories in the world of *Kolchak, the Night Stalker*. Daughtee created Kymera Press, a comic-book publishing company that supports women in comics. She writes the comic series *Gates of Midnight*, which won the 2019 Irwin Award, and she publishes the Bram Stoker Award-winning *Mary Shelley Presents Tales of the Supernatural*.

SEAN WILLIAMS

How did you get into writing tie-ins? I was approached because of work I was doing in related fields, first for a series from a small press in Australia (the editor saw potential in original short stories I'd had published in the early 1990s) and then to write for *Star Wars* (thanks to space opera novels loosely connected to that other independent franchise). So really, it all goes back to me writing work I loved and standing out from the field as someone who could write quickly and well.

What do you like about writing tie-ins? What are the rewards for you? I like writing tie-ins for the same reason that I like other forms of collaboration: it gets me out of my head. While I do like having total control over work I've developed and brought into being myself, there's something refreshing about being handed a world that already exists and being told to play in it, or to give existing characters something new to do. I'm able to focus on certain aspects of the creative process while letting others slide in ways that wouldn't be possible if it was all on me. I also like being part of a team, and I enjoy the unexpected ways that other people can elevate ideas I've half-had into something unexpectedly new and amazing.

What challenges have you faced in your career as a tie-in writer? Well, the challenges are the flipsides of everything I've mentioned above. When creative visions don't match, when communication fails, when team-members behave unpredictably—all these things can make writing tie-ins enormously difficult. Not to mention the fact that the deadlines always seem stupidly short. Yes, I can deliver a novel in four weeks, but wouldn't it be better if I didn't have to? (The challenge is definitely part of the fun, though.)

Does writing tie-ins require a different skill set than other types of writing? If so what are these skills? I think the skill sets are broadly similar, in that even original work takes place in an environment of genres, tropes, and an industry full of people to work with (and occasionally against). But writing tie-ins definitely requires an author to hone some skills more keenly than when they're working on original work. The ability to communicate their abilities, needs, and expectations, for one. To be flexible with plans, generous with ideas, and patient with collaborators, for two. What would be three? To be able to let go, I guess, remembering that you're giving this thing your best work, but that at any moment it could be overwritten or even deleted outright if the bigger picture shifts. This act of committing totally while at the same abandoning all investment is some kind of Zen puzzle that not every writer is built for, although it can come with practice.

Do you think it's possible to be pigeonholed as a tie-in writer, making it more difficult to publish your own work? If so, how do you deal with this? I've never had an issue with this, and other authors I know haven't, but I suppose it's possible, in the same way that some authors get "stuck" in particular genres. The solutions are the same for both, I imagine: keep writing what you love and hope the market will figure it out. There's no reason why an author can't do both, as long as the work is good. I like to believe that the cream eventually rises, but there's luck involved, of course, and that's impossible to plan for.

What advice do you have for writers who want to break into the media tie-in field? Don't write anything you wouldn't be proud to put your real name on.

SEAN WILLIAMS' novelization of *Star Wars: The Force Unleashed* was the first computer game tie-in in history to debut at number one on the *New York Times* bestseller list. He is a multi-award-winning author of over sixty books and 120 shorter publications for readers of all ages. His original works include series, novels, stories, and poems that have been translated into numerous languages for readers around the world. He has collaborated with other authors, including Garth Nix, makes music as a side hustle, and is Discipline Lead of Creative Writing at Flinders University, South Australia. Websites: seanwilliams.com and theadelaidean.com.

BRYAN YOUNG

How did you get into writing tie-ins? My first start with tie-in writing was the Robotech: Roleplaying Game Strange Machine Games put out. I had a friend who knew I loved the property refer me to the current licensor and they snatched me up for 40k words of fiction and scenarios for the game and I was off to the races. Then, it wasn't long before another friend (Michael A. Stackpole) recommended me to the folks handling BattleTech and Shadowrun and I started writing for them. But that was all on the heels of a lot of professional writing and publishing other books—mostly at small presses—that had nothing to do with tie-ins.

What do you like about writing tie-ins? What are the rewards for you? I really love the constraints of tie-in work. I love being told, "Here's a sandbox, here are the borders of that sandbox, what creativity can you come up with?" and I find the rewards of that style of writing are similar to writing my own original fiction. At least on a metaphysical level. Monetarily, I've found that my own work pays more.

What challenges have you faced in your career as a tie-in writer? Just trying to find the right foot in the door can be hard. But once you're in, then it becomes a little easier. There are still licenses and franchises I really want to write in and still find closed doors and that continues to be a struggle.

Does writing tie-ins require a different skill set than other types of writing? If so what are these skills? I think it requires something more collaborative. Your goal is to help sell whatever product you're tying into, as well as selling the book. There are more cooks in that kitchen and it requires more soft skills in that direction. I think that's actually my favorite part about it, too.

Do you think it's possible to be pigeonholed as a tie-in writer, making it more difficult to publish your own work? If so, how do you deal with this? I haven't experienced this issue yet ... I hope it's not a problem. So far, I just write what makes me happy and pays the bills and it's worked out.

What advice do you have for writers who want to break into the media tie-in field? Don't think you can start with having someone hand you their beloved property. Licenses for these universes and franchises are often expensive. They want to know you can deliver a book first. Learn to be a good writer. Most places I've worked for are looking for a good writer first and being a fan of the property is much lower down on the list. They have teams to help you get your details right and it's easier to get to that point with a writer who already knows their craft.

BRYAN YOUNG (he/they) works across many different media. His work as a writer and producer has been called "filmmaking gold" by *The New York Times*. He's also published comic books with Slave Labor Graphics and Image Comics. He's been a regular contributor for the *Huffington Post*, StarWars.com,

Star Wars Insider magazine, SYFY, SlashFilm, and was the founder and editor-in-chief of the geek news and review site Big Shiny Robot! In 2014, he wrote the critically acclaimed history book, *A Children's Illustrated History of Presidential Assassination.* He co-authored *Robotech: The Macross Saga* RPG and has written two books in the BattleTech Universe: *Honor's Gauntlet* and *A Question of Survival.* His latest book, *The Big Bang Theory Book of Lists*, is a #1 bestseller on Amazon. His work has won two Diamond Quill awards, and in 2023, he was named Writer of the Year by the League of Utah Writers. He teaches writing for *Writer's Digest, Script Magazine*, and the University of Utah. Visit him at swankmotron.com.

CHAPTER THREE
MY PULSE-POUNDING ADVENTURES IN MEDIA TIE-IN LAND
2006-2010

Blade of the Flame 1: Thieves of Blood
Blade of the Flame 2: Forge of the Mindslayers
Blade of the Flame 3: Sea of Death
Wizards of the Coast (2006, 2007, 2008)

I'm going to cover these three books as a group, which seems only appropriate since they're a trilogy. While I'd written two volumes of the YA *Dragonlance* series, the *Blade of the Flame* books felt like the first true series I'd written. When WotC was in the process of bringing out their Eberron game setting, I wasn't sure whether to continue writing *Dragonlance* novels or get in on the ground floor of Eberron. I asked both Dennis McKiernan and Mike Stackpole what they thought I should do, and they both said the same thing. *Dragonlance* was a long-running series, and it would be more difficult for me to stand out from the pack if I continued writing them. But Eberron was new, and thus there was a greater chance the books I wrote for that setting would get more notice. So I switched to Eberron.

Mark Sehestedt was my editor for the trilogy, and we worked together well. The Eberron sourcebook was still in process, so Mark sent me a binder containing printouts of what had been done so far for reference. Throughout my tie-in writing career, publishers almost never gave me any kind of materials to help me write books, but WotC was the exception. They sent me all kinds of books for reference—*Monster Manuals, Dungeon Master's Guide*, and more—and I was grateful to have so much to work with.

I created my main character, reformed assassin Diran Bastain, and gave him a partner, a half-orc warrior named Ghaji, and they worked so well together that I've revisited the partnership dynamic in other books of mine, such as my two *Shadow Watch* books and most recently in my *Custodians of the Cosmos* trilogy. Eberron wasn't a horror setting, but it took place after the Last War, which gave it a post WWI feeling, and Diran's order, the Blade of the Flame, had hunted lycanthropes in Eberron to extinction. Add to this Diran's past as a deadly assassin, and these elements gave the setting a darker atmosphere than Dragonlance, so I decided to take a horror-adventure approach to the books and base them on my love for the Universal Monsters. *Thieves of Blood* featured a vampire pirate crew. *Forge of the Mindslayers* featured a Frankenstein-like sentient golem—one of the Warforged created to be soldiers in the Last War—who possessed psychic abilities, along with a mummy-like undead witch and a barghest, a werewolf-like creature that wasn't *technically* a werewolf. *Sea of Death* featured a lycanthrope that had survived the Silver Flame's purge, as well as weresharks, which I used as a Creature from the Black Lagoon analogue. (I figured the Silver Flame might've gotten rid of lycanthropes on land, but they wouldn't have been able to do anything about the shapeshifters in the sea.)

I had a ton of fun writing these books, and reader response was quite favorable. They're still available today if you'd like to check them out.

Some (hopefully) interesting tidbits about these books …

Since the Eberron setting was still in flux when I started the first book, there weren't always detailed descriptions of certain elements. For example, there was an island prison in the setting, and since it hadn't been designed yet, and I wanted to use it in the story, I created it myself, basing it on Alcatraz. Mark was fine with that, although I'm sure the official prison design, once it was finished, was different than mine. Sometimes you have to fill in the blanks regarding setting or character when you write tie-ins, even if what you come up with will eventually be contradicted by official source material.

In the game, the chosen weapon of priests of the Silver Flame was a bow and arrow. A silver arrowhead wreathed by silver flame was even their symbol. Diran's weapons of choice were daggers, and he was an absolute genius at using them, throwing them with unearthly accuracy. Mark said that we should probably have Diran start using a bow so he'd fit better with the game lore, but I didn't want to make the switch. I loved Diran just the way he was, so in one of the books—*Sea of Death*, maybe—I showed Diran trying to master the bow and finding out his skill with daggers did not automatically translate into skill with other weapons. He was no better than any other beginner, and he found this extremely frustrating. In my imagination, Diran eventually got okay with a bow, but he primarily stuck to using his daggers for the rest of his adventuring career.

Since Ghaji was a half-orc, I decided to explore what it was like for him to be bi-racial in a setting where orcs aren't even considered human. He faced prejudice, and he had conflicting feelings about being part of two worlds but not fully belonging to either. He certainly wasn't above playing the dangerous, bestial half-orc when necessary, though. Just because we tie-in writers create our fiction for entertainment doesn't mean we can't write about important issues as well.

I came up with what I thought was a cool concept for the villain of *Thieves of Blood*. Once a person becomes a vampire they retain their human personality, but they become more inhuman as time passes, and after several decades—basically the extent of a human lifetime—their human self "dies" and all that remains is a cold, calculating, predator. The vampire pirate captain in the book is coming to the end of his human lifespan and on the verge of becoming a full-fledged monster.

When I pitched using a psionic Warforged in *Forge of the Mindslayers*, Mark told me that no such creature existed in the game. I told him the page number in the Eberron guide (which had been published by this point) where I found the character, and he looked it up and then laughed. He said the games WotC dealt with were so complicated and had so much lore, it was impossible for any one person to know it all off the top of their head.

Both Mark and I thought *Forge of the Mindslayers* was a good title for the book. It was only after the novel came out that we discovered D&D fans were misreading the title as *Forge of the Mind Flayers*. Mind Flayers were iconic D&D monsters, and some readers were disappointed the book wasn't about them. Maybe we should've titled the book *Forge of the Mindkillers* instead.

I would've loved to revisit the characters in a follow-up trilogy, but WotC was eventually acquired by Hasbro, and their new corporate masters decided they should focus entirely on their games and stop producing fiction. I sometimes wonder what would've happened with my career if they'd continued to publish fiction. Would I have been primarily known as a D&D novelist? Would I be satisfied with that? I'll never know, of course, and that's often the lot of a tie-in writer. Publishers come and go, your career takes various twists and turns, and sometimes it feels like surfing. You take the waves that come and ride them the best you can.

Unlike with my *Dragonlance* characters, no one else has ever written about Diran and Ghaji, and I'm glad. They're *my* boys, even if they are technically owned by WotC.

What I learned from writing the *Blade of the Flame* books:

- **I continued to get better at action sequences.** Although my daughters would laugh at me when I would get up to act them out so I could more clearly envision how to write them. Artists are never fully appreciated in their own lifetime.
- **I learned to get comfortable with making up some aspects of the story when there isn't established reference material.** This is an important aspect of being a tie-in writer. You need to know when to follow what's been established, when not to, when to fudge things, and when to ignore established lore. For me, that was a skill that only came with practice and seeing how editors and readers responded.
- **I really liked the partnership dynamic.** Diran and Ghaji were two of the most successful characters I ever created, and in some ways, I've been trying to find a way to replicate that success by employing the partnership dynamic in my original fiction. I'll probably keep returning to this throughout the rest of my career. Discovering your strengths as a writer and working to make them even stronger is important, but it's just as important not to become so bound to a certain type of story or technique that it limits your growth as an artist.
- **Sometimes even employees of the license holder don't know everything about the IP.** The license holder may have the final word on what you can and can't do in a tie-in novel, but that doesn't mean they're infallible. If you think they made a mistake, it's okay to check—politely and professionally, of course.

- **I don't particularly like writing trilogies.** This surprised me. I wrote the three *Blade of the Flame* books one after the other. The first book went smoothly, the second was more work, and the third was a bit of a slog at times. The same thing has happened whenever I've written a series. By the third book, I'm looking forward to being done with the characters and setting. I'm not exactly sick of them, but I definitely need a break. I'm not sure why this is since I love the characters and settings I create, but it happens. I guess the thrill of discovery starts to wear thin the further into a series I get. Knowing this about myself is important, since it tells me not to commit to writing a series unless I really want to do it, and to expect the third book slog to happen and be prepared to push through it. That's what a professional does, right?

Stargate SG-1: Valhalla
Fandemonium Books (2009)

I'd seen writers announcing online that they'd sold *Stargate* books to Fandemonium, and I decided to give it a try. I think publisher Sally Malcolm put out an open call for pitches, but maybe I contacted her directly. I was divorced and living on my own at this time, and while my ex and I had shared custody of our daughters, I had a lot of extra time on my hands, so I watched far more TV than usual. I was already a fan of *SG-1,* and I'd been watching reruns on cable. I'd never gotten into *Stargate: Atlantis* before, but I borrowed DVDs of the series from the library and binged it. I really like the characters in Atlantis, as well as the expansiveness of its setting, so I hoped I'd get to write an *Atlantis* novel. Sally had plenty of *Atlantis* novels lined up already, but she needed some *SG-1* stories, so—only a little disappointed—that's what I pitched.

This was my first time writing a tie-in for a TV series, and it was great having many different characters I could use in addition to the main heroes and so much lore to draw on. An embarrassment of riches, really. I decided to use a member of the alien race called the Asgard as the main antagonist. I've loved Norse myth since I was kid reading *Thor* comics, so it was only natural that I gravitated toward this race. For years, I'd been mulling over writing a horror novel based on the myth of Valhalla about a town where everyone fought and killed each other during the day and were resurrected in the morning to do it all over again. I hadn't done anything with this idea yet, so I decided to use it for my SG-1 novel, which I cleverly titled *Valhalla*. The Asgard were an old race with a failing genetic structure. Some of their scientists sought to find biological ways to save their species, but what if one scientist took a different route and tried to discover a way for the Asgard to be preserved as virtual entities? I named the scientist Odin, and he'd created a Valhalla on a distant world, populated with Vikings whose brain patterns he'd recorded as they lay dying on a battlefield. He had them fight as solid, three-dimensional holograms of their former selves and rebooted them at dawn as he worked on perfecting his holo technology. The main SG-1 crew arrives to what seems to them a colony of Viking warriors who perpetually slaughter one another each day, and they investigate this mystery.

I used to be hesitant about using my best ideas for tie-ins—surely I should save them for my original fiction, right? Writing *Stargate SG-1: Valhalla* taught me not to hoard my ideas, saving them for a magical Someday that might never come.

This was my second SF tie-in (second SF novel of any type), and my experience with *Defender* made me feel confident about tackling it.

I didn't think the Valhalla storyline would be enough to fill an entire novel, so I decided to have a second storyline running concurrently with the first and alternate between them—and I'd have the storylines impact each other at the end. I used Jonas—who'd only been a member of SG-1 for a single season—as the main character in the second storyline. He'd been working on creating a huge AI called the Lattice that would orbit his world and run the planet's high-tech cities. Of course, this Does Not Go as Planned, and Jonas must find a way to stop the Lattice when it goes rogue. His storyline ended first, and he was able to come to the aid of his former teammates and use what he learned from dealing with the Lattice to help them defeat Odin and his holo-Vikings.

I'd used a parallel structure like this in my short fiction many times before, but I'd never used it at novel length before. I commonly used multiple viewpoint characters in my books, but I'd never had truly separate storylines which merged in the end, with one affecting the outcome of the other. It was a great way to expand the novel to the length I needed while adding more cool stuff to the book.

My second wife and I had begun dating at the time, so I named a character after her and dedicated the book to her as well. What was weird (in a good way) was that her mother was a huge SF/F fan and had read a number of my books before we met, and she was far more excited about me writing the book than her daughter was!

Sally liked the finished book, and her suggested edits were minimal and easily dealt with. I looked forward to the book coming out and learning what fans thought of it. In the meantime, I moved on to the next project. When the book was released, Jonas was featured prominently on the cover, and that's when I learned that a lot of *Stargate* fans hated him. We're talking hate as powerful as a thousand blazing suns. I was a fan of both *Stargate* series, but I wasn't connected to the show's fandom, and I had no idea how much they—or at least a significant contingent—loathed Jonas. Since none of the previous *Stargate SG-1* novels had included Jonas, I'd thought mine would fill that gap. Now I was thinking I'd made a huge mistake, and I wondered if Sally had been aware that using Jonas in the book would be poorly received, and if so, why'd she given me the greenlight to use his character? Over time, the reviews evened out and there was less Jonas hate in them. The book now has an aggregate score of four stars on Amazon and 3.8 stars on Goodreads. This was my first time experiencing negative fan reaction to a tie-in I wrote, and it was instructional, if not much fun.

I never tried to write another *Stargate* book, and I'm not sure why. I don't think the fans' Jonas hate scared me off, but maybe on some level it did. It's more likely that I needed to focus on other projects for a while and was always too busy to return to *Stargate*. Since I have a dual career writing original and tie-in fiction, sometimes I find myself feeling that I should make one or the other my main focus, and

I'll spend more time writing one type of fiction than the other. That might've happened here, too. At any rate, I enjoyed writing the book, and I'm proud of it, and I'd be happy to write another (hopefully an *Atlantis* one next time!).

What I learned from writing *Stargate SG-1 Valhalla*:

- **Don't save ideas. Use them when you need them.** You could get hit by a bus at any time or keel over dead from a sudden heart attack, and then your best ideas will die with you. Don't be stingy with them. Use them. You can always come up with more.
- **The parallel plot structure can work for any type of novel, but it really helps me flesh out tie-ins.** Sometimes giving the villain their own storyline that is interwoven with the heroes' works well, too.
- **FANS! You can't kill 'em, so you might as well love 'em (or at least learn to live with them).** But seriously, this experience taught me to be aware of fan expectations but not to be beholden to them. I need to write what I think the best story will be. For some writers, it might be easier to avoid reviews of their tie-in fiction, but I always read reviews so I can learn from them. Although if I come across one that's basically just a fan rant with no substantive feedback, I usually skip it. (Unless the review is psychotically mean, and then I read it for fun.)

Lady Ruin
Wizards of the Coast (2010)

I didn't know it at the time, but this would be my last novel for WotC.

It was supposed to be the first of a two-book contract, and at the time, I found that odd. Three-book contracts were more standard for established authors. I didn't realize then that the entire publishing industry was moving to offering only two-book contracts. Publishers wanted to hedge their bets, and if the first two books weren't successful enough, they didn't want to be stuck publishing a third unprofitable one. It was kind of a bummer, especially after writing the *Blade of the Flame* books, but I told myself that if these two new books did well, maybe I'd get to do more.

Mark Sehestedt wanted me to pitch a new character, and he suggested I try an Impure Prince. These were humans who'd become bonded with a magically corrupted symbiote which gave them certain abilities but which slowly turned them evil bit by bit. After reading up on Impure Princes, I thought the concept would work well for a more cosmic horror-oriented story, so I was excited to use it and write what would essentially be a Lovecraftian D&D novel. I decided to make the main character a woman since two males were the leads in my last series, and she'd one day become a legendary figure in the land known as Lady Ruin. These two novels would be her original story and her first steps toward becoming a fearsome legend. I wrote my outline, Mark liked it, and it was time to get writing.

Mark left WotC shortly after this, and I was assigned another editor. I was sad to see Mark go. He was a great guy and I really enjoyed working with him, but I hoped the new editor and I would work well together, too. I wrote my draft, had fun doing it (as usual), emailed it to the editor … and she tore it to shreds.

By this point in my career, I'd never had an editor provide such *voluminous* and *intense* feedback, and I was shocked. Not because I think my work is too good to be edited. As someone who'd always traditionally published, I understand that the relationship between author and publisher is essentially a collaborative one with a mutual goal of making a book the very best it can be before it goes out into the world. But the only other time I'd gotten feedback like this was years earlier, when I'd been in a writers' group with Dennis L. McKiernan and Lois McMaster Bujold. The other would-be writers in the group usually looked to Dennis and Lois to see how they should respond to a draft. If Dennis and Lois liked it, they did too. Lois and Dennis were pros, so their assessment mattered the most to the other members. Lois and Dennis did absolutely nothing to create this dynamic. It just happened. Dennis and Lois always gave me great feedback, and they both saw a lot of promise in me and would say so. Lois eventually moved in Minnesota, but the group continued. One evening Dennis couldn't come, and this was the evening when the other members of the group tore into my work with the savagery of a pack of starving wolves. Maybe the selection I read that night was especially bad, but I don't think so. I think a lot of hidden resentment came to the fore and influenced their feedback. Next time, Dennis was back, and the rest of the group returned to giving me mostly positive feedback. I eventually moved to take the college teaching job I still hold, and Dennis and his wife moved to Tucson. That was twenty-five years ago, and I've never been in a writers' group since. I'm not knocking them for other people, but I don't feel they're necessary for me.

Knowing that I shouldn't let my ego get in the way, and also knowing this was a tie-in situation, and the editor represented the license holder, I told myself to calm down and go through her feedback with a professional mindset.

It didn't help.

Some of the comments were really useful. I'd personified the Big Bad at the end of the story, and the editor thought I should make it more of an evil force, kind of like Sauron, and that worked much better. But she'd make weird, almost insulting comments at times. At one point she said, "This is a very rough draft, but I think you already know that." I was like, what the hell? I did my best to write a good first draft. I revise and edit as I go, and editors often comment on how clean my drafts are. It's not uncommon for me to be able to make changes editors request for one of my novels in a half hour or less, that's how few revisions they want. But maybe for whatever reason, this draft *had* turned out really rough. But other comments didn't make sense. I'd included some humorous touches in some of the scenes, and the editor wrote that "Fantasy shouldn't contain humor." I found this comment absolutely baffling. There were lots of places where she made lengthy suggested changes, almost as if she saw herself as a co-writer instead of an editor.

I then did something I've never done before or since. I went over her head. I emailed head editor Philip Athans, explained the situation, and shared the editor's comments with him. Phil went over them and got back to me the next day. He said the editor was young and new at the job, and she hadn't yet learned how to point out an issue to a writer and then trust them to fix it on their own. He told me to not worry so much about what she specifically suggested, but to try to figure out what the issue was that prompted a comment from her, then find my own way to address it. This was the most valuable advice I've ever received from an editor.

I returned to my editor's comments and did the best I could to interpret them. For the "fantasy shouldn't contain humor" comment, I decided to go over every humorous bit I included in the draft and tone it down. When the editor got the revised draft, she must've been satisfied with my humor correction because she said nothing more about that aspect of the book. In fact, she must've been happy with my overall revisions because the book moved into production after that.

Before I could even come up with an idea for the second adventure of Lady Ruin, the editor contacted me to let me know that WotC's new owner Hasbro was shutting down their fiction line. She said I didn't have to repay my advance for the second book, which was nice, but I was sad that I'd never get to write more books for WotC. They still published a few novels after this, and one of them was written by my editor. I then had a better understanding of what had been going on. My editor wasn't an editor; she was a *writer*.

I'm not saying writers can't be good editors and vice versa, but I learned something extremely important about the difference between the two mindsets when I first started teaching. I have a bachelor's degree in education, specifically teaching high school and middle school. By the time I graduated, I knew I didn't want to teach at that level, so I started graduate school to get a master's in English with a creative writing concentration. I financed my grad school education by being a teaching assistant, which required me to teach four sections of freshman comp each year for two years. Whenever I gave feedback on student drafts, I sensed I was doing something wrong, but I didn't know what. After I had a few classes under my belt, I realized that I was responding to drafts *creatively*. I would read a draft and then tell the student how *I* would've written it instead of giving them advice on how they could better communicate *their* ideas. It only makes sense that creative people engage with drafts creatively when they give feedback, but it's so natural to them that they don't realize how limited (almost useless, really) their feedback is for the writer. Their feedback is *self-focused* instead of being *writer-focused*, and I was just as guilty of it as anyone. (But cut me some slack—I was only in my mid-twenties at the time.) With each class I taught, I got better at providing writer-focused feedback until it became second nature to me.

Phil had said the editor was new, and my guess is that her feedback was still self-focused. *Lady Ruin* was the only time we worked together, so I don't know if she ever learned how to give writer-focused feedback. I don't even know if she's still editing. She is still writing and publishing books, though, which is great. Who knows? If she works solely as a writer these days, maybe she's happier.

I moved on to new projects after this, and I figured I'd probably never encounter an editor like this again. I mean, what were the odds? (He said ominously.)

Lessons learned from writing *Lady Ruin*:

- **A reminder to keep my ego in check when considering editorial feedback on my work.** This is a lesson writers need to re-learn periodically throughout their careers.
- **Avoid working with editors who provide self-focused feedback (especially if they'd rather be a writer themselves).** And if you do end up working with one, understand the mindset where their feedback originates from—don't blame them for it; it's part of a natural growth process for a writer/editor/teacher—and try to get them to provide writer-focused feedback. You could ask questions like, "What do you mean when you say fantasy novels shouldn't contain humor? Can you point to specific instances in the novel that prompted you to feel this way? What specifically would've made those scenes work for you?" (I wish I'd thought to ask such questions back then, but remember, I suck at asking editors questions.) If you find yourself working with a problematic editor, you can always follow the advice I heard from some old pros back in the day. They said they would purposely add a few less-than-stellar elements to their novels—a questionable idea, a poorly written scene, large chunks of unnecessary exposition, wooden dialogue in places, a confusing chapter—to draw the editor's attention away from the rest of the manuscript, give them something to ask you to revise, and make them feel as if they did their job. I've never tried outwitting editors with this strategy, but I wouldn't be surprised if it works.
- **I get knocked down, I get up again, you're never gonna keep me down.** Writing *Lady Ruin* was another reminder of the importance of psychological resilience. Not just because of the difficulty I had working with my editor, but because of WotC canceling the second Lady Ruin book and shuttering their fiction line.

EXERCISES

1. Take the tie-in story idea you developed for last chapter's exercise or come up with a new one. Consider ways you might be able to use parallel plot structure if you were to develop the idea into a novel.
2. Think about times you've given and gotten feedback. How would you describe the kind of feedback you tend to give to others? What sort of feedback do you find most useful? Least useful? What kind would send you into a white-hot rage? Getting a better idea of how you feel about feedback can help prepare you for the highly collaborative nature of tie-in work.

VOICES FROM THE TRENCHES

JEFFREY MARIOTTE

How did you get into writing tie-ins? I was a staffer at WildStorm Productions, comic artist Jim Lee's studio under the Image Comics umbrella. I'd written some comics about our very popular superhero team Gen13, as had my friend Christopher Golden. We produced an animated feature film about the characters and sold it to Disney, and on the strength of that, Ace (through book packager Byron Preiss, with IAMTW's own Keith DeCandido editing) acquired the rights to publish three Gen13 novels. Keith offered the first one to Chris, but as Chris was overloaded, he asked me to write it with him. I wrote about 2/3 of it and Chris wrote the other third, and of course we both went over it to smooth out the wrinkles. For the second one, Keith asked me to take the lead, and I brought in my pal, the late Scott Ciencin, to pay forward the favor Chris had done for me. Chris introduced me to his *Buffy the Vampire Slayer* editor at Simon & Schuster, and I was on my way.

What do you like about writing tie-ins? What are the rewards for you? The facile answer is, of course, getting paid for something before you write it. But the real answer is that I'm a prolific reader of multiple genres, and I like to write in all of them as well. Through tie-ins, I've been able to write horror (Buffy, Angel, *30 Days of Night*), sword & sorcery (Conan, Dark Sun), mystery/thriller (*CSI, NCIS, Narcos*), adventure (Tarzan, the Phantom, Zorro), superheroes (Superman, Spider-Man, Gen 13), and much, much more. I've written in more than 30 separate properties, and getting to play in so many beloved sandboxes has been great fun.

What challenges have you faced in your career as a tie-in writer? The challenges are unique to each project. For example, writing a comic book miniseries for the great TV crime series *The Shield*, someone in the production office complained about my proposal because I had police officers breaking the law. This was, of course, the series in which—in the first episode—some of them killed a fellow cop. Shawn Ryan, the show-runner, interceded and told the office to let me do what I wanted, because clearly, I understood the property. In another case, writing a movie tie-in for *Boogeyman*, I was given an old copy of the script, which had been rewritten a few times. Fortunately I figured it out (after wasting several weeks writing unusable material).

Does writing tie-ins require a different skill set than other types of writing? If so what are these skills? Absolutely. A tie-in writer has to be able to grasp what makes a property unique and what the fans are looking for from the material. Another important skill is being able to capture the voices of existing characters (particularly in TV or movie properties, where the fans have heard those voices and not just read them). It's also important to be able to come up with a story that feels like it has real stakes, but that leaves the property intact at the end. If you kill a beloved character, you'd better know how to bring them back to life.

Do you think it's possible to be pigeonholed as a tie-in writer, making it more difficult to publish your own work? If so, how do you deal with this? It definitely is. There's a stigma attached to tie-in writing, at least in certain circles. One can get a reputation as a hack, willing to write anything for a buck. (If only they knew how hard it is to make a buck as a writer, they might be more forgiving.) For me, because I've written in so many genres, my fan base is scattered. Some people like my horror but won't read a western or a mystery from me, etc., so any time I move to a different genre, although I might pick up a few new readers, I might also leave some behind. Career-wise, it'd be more helpful to write in the same genre in tie-in work and original work. But I'd find that boring.

What advice do you have for writers who want to break into the media tie-in field? Write something and get it published. I've edited licensed work for various publishers, mostly in the comics field. People often think they can write tie-ins to properties they love, but unless they've been published, an editor can't know that they can really do the job—write something good enough to be published, finish it, and maintain acceptable quality throughout. I've had other editors tell me they don't necessarily look for somebody who loves the property—because those writers might be bringing their own prejudices to it, rather than reflecting the actual nature of the property. Someone who can tell a good story and capture the essence of the property is most important.

JEFFREY J. MARIOTTE is the award-winning author of dozens of books, including the *Major Crimes Squad: Phoenix* procedural thriller series, the historical Western epic *Blood and Gold: The Legend of Joaquin Murrieta* (with Peter Murrieta), the Cody Cavanaugh Western series *Tarzan and the Forest of Stone*, and many more in various genres. He's also known for his comics and graphic-novel work, especially the long-running Weird Western series *Desperadoes*. Three of his novels have won Scribe Awards. He's also won the Inkpot Award from the San Diego Comic-Con, is a co-winner of the Raven Award from the Mystery Writers of America, and he has been a finalist for the Bram Stoker Award, the International Horror Guild Award, the Spur Award, and the Peacemaker Award, among others. Mariotte has worked in virtually every aspect of the book business, including bookselling, editing, and publishing. He lives in the desert with his wife, author Marsheila Rockwell, and their family and pets.

DAVID BOOP

How did you get into writing tie-ins? I was a *Star Wars* kid, and while the tie-ins for that made me want to write in that world, my first ever media tie-in book was *Six Million Dollar Man: Secret of Bigfoot Pass*. While other authors read Heinlein, Asimov, and Clark, I read (Alan Dean) Foster, (Kevin J), Anderson, and (Mike) Stackpole. Playing with various action figures, I created long-form stories I'd invite my best friend over to watch be acted out. I always knew I would write media tie-ins, but it wasn't until Win Scott Eckart gave me a chance with a Green Hornet anthology that I finally made it.

What do you like about writing tie-ins? What are the rewards for you? There is a challenge and a freedom that comes with writing tie-ins that I'm addicted to. The challenge is being true to the voice and characterizations created by someone else. It's a form of licensed plagiarism that means you need to copy the original, but alter it just enough to add your own style to it. The freedom is, most everything in a world-building sense is created for you, so you can focus more on things like character depth and plot while just looking up the details of religion, society, magic, science, etc.

What challenges have you faced in your career as a tie-in writer? Having that really cool line or idea that the publisher scraps. For example, in Green Hornet, I had Kato drive a hydrofoil called the Black Barracuda. The Hornet says it "looks like something the Bat would drive" meaning Batman, since they know each other. Publisher deleted it, even though it didn't specifically mention Batman by name. The "Kill Your Darlings" idea is fine when you're doing it, but it still hurts when the editor does.

Does writing tie-ins require a different skill set than other types of writing? If so what are these skills?
Skill #1: Research. Don't go in blind.
Skill #2: Thick skin. (See the previous answer.)
Skill #3: Be comfortable writing all different types of characters including other races, genders, and even non-humans. If you have any biases, they will come through in the writing.
Skill #4: Being a fan of the property is fine, but don't become obsessed with the "perfect" version of the IP that exists in your head. Other people will also be playing in this world and they will also have their visions. It's best to play well with others.

Do you think it's possible to be pigeonholed as a tie-in writer, making it more difficult to publish your own work? If so, how do you deal with this? The myth is that doing media tie-in will bring more attention to your original work, but that doesn't always work out. Fans of an IP may not be a fan of your original stories, unless they, too, are being adapted into another media. That doesn't mean it's not beneficial. Some will follow you everywhere and those are the fans for life.

What advice do you have for writers who want to break into the media tie-in field? Go to conventions. Meet media tie-in authors. Meet media tie-in editors and publishers. Listen more, talk less. Be professional. Prove you can be edited by professionals. Wait for your chance. Follow the rules. Turn in your best work.

DAVID BOOP is a Denver-based, award-winning author, editor, essayist, and screenwriter. Before turning to fiction, he worked as a DJ, film critic, journalist, and actor.

Boop's novels run the gamut, such as the sci-fi/noir *She Murdered Me with Science*; *The Soul Changers*, a historical dark-fantasy tie-in to *Rippers Resurrected*; and the Weird Western *The Drowned Horse Chronicle: Volume 1*. He edited the bestselling, award-nominated Weird Western anthology series

Straight Outta Tombstone, Straight Outta Deadwood, and *Straight Outta Dodge City*. He's currently working on a trio of Space Western anthologies, starting with *Gunfight on Europa Station, High Noon on Proxima B,* and *Last Train Outta Keplar-321c.* He's also edited several pulp anthologies, including *Green Hornet & Kato: Detroit Noir.*

Boop is prolific in short fiction and has composed media tie-ins for *Predator* (nominated for the 2018 Scribe Award), *Kolchak the Night Stalker, The Green Hornet,* and *Veronica Mars.* His first comic, *Travailiant Rising,* co-authored with NYT bestseller Kevin J. Anderson, is a giant-mech series. He works in game design, too, and he's written for the *Savage Worlds* RPG for their *Flash Gordon* (nominated for an Origins Award) and *Deadlands: Noir* titles.

A Summa Cum Laude graduate from UC-Denver in the Creative Writing program, Boop temps, collects Funko Pops, and is a believer. His hobbies include film noir, anime, the Blues, and history. You can find out more at davidboop.com.

JOSHUA PRUETT

How did you get into writing tie-ins? My intro into tie-ins was co-writing an adaptation of Jon Favreau's *Jungle Book* remake titled *The Jungle Book: The Strength of the Wolf is the Pack* for Disney Press with Scott Peterson. We'd been eyeballing an opportunity to write some original *Haunted Mansion* books and wanted to create an avenue where we could also pitch original books to the team at Disney and this seemed like a great way to "introduce" ourselves to those editors. Scott had done quite a bit of work for *Phineas and Ferb* tie-ins and when he was offered *Jungle Book,* he brought me on board. We took the screenplay by Justin Marks that blended the original Disney animated feature and Kipling's original text and split it in half; I took the front half, and Scott the back, then we switched and re-wrote each other.

I'd written short stories and one original middle grade novel before that (in addition to TV animation work), which gave me just enough confidence to jump in. The studio wanted to get more into Mowgli's head and inner life like a lot of middle grade books do, so I felt like I could offer something there. We also added a prologue (that I'm particularly proud of) and changed the ending so that we could pull the themes together a bit more.

And while the *Haunted Mansion* opportunity vanished like a phantom (a story for another book, perhaps) our *Jungle Book* tie-in proved successful enough that they wanted more from us and we pitched and sold our first original middle-grade to Disney Hyperion, *Shipwreckers: The Curse of the Cursed Temple of Curses—Or—We Nearly Died. A Lot.* So, our plan worked (almost) perfectly!

What do you like about writing tie-ins? What are the rewards for you? Getting the chance to play with other people's toys/in other people's sandboxes feels like a dream come true. I've since written tie-in material for *Avatar: The Last Airbender, How to Train Your Dragon, Toy Story, Predator* and (dream of dreams) *Doctor Who* (for Big Finish Productions). On the best days, it feels like you're getting to make all your boyhood fan fiction fantasies come true, but as a pro, you're trying to balance those ungainly geek-out moments with craft and discipline too—as a fan, you want to ensure that your story doesn't just count, but that it's great! And that it delivers for fans just like yourself! That feels like a very specific and unique creative challenge to tie-in writing that I've not found in any other part of my writing work. And the reward of not only pulling it off, but hopefully contributing to those worlds and characters can be quite a heady elixir.

What challenges have you faced in your career as a tie-in writer? The biggest challenges I've faced and still face is proving to folks/potential editors that I've got what it takes. I feel like it never completely goes away. I've now written two full length audio books for *Doctor Who*, and would love to do much more (forever), but it's not a guarantee that I'll get to or have earned that opportunity, by any means. In some instances, I may not have the right kind of tie-in experience for certain editors or producers, or that I don't have books with a high enough page count under my belt, or the right genre. So, at the moment, part of my journey is creating and writing those kinds of projects for myself and trying to build out not just my skill set but my perceived skill set. Maybe one day, the work will speak for itself, but in the meantime, my plan is to keep stretching until my reach exceeds grasp.

Does writing tie-ins require a different skill set than other types of writing? If so what are these skills? As I mentioned, I think balancing or better yet uniting your inner fan and the craftsperson is key to writing tie-in work that really sings. It also requires the ability to work within pre-established rules and world/character guidelines with a deft hand and a certain amount of grace. It's easy to grouse about the often restrictive or strange parameters tie-in writers get handed, but I think part of our skillset is not just playing nice in that sandbox and respecting its borders but staying inspired and creative within those walls. The job is to stay inside the sandbox we're given; the opportunity is that we can climb high above that sandbox and dig far beneath that sandbox, uncovering buried treasures in the process.

Do you think it's possible to be pigeonholed as a tie-in writer, making it more difficult to publish your own work? If so, how do you deal with this? I've been very fortunate in that I've bounced back and forth between original and tie-in work for most of my career, but I have noticed that not all of our tie-readers will follow us to our originals, nor is it safe to assume the folks reading our originals will pick up our tie-in work. Part of the solution I think is to be strategic with both and having a sense of our superpowers; it seems like good strategy to pigeon-hole yourself for a stretch in order to establish a bit of a brand, so that readers can follow us down one genre or another, whether that's original or tie-in.

What advice do you have for writers who want to break into the media tie-in field? I think the best advice is to write in the genre you love, the same genre or genres of the tie-in material you love, so that you make it easy for editors and publishers to imagine you writing work for their tie-in worlds and characters. My TV animation work doesn't necessarily scream, "Guy who would kill to write an *Aliens* book for Titan," but adding original horror books to my resume could at least start me on that path. In my experience, writing the thing you hope to write one day before anyone wants it, is far more convincing than trying to convince someone you're worth rolling the dice on. We're the only person who cares how long this takes; no one reads a book and says, "I'm so glad they only worked hard for two years on this," or, "I'm so glad they spent ten years paying their dues." Readers just want good stuff. Give yourself permission to write the first one. It's the only way there'll be a second one.

JOSHUA PRUETT is a *New York Times* bestselling author and Emmy Award winner as well as the only human being on Earth to have written for both *Mystery Science Theater 3000* and *Doctor Who*. Best known as a TV writer on shows like *Phineas and Ferb* for Disney TV Animation, Pruett is also co-author of the graphic-novel series *The Last Comics on Earth*, specializing in books for all ages, including *Shipwreckers: The Curse of the Cursed Temple of Curses* (with Scott Peterson from Disney/Hyperion). He's written tie-in material for *How to Train Your Dragon* and *Avatar: The Last Airbender,* and he's contributed a story to *Predator: Eyes of the Demon* for Titan Books. Pruett's *Gyro and the Argonauts*, pitched as "The Hitchhiker's Guide to Greek Mythology," where monsters become the heroes they were always meant to be, debuts in 2025 from Andrews McMeel Kids. You can follow him on Twitter/Instagram at @zombietardis.

CHAPTER FOUR
MY PULSE-POUNDING ADVENTURES IN MEDIA TIE-IN LAND
2013-2019

Supernatural: Carved in Flesh
Supernatural: Mythmaker
Supernatural: Children of Anubis
Titan Books (2013, 2016, 2019)

As I did with the *Blade of the Flame* books, I'm going to cover my *Supernatural* novels in one entry.

I started watching *Supernatural* when the first episode came out. A show about two brothers hunting monsters? Yes, please. The early publicity for the series made it sound like Sam and Dean were going to be confronting a different urban legend—such as Bloody Mary—every week. It didn't seem like a premise that could be extended for an entire season, let alone multiple seasons, but I tuned in anyway. Eventually the premise broadened to the brothers combatting any and all supernatural entities, and the series took off. After watching the first few episodes of *X-Files* when it came out, I thought every episode would follow the same pattern: Mulder thinks something paranormal happened, Scully doesn't, and the truth would lie somewhere in between. It seemed really boring to me, but the show eventually found its feet and became one of my favorites. Sometimes I think the faster a show can adjust and find a way to make an initially dull and confining premise into something that's actually interesting, the better chance at longevity it'll have. (That's probably a good tactic for keeping a long-running book series fresh, too.)

Eventually, *Supernatural* tie-in books began to appear, and I was jealous of the authors. I decided to see if I could snag a gig with the franchise, but I had no idea who to contact. By this point in time, social media had made interacting with other writers much easier (it reminded me of the old GEnie days, actually), and I decided to ask Keith DeCandido—who'd written several *Supernatural* novels—if he would be comfortable sharing the name of his editor with me. I'd spoken with Keith a few times at conventions, and I knew he was a good guy. I didn't think he'd be offended by my request, even if he decided for whatever reasons to turn me down. Keith was happy to share the name of his editor at Titan Books, I thanked him, and then I immediately emailed her to introduce myself, list my tie-in writing credits, and ask if she was currently looking for any authors for future *Supernatural* books.

A quick aside here. During the time I was writing my *Supernatural* novels, a number of writers emailed to ask if I could help them get a gig writing Sam and Dean's prose adventures. I tried to help, but none of them ever got a contract to write a *Supernatural* book. Having a deep desire to write for a franchise you love with every fiber of your being isn't important to editors. Having a substantial track record as a traditionally published novelist is. As I said earlier in this book, tie-in writing is not an entry-level position.

The editor was kind enough to reply. She said she had no openings at the moment, but she'd keep me in mind. I was disappointed, of course, but I'd long ago become used to getting rejections. If you can't handle rejection, you can't survive as a writer. (The most important quality any artist can have is psychological resilience, the ability to take a hit, bounce back, and keep on going.) So that's what I did—I sighed and moved on.

Several months later, she emailed me to tell me one of the writers that had been scheduled to do a *Supernatural* novel for Titan had to drop out. Would I be interested in taking their place? Yes. Yes, I would.

I've told you before that license holders rarely provide you with any resource material when you write a novel for one of their properties. Well, the good folks at *Supernatural* HQ sent me all the scripts for the entire upcoming season of the show. Every. Damn. One. Of. Them. And they didn't ask me to sign a nondisclosure form. If I'd been a dick, I could've shared the scripts on the Internet or sold them to fans eager to find out what was going to happen to next to their beloved heroes. As it was, I never read them. I'd already decided to set my novel in the previous season, shoehorned between two episodes. This way I'd know exactly where Sam and Dean were at mentally and emotionally, and what the current state of their relationship was. If you've watched the show, you understand what I'm talking about. I didn't want to know the boys' future.

I was only given one restriction. Bobbie Singer had died in the previous season, and I was told that they had "plans" for Bobbie coming up and that I couldn't use him in my book. As a fan, I was like, I KNEW THEY'D BRING HIM BACK! As a professional writer, I merely said, "Okay."

Since at that time the show hadn't covered anything to do with Frankenstein, I decided to use that as inspiration for my plot. In a later season, they introduced the Styne family, which was a very different take on the Frankenstein legend. (When I wrote *The Men of Letters Bestiary*, in the entry on the Styne family, I suggested a connection between them and the bad guy in *Carved in Flesh*.)

When I started writing *Carved in Flesh*, I was acutely aware of the thousands—perhaps millions—of hardcore *Supernatural* fans in the world metaphorically looking over my shoulder, scrutinizing every word I wrote, and shouting, *Dean would NEVER say something like that!* As I've mentioned before, you need to keep the fans in mind while at the same time forgetting about them when you write a tie-in novel based on a popular and beloved IP. It's a tricky balancing act, but I'd learned how to do it by this point in my career, and I managed to maintain that mindset throughout the writing of the book. I had to work harder at it this time, though.

I used my parallel plot technique in the book, detailing an adventure Sam and Dean had when they were young and just beginning to learn what it meant to be Hunters—an adventure that would tie back into the main plot. I decided to write about Sam and Dean as kids for a couple reasons. I doubted the series would ever detail the brothers' childhood and young adulthood, so there was opportunity to make up whatever I wanted (within reason, of course). As adults, the brothers were highly skilled Hunters who could easily defeat average, run-of-the-mill supernatural threats, but they'd know next to nothing as kids, which would make it harder for them to deal with a threat and create more suspense. But the main reason was that series characters don't change. The audience doesn't want them too. Yeah, the Winchesters went through all kinds of weird shit throughout the series—Sam being addicted to demon blood, Sam losing his soul and basically becoming a sociopath, Dean spending time fighting monsters in Purgatory, Dean spending years as a torturer in Hell … But all of these events had no real lasting effect on the boys. Eventually, those changes would be undone (or glossed over), and Sam and Dean would basically return to their old selves. It's impossible to have a big character arc in a tie-in novel if the characters aren't allowed to substantially change. But Kid Dean and Kid Sam could change and grow.

Six years earlier, I had the opportunity to write a Doctor Who story for an anthology called *Destination Prague*. Each story would be about a different Doctor (up to Number Eight, since that's all the publisher had the rights to use), and the stories had to somehow connect to the city of Prague. I thought it kind of an odd theme (and one I feared might become repetitive to readers as they made their way through the book), but I was ecstatic to write a Doctor story. Americans don't often get the chance. Usually, British writers are chosen to write Doctor Who fiction, so I felt doubly lucky to be invited to contribute. I originally chose to use Number Six in my story, but the editor said there were already a couple stories featuring that Doctor, and he asked if I would mind writing a tale about Number Two. I love all the Doctors, so it was cool with me. By this point, the show had been revived, and new Doctors were appearing. The character had gone through so many changes since his days as Number Two—all of them documented in the series—that I couldn't see how to make him change by the end of my story. And having a character change by the end of the story is one of fiction's most sacred laws.

Eventually, I figured out what I needed to do. Series characters can't undergo huge changes during the course of a story, but they *can* learn a lesson, one that results in a small change. I decided Number Two was a (relatively) young Doctor and was still somewhat new to adventuring. I gave him a dilemma toward the story's end. In order to save billions of lives, he had to allow several thousand people to die. He couldn't find any other way. Number Two learned that he couldn't always save everyone (a lesson the Doctor needs to relearn from time to time), and that he sometimes had to make some very hard choices in his adventuring life. This "character learns an important lesson as a substitute to more substantial change" is a technique that has served me well whenever I write a new adventure for an established IP character.

I used this technique with the kid versions of the Winchesters in *Carved in Flesh*, but I also had the adult versions learn lessons, too. I didn't invent this technique. TV series have done it since the inception of the medium, but once I realized I could do the same thing with tie-in fiction, I was able to make the stories read more like actual stories, rather than a series of events that didn't have much impact on the characters in the end.

I didn't ask permission of the studio to write about Sam and Dean as kids. I included that aspect of the story in my outline, the studio approved it, and I started writing. Over the course of my tie-in writing career, I've learned it's best to just go for your weird/cool idea and see what the license holder will let you get away with. It doesn't always work (it didn't for my novelization of *xXx: The Return of Xander Cage*, which I'll tell you about later), but it works more often than you'd expect.

I had young Sam and Dean parallel plots in both *Mythmaker* and *Children of Anubis,* and since the adult Winchesters moved forward in time with each book, I made young Sam and Dean age as well, and by *Children of Anubis*, they're in their late teens.

I didn't have to do much revision on *Carved in Flesh*. I'd included a Reaper in the story, and I gave him some abilities that it seemed to me a Reaper *could* have, but the studio made me take them out. (Like I said, just going for it doesn't always work.) The studio people and my editor all thought I did a good job depicting the brothers. I'd started college as an acting major, but soon switched to theater education with a concentration in English. I still had to take acting classes for two years, though, and everything I learned in them has helped my writing tremendously over the years. When I write fiction—tie-in or original—I try to inhabit the characters the same way I would inhabit a character on stage. With established characters like Sam and Dean, I imagine that I'm acting their roles, the same way so many actors have portrayed Hamlet, Macbeth, etc. over the years. I try to find my way to "act" the characters while also infusing them with the original actors' performances. I'd done this with Freddy Krueger, as well as the Winchesters, and based on reader reviews, most people seem to think I succeeded.

For *Mythmaker*, I used an old concept that I'd never gotten around to writing, once more not hoarding a good idea. In my twenties, I wondered why the horror genre didn't take more advantage of all the things the supernatural (in other words, magic) could do, and I wondered why the fantasy genre didn't lean more into the horrific aspect of magic power and strange creatures. (Clive Barker hadn't shifted from horror to dark fantasy yet, and it would be a few more years before I read Jonathan Carroll's novels). I thought a fusion of horror and fantasy would make a powerful genre of its own, but the best example I could think of was the work of Charles DeLint, although the horror and fantasy elements in his fiction were often kept apart and not truly fused.

I pondered writing a book called *Mythmaker*, about a person who could literally create new mythic gods and creatures, ones more suited for the modern age. I envisioned it as a horror novel with a fantasy foundation, but I never wrote it. The idea did keep returning to me throughout the years, though, and I finally decided to give it a home in the *Supernatural* universe.

For *Children of Anubis*, I decided to have a clan of werewolves clash with a clan of related shapeshifters called Jakkals. The Jakkals were my creation, and they were of Egyptian descent and tended to the sleeping mummified form of their god Anubis (who of course would eventually be awakened to cause trouble). I loved the character of Garth, and since he'd become a werewolf by this point in *Supernatural*, I decided to add him into the mix. I'd never written a full novel about werewolves before, and I loved writing about the Jakkals, so all in all, this book was ton of fun to write.

I originally had Anubis' spirit possess one of the Jakkals at the climax and use his body to fight. My editor told me to have the actual Anubis—with his jackal features, teeth, and claws—come to life and attack during the climax, and her suggestion greatly improved the novel.

There were two things I did *not* do in my three *Supernatural* books. First, I made sure that each adventure would be a down-to-earth one, and I portrayed the boys as highly skilled Hunters but not as the Ultimate Hunter Badasses that could go toe-to-toe against Satan and God. I found it ridiculous that Sam and Dean would be fighting some of the most powerful beings in existence one week, and the next they would have trouble taking out a nest of ghouls. When characters become too powerful, there's no real tension in a story.

Second, I refused to use Castiel in my stories. I loved the character, but he was too often used to get Sam and Dean out of trouble with his angel powers. How can there be any real tension in a story when the human characters are best friends with a being who's basically a god? And I thought it was a cop-out when Dean would try to telepathically contact Castiel for help, but would get no answer, usually without any reason given. (The real reason was the writers didn't want Castiel in the story that week because he'd wave a hand and fix everything within the first couple moments of the episode.) As I said, I loved Castiel, but the truth was—narratively speaking at least—he was a literal *deus ex machina*, and he made everything too damn easy.

Lessons learned from riding down the road in the Impala with Sam and Dean:

- *Really* learning how to keep fan expectations in mind while at the same time ignoring them.
- I gained a deeper understanding of the power of the parallel storyline, since I used the technique for three different books.
- I obtained more experience with the "learning a lesson" technique at novel length.
- I had another opportunity to use a good idea instead of saving it for a future project that might never be realized.
- If your characters are best friends with someone who's basically Superman, keep that character far, far away from your story.

Supernatural: The Roads Not Taken
Insight Editions (2013)

Insight Editions wanted to publish a choose-your-own adventure book featuring Sam and Dean. (Choose Your Own Adventure is copyrighted, so you're supposed to say *interactive story*, but nobody knows what the hell that means, so I'm sticking with *choose your own adventure*.) The publisher had hired a pair of writers for the project, but they dropped out. The editor for the project contacted my editor at Titan and asked if she could recommend someone, and she recommended me. I was grateful for the rec, and I was excited about writing a choose-your-own adventure story as I'd never done anything like that before.

The original authors had wanted to write three separate stories for the book, so I decided to keep that structure, but I'd link the stories together so that they told one larger story. Since this was *Supernatural*, Sam and Dean could literally be experiencing the alternate choices in the stories. I decided it would all be part of a plot by the Roman deity Janus, the god of gates, doors, and transitions in life. In other words, the god of *choices*. I decided to set the story not long after the boys had closed the gateway to Hell. Janus was angry they'd closed a door *and* closed off so many different choices/pathways for both humans and demons by doing so. He wanted to punish Sam and Dean, but of course they defeated the two-faced god in the end.

I had two editors for this project, and they made me take out the reference to the closing of Hell's gateway since the series had moved past that point. I was disappointed because Janus' main motivation for his scheme disappeared from the story, weakening it, but whaddaya gonna do? It's Tie-In Town, Jake.

I had an obscene amount of fun killing the brothers in the various wrong turns in the stories. For variety, in one wrong turn, Dean slipped on ice and broke a leg. He and Sam had to let the creature they were chasing escape, and Sam took Dean to the hospital. One editor thought that wrong path was underwhelming, but the other editor liked it and let it stay.

I had no idea how to arrange the manuscript, so I wrote the "correct" version of each story, indicated the places where a wrong choice could be made, then I placed the wrong paths at the end of each story and told the editors to put them wherever they wanted in the finished book. There's never been an eBook edition of *The Roads Not Taken*. I have no idea how you'd structure one.

What I learned from writing this book:

- **How to write a choose-your-own adventure book.** That's really about it, but that's enough, don't you think? I've never written another one, but I'd love to. Maybe someday.

The Men of Letters Bestiary: Winchester Family Edition
Insight Editions (2017)

I'm going to talk about this project here to keep it with the other *Supernatural* books.

The editors at Insight Editions decided to bring me back for this book, which they originally envisioned as a monster manual for the series written by Sam and Dean's grandfather, Henry Winchester, who belonged to the Men of Letters, a group that believed in fighting supernatural threats with knowledge rather than brute force. Essentially, the book would be written as if it was a nonfiction guide, but since it was about fictional monsters in a fictional universe being presented as if it had been written by a fictional person, it was a work of fiction as well. This hybrid approach sounded intriguing to me, and I happily took the job.

The editors sent me a list of creatures that had appeared in the series, and I scoured the Internet for articles and fan wikis for detailed information about them. I also checked for creatures that had been left off the list for whatever reason. I wrote entries on each creature, arranged in alphabetical order. I decided that Henry's motivation for writing the guide was to pass on knowledge on the habits, strengths, and weaknesses of the various threats to prepare the reader for finding and defeating them. I had a lot of fun writing it, and when I was finished, I submitted it to my editor.

Once my editor read the manuscript, he changed his mind about the focus. He said it should be written from Sam's point of view because readers would expect one of the boys to be the "main character." So I rewrote the entries to make them sound as if Sam had written them as an update to the Men of Letters' records. I sent the new draft to my editor, who then decided Dean's voice needed to be a part of the book, too. I couldn't imagine Dean writing a lot of entries (although I did have him write a couple). What I *could* imagine was Dean reading over Sam's work and writing comments on the pages, so that's what I did. I sent this draft to the editor, and he asked if I could include Castiel's voice too, so I added Cass' point of view in a couple entries. After that, the editor was satisfied, and the book went to press.

The finished book was gorgeous, with awesome illustrations by Kyle Hotz. Dean's comments were presented as if they been handwritten on Sam's pages, and I thought that was a nice touch. I added some of my own speculation into the entries as if they were comments from Sam or Dean. I already told you that I connected the Styne family to my novel *Carved in Flesh*. The bit I added that I'm most proud of was in the entry on Chuck (aka God). I had the brothers speculate that in the end, God might be the biggest monster of them all. I had no special insight that Chuck would eventually become the Biggest Bad of the series, but I had a feeling the show might be heading in that direction. That was a gamble that really paid off!

What did I learn?

- **One of the most difficult tie-in situations is when the editor or license holder doesn't know what they want.** They have kind of a vague sense of what they're looking for, but they won't know for sure until they see a draft. When this happens, you might end up writing one draft after another until they finally say, "That's it!" The more writing you need to do on a project, the less you earn per hour of effort. If you make your living solely as a writer, this is an important consideration. In that case, you might pass on jobs where it's clear the editor or license holder aren't entirely sure what they want you to do.
- **Combining the forms of fiction and nonfiction was fun.** And I acquired more skills for my authorial arsenal.
- **Without the cool illustrations, my text would've had almost zero impact on readers.** This was Kyle Hotz's book as much as mine. Maybe more so.
- **Thank god for fan wikis!**

Grimm: The Killing Time
Titan Books (2014)

I was insanely busy at the time when *Grimm* premiered on television, so I didn't have time to watch it. I figured I didn't need to as far as my writing career was concerned. What were the odds I'd be asked to do a *Grimm* tie-in novel? (You can see where this is headed, can't you?)

My editor at Titan emailed me to ask if I was familiar with the show, and if so, would I like to write a tie-in novel. I told her I'd been watching the show, and I enjoyed it. Then I got in my car, hauled ass to Best Buy, bought the first season on DVD, rushed home, binged it, and came up with several novel ideas to pitch. My editor and the studio decided to go with *The Killing Time,* a story about a doppelganger creature that the entire Wesen community fears. The doppelganger assumes the shape of its latest victim, but that form can only last a few days. I called the creature a Wechselbalg, which means *changeling* in German. Nick encounters the Wechselbalg early in the story, and during the fight it assumes his form, but without killing him. Grimms are special that way, you know? The Wechselbalg finds itself increasingly becoming more like Nick, giving it empathy for others, which it never had before and which makes it difficult for the creature to kill anyone.

I don't recall being asked to do any major revisions for the book. I used the lesson learned technique again. I set the story during the first season of the show, during a time when Nick still viewed Wesen as monsters and the Wesen community viewed him as a pitiless killer of their kind. I wanted to show Nick and the Wesen take an important first step toward a better understanding of who the other was.

I really came to like the show and its mythology, although some its rules about what Wesen were and how they functioned were contradictory. Supposedly their shapeshifting powers and other abilities were solely the result of biology, but their abilities often functioned more like magic (and they would've made a lot more sense if they *were* magic). I avoided that issue in my story and just had the Wesen do their thing without going into much explanation. I also liked that the series was a true blend of fantasy and horror, if not an actual fusion, which was what I'd been exploring in my original work for some time.

What did I learn?

- **To lie to an editor.** I do my best to keep up with genre TV shows now, even if I only read an article explaining their basic premise or check out a Wikipedia article or fan wiki about the show. This way, I'm at least somewhat familiar with TV IPs and don't have to lie. And thanks to the advent of streaming services, I don't need to buy DVDs of TV series anymore.

EXERCISES

1. Watch an episode of a favorite TV show. Pay attention to how the characters change from the beginning of the episode to the end. How big or small are these changes? Did the episode use the lesson learned technique? If so, did you think it was effective?

2. Do you have a good idea (or several) that you've been carrying around for years? If so, what would make you willing to use this idea in a piece of tie-in fiction? Pick a media property and make notes about how you'd adapt your idea to make it work for the property.

VOICES FROM THE TRENCHES

RICK HOSKIN

How did you get into writing tie-ins? I came in as a comic book writer, where I think the sense of what constitutes a tie-in is slightly different—writing for *Superman* or the *X-Men*, say, is seen more as "adding to the established mythos" than elaborating upon it in the way that writing stories based around a movie or TV show might be. I went from that into writing books as myself and under a house pen-name. I think I've written something like 45 novels, and countless comic books to date, as well as animation and video games.

What do you like about writing tie-ins? What are the rewards for you? Writing for characters that I love. For example, writing for *Star Wars* was huge for me, writing comic strips for Han Solo and Chewbacca felt like I was being paid to do the same thing I'd done for free at age seven! I could give dozens of examples like that, and it's usually writing for things I loved as a child (and probably never grew out of!)—*Star Wars, Doctor Who, Spider-Man* … the list goes on and on. I've enjoyed and continue to enjoy working with so many properties, and shaping the lives of these characters.

What challenges have you faced in your career as a tie-in writer? I can't really call them challenges, but you have to remember it is a job. The biggest challenge for any freelance writer is if the editor changes, and you're left out in the cold, or if a project you've worked on for a while doesn't actually move forward through no fault of your own.

Does writing tie-ins require a different skill set than other types of writing? If so what are these skills? Broadly speaking, no. I always say, writing is writing—that's what I do, that's what I enjoy. But you do have to become familiar with the world in question, and get into that style, and you need to be able to work with licensors and deliver on what they expect for a particular franchise.

I think also you need to remember that the franchise is more important than you are to the readership. If you do a good job, they shouldn't notice you—it should be seamless and faithful to the franchise.

Do you think it's possible to be pigeonholed as a tie-in writer, making it more difficult to publish your own work? If so, how do you deal with this? That's a question I find hard to answer, because what constitutes tie-in fiction is so broad. I've written comic books, novels, video games, animation, and I've worked on everything from *Superman* to *Shrek*, Disney Princesses to *Deathlands* … often in the same week!

I've had original material published, too, and, to be honest, the biggest hurdle is finding time to write it between tie-in assignments. Writing your own material is usually on spec, which is to say you're not paid until you land a publisher for it.

When people ask me what I've written, they're more interested to hear I've written *Star Wars* or *Peppa Pig* than an original book like *Bystander 27*, because they have brand recognition for the former.

What advice do you have for writers who want to break into the media tie-in field? I don't have any clever advice, I really don't know how I came to be here!

As more general advice for writing I would say finish what you start, that manuscript you're working on is only a book when you've completed it. And also, don't view it as a competition—just be the best you can be.

RIK HOSKIN is a multi-award-winning writer of novels, graphic novels, video games, and animation. He's written comics for *Superman, Star Wars, Doctor Who*, and various other properties, and he's won the Dragon Award for Best Graphic Novel for *White Sand*, which also made the *New York Times* bestseller list. He writes SF and horror novels and short stories under his own name and as "James Axler." He also writes video games and animation for BBC television in the UK.

STACIA DEUTSCH

How did you get into writing tie-ins? When I was working on my first novel, I saw an ad for writing Strawberry Shortcake books and thought "I can do that!" I emailed and they asked me about my experience. Huh? I thought: How do you get experience so you can have experience? Fast forward a few more years after I sold *Blast to the Past*, an original children's book series to Simon and Schuster. The editor said that they were looking for people to write young Nancy Drew. Did I know how to write mysteries? I immediately said "I can do that!" And lucky me, they let me learn along the way. Once I was in the world of licensed properties, I found that I loved working in other people's sandboxes, with known characters—adding my own twists. There was no going back. It's been 20 plus years that I've been doing this. More than 350 books. I've worked for nearly every publisher. Now, if only someone needed me for Strawberry Shortcake!

What do you like about writing tie-ins? What are the rewards for you? Tie-in writing is not for everyone. The deadlines are fast, sometimes ridiculously so. The pay can be adequate, but it can also be pennies. All said, however, a writer does get paid for writing. When I get a check, I am always stunned that this is my career. I have original midgrade books that my agent has been trying to sell for years (eight in one case). With hire work, there's no waiting. There's no depending on my agent, who I love, but is tied to the whims of the greater publishing market. And because I have picked this path—I write all the time!

What challenges have you faced in your career as a tie-in writer? It breaks my soul, just a little, when a book gets cancelled before it comes out, or when I write and write and we just can't get the work to a place where the licensor signs off. It happens. I try not to take these experiences personally, but in those moments it's hard not to think that a regular career with a regular check would be easier and less of a slam to my ego. The other part that I find hard is figuring out what to do in the spaces between projects. Freelance sites for indie projects have been helpful, but there are still weeks when I watch a lot of Netflix before the next thing rolls in with a slamming fast due date to consume my time. It's feast or famine.

Does writing tie-ins require a different skill set than other types of writing? If so what are these skills? Good writing is the same for anyone. The nuts and bolts of storytelling don't change—I mean look how many of us started with Robert McKee or Chris Vogler as our guides. What differs is the research. Am I creating my own characters from top to bottom, obstacles and motivations, or are those provided? Am I creating the setting details? Or is my world crafted by someone else, perhaps even a team of professionals? I think a tie-in novel is a little like baking a cake from a mix—I can follow the recipe on the box and it's going to be yummy or I can embellish and it will be a different kind of yummy. Still good cake.

The one thing I would advise new writers though is to check your ego at the door. I often don't get my name on my work. Editors will sometimes change things after I turn them in, before publication, without consulting me. If you are bonded to each of your words, or want a big book signing, this kind of work might not be for you. I never mind. I just want to write.

Do you think it's possible to be pigeonholed as a tie-in writer, making it more difficult to publish your own work? If so, how do you deal with this? I try not to think that an editor wouldn't take my original work because I write tie-in. That just feels silly. I mean, I'm racking up experience working for different editors, in diverse genres. I'd think that would be a bonus. Then again, I do have trouble selling my original stuff—I tell myself it's more about the kinds of originals I want to write and timing the market—which we all know is impossible. What I find difficult is that agents generally don't want to manage this kind of a portfolio. I don't really understand why. I mean they have tons of writers on their list, bringing in no money, and I am bringing in a constant flow. It might not be the great riches that might be attached to a book that could possibly have its own movie, or foreign rights, but it's constant.

My agent, thankfully, is all in. And when she hears about potential projects, she lets me know. Mostly, though, new writers should know that I bring my contracts to her for negotiation and settlement.

What advice do you have for writers who want to break into the media tie-in field? Be nice. Be fast. Get the work done. Listen to the licensor—it's their vision. Set realistic expectations. Hire writing is awesome, but I also like to remind myself that there are hundreds (more) of other writers who would gladly I what I do, probably for less. I want to be the one that editors think of when they need a children's writer. In order for that to happen, I need to be my best self, and consistently show them what I can do!

All said, if you think that this is for you—there are ways to break in and it takes determination. Tell everyone on the planet that this is what you want: you gotta plant those seeds and you never know who out there knows someone who knows someone. Look at educational presses as a way to sharpen your skills and build a resume. Walk the halls at conferences and meet editors in licensed properties. Oh, and if they ask for samples, based on their own prompt, go for it. I think that any writing is worth the time at the computer. Breaking in is hard, but once you have a few projects under your belt, it gets easier. Remember the Strawberry Shortcake conundrum—I wanted it, but didn't have the experience, so I found a way to get that experience. If work for hire is your dream—dig in. You've got this.

STACIA DEUTSCH is the *New York Times* bestselling author of more than 350 children's books. Her career started with the original award-winning *Blast to the Past* series about four kids who time travel and meet famous people in history. Now, she writes mostly chapter books and mid-grade for licensed characters. Deutsch loves playing with known characters in worlds that already exist. Her first movie novelization was *Batman: The Dark Knight*, and since then she has written many more movie and TV tie-ins. Recent books include *The Friendship Code for Girls Who Code* (Penguin), seven novels for *Spirit: Riding Free* (Little Brown/Dreamworks), ghost stories for Arcadia, and LEGO shorts. She's deep, deep into Ninjago. Under pseudonyms, Deutsch has been quietly behind *Nancy Drew*, *Boxcar Children*, and a nonfiction book about Barbie. When she isn't writing, she lives on a Temecula, CA, ranch with four horses and two dogs. Website: staciadeutsch.com.

GRAHAM MCNEILL

How did you get into writing tie-ins? I'd been a fan of Warhammer for many years before Games Workshop hired me as a Staff Writer for the Design Studio. I started off writing articles for *White Dwarf* magazine, mostly hobby articles, background pieces for the various factions in the game, and the occasional (very) short story. The readers really responded to them, so I expanded some of the pieces into short stories for Black Library's fiction magazine, *Inferno!* Again, the readers seemed to like them, so the editors asked if I wanted to write a novel and I seized the opportunity with both hands. A second novel soon followed, then a third, and we were off to the races.

What do you like about writing tie-ins? What are the rewards for you? Pretty much all the tie-ins I've done have been in franchises I had already loved for years, so getting to tell stories in those universes are, in many cases, dreams come true. To get to play with the characters, settings, and storylines that enthralled me and take them to new places is tremendously exciting. As to rewards, beyond the getting paid up-front part, it's always great to be part of the communities of fans, as the interactions I've had have been almost universally positive. Doing tie-in writing immediately connects you to fans of the work, and you get to see it impact them very quickly.

What challenges have you faced in your career as a tie-in writer? The most obvious one is becoming intimately familiar with an IP if it's not one you're already a fan of. I'm a quick study, but it's always challenging working with a setting that requires a deeper, nuanced understanding, as there can be a lot of material to catch up on and a lot of established storylines and characters to whom the readers are deeply attached. Mess with a reader's favourite character or write something they don't like or agree with and you'll soon know all about it. Also, the license holders of each property are—rightly—very protective of their IP, and it can be hard to push the envelope if the idea of change or things that stretch what they've done before are too scary for them. Added to that, you can be entering into an already crowded field with a lot of stellar authors having made their mark and trying to find your own voice. That can be doubly difficult because there's often a certain expectation of conventions you might be expected to hit; that characters feel like they're the same as they were previously, while still allowing for character growth and development. That, and you can't just blow up the world or have the stakes so high that the readers absolutely know you're not going to let it happen because the property has to go on beyond your book.

Does writing tie-ins require a different skill set than other types of writing? If so what are these skills? It requires an adaptability and the ability to work in deep collaboration with an editor who knows the IP as well as or better than you do. There are going to be limits on what you can and can't do, and there will be moments where you have to change something you absolutely love because it either doesn't quite work with the IP or someone else is (or has) done something similar to what you're proposing. Tie-in writing requires an open mind and one that's made peace with the idea that you can't always do what you want.

Do you think it's possible to be pigeonholed as a tie-in writer, making it more difficult to publish your own work? If so, how do you deal with this? It absolutely is. I've been called "The Warhammer Writer" though I've written plenty of other stuff, but that's fine. I don't mind that, as I've established a good reputation among that fanbase, so if I can pull them over to other genres, other IPs, or other styles of storytelling, that's all good. I think there is a real perception that you're not a "proper" writer, that you can only do the job if you're leaning on the crutch of someone else's IP and can't do anything original. When the *Horus Heresy* novels from Black Library started appearing on the *New York Times* bestseller lists, folk started taking books from that imprint more seriously. So far, I haven't found it more difficult to publish my own original fiction, as I've hopped genres, IPs, styles so often that prospective editors know I can work without that perceived "crutch."

What advice do you have for writers who want to break into the media tie-in field? So the likelihood is that you're first targeting a property you already love, but perhaps that's not always the case. Read a bunch of the novels in the series, watch the TV show/film and really understand what's at the core of it, what's given it the longevity it has and why readers want more of it. Treat the material seriously and know that you're playing in a field that a huge amount of people absolutely love, so you owe it to them to do the best job you can. Write something in that genre/IP and have a portfolio of work that shows you can write in the voice of the show or IP, that you deeply understand it, and can be trusted not to break it.

GRAHAM MCNEILL hails from Scotland and worked as a games developer and writer for Games Workshop, writing rulebooks, and background lore while developing new ranges for the *Warhammer*, *Warhammer 40K*, and *Lord of the Rings* outfits. After leaving GW, he become a fulltime author, penning novels in the *Warhammer* universes and many others. To date, he's written forty-five novels, four of which went on to become *New York Times* bestsellers, and one that took home the Legend Award for Best Fantasy Novel in 2010. During his eight-and-a-half years as Principal Narrative Writer for Riot Games in Los Angeles, Graham played in all kinds of storytelling spaces: he wrote short stories, cinematic treatments, and scripts, and he directed VO sessions, champ bios, and colour stories. Most recently, he worked in the writer's room for the Emmy Award-winning show *Arcane*. He also wrote a feature adaptation for the rock band, Coheed and Cambria, based on their album *Vaxis: The Unheavenly Creatures*.

CHAPTER FIVE
MY PULSE-POUNDING ADVENTURES IN MEDIA TIE-IN LAND
2017-2019

Resident Evil: The Final Chapter
Titan Books (2017)

I'd always wanted to do a novelization, and when Titan contacted my agent to ask if I'd be interested in writing the novelization of the latest *Resident Evil* movie, I got my chance. I'd seen the previous films in the series and owned them on DVD, so I was well versed in the franchise. I was looking forward to the challenge of bringing a script to life as prose and expanding it into a full-length novel. I had to sign an NDA (non-disclosure agreement), and then Titan mailed a print-out of the script to me. I was surprised they shipped it via mail. What if someone intercepted it along the way? But it arrived safe and sound, and I opened the package, removed the pages, and started reading—

—and I was horrified. The previous film in the franchise ended with the franchise's hero, Alice, standing atop the White House alongside allies and an old foe, as thousands of mutated monstrosities fought to break through the protective barrier around the building to get at them. This was to be the Final Battle against the forces of darkness. Naturally, I expected *The Final Chapter* to begin with that battle. Instead, it began with Alice crawling out of an underground bunker in D.C., the battle over, with none of her companions in sight (and no corpses of defeated mutations anywhere). Plus, in the previous film, Alice had unofficially adopted a young deaf girl named Becky. Their relationship was a core component of that movie, but Becky wasn't around either. And as I continued reading, I discovered she was never mentioned in the script. It was like Becky had never existed. It's not like I'd never encountered a film series where the different installments didn't match one hundred percent, but I'd never seen anything like this. As a fan of the franchise, I was disappointed, and as a writer, I imagined other fans reading my novelization and feeling cheated. The main villain of the films—Albert Wesker—had become something of an ally in the previous installment, but now he was back to being a bad guy, and even worse, he was nowhere near as powerful and important to the plot this time. In fact, he functioned as an assistant to an entirely new villain. I imagined big fan rage over this.

As I read, I made notes on scenes that I could expand and wrote down ideas for new scenes I could add. A film script doesn't contain enough story to fill a whole novel, so you have to find ways to make it bigger. Hence the word *novelize*.

When I finished reading the script, I didn't know what the hell to do about the disconnect between the previous installment and this one, so I decided not to worry about it for the time being. Generally, novelizations are scheduled to come out one week after the film hits theaters, so the book's deadline was set in stone, and I needed to get to work right away. As I've said earlier, no one (except WotC) gives you any material to help you write tie-ins, so I hit the Internet to read interviews with Paul W. S Anderson—the writer, director, and producer of the film—to learn more about the movie, and see if I could discover if there had been any changes to the final film from the script. I searched for every promotional photo I could find from the film so I could better visualize characters, scenes, monsters, locations, etc. There were weapons and vehicles in the script, but few details were given about them, so I searched for photos of these, and when I couldn't identify the exact make and model of equipment, I researched likely equivalents.

Remember when I talked about the cover to my *Defender* novel and how I made sure the story matched the image? I wanted to do the same with the *Resident Evil* book. I wanted my novel to match the finished movie as much as possible. For example, the script had Alice meeting a group of survivors who all had skull tattoos on their faces. I couldn't find a single image online of actors who looked like this, but I found some of Alice talking to people who looked like a group of survivors, but with no facial tattoos. I left the tattoos out of my book, and when I saw the finished film, I discovered my guess was right. (If the script had given an explanation for their skull tattoos—say, the survivors were part of a death cult of some kind—I'd have left them in, because they would've served a story purpose then instead of being meaningless decoration.)

I also checked out the previous novelizations so I could align mine with them as much as possible. That way, readers who read the whole set would get a more coherent—and I hoped richer—experience.

After that, it was time to start writing, and I'd decided on a couple additions/changes to the script. I was going to make Wesker more badass, to keep him more in line with how he was portrayed in the previous films. I also decided to do something risky. I wrote a sixty-page opening sequence that bridged the gap between the two films. I created the big battle that fans were promised but never got, and—since there were no bodies at the beginning of the *Final Chapter*, I came up with a reason for that. I also came up with an explanation for what happened to Becky. I made Alice's feelings as a surrogate mother for Becky part of the overall narrative, and at the end I reunited the two. Since I generally think it's better to ask for forgiveness than permission, I didn't check with the studio to see what they thought about these additions. I just wrote them. As I said, it was a risky move, especially for my first novelization, but I'd written the book so the additions could easily be removed if necessary. (That modular technique again.)

Resident Evil: The Final Chapter was the sixth film in the franchise and, as of this writing, it really is the final one. I did my best to connect my novel to the other books and films as much as possible without clogging the narrative with a bunch of extraneous detail.

I developed a technique for drafting a novelization with this book. First, I typed up all the dialogue in the script, figuring it would definitely go in the book. Then I wrote scenes around the dialogue, using as much of the script's descriptions and imagery as I could. I wanted Anderson's voice to be part of the finished book along with mine. I viewed this process as collaborating with another writer who I'd most likely never meet or talk to. I've used this technique for all five of the novelizations I've done so far, and it's worked well for me.

I don't recall how long it took me to write the book once I started. A month maybe? I sent the book off to my editor, and she sent it to the studio. I waited nervously to hear what everyone thought about the mini movie I'd added to the beginning of the book. My editor liked it and the studio approved the book without comment, and I was relieved. (Well, they had me change *one* small detail. Alice loses a finger in the movie, and they changed which finger in the final film. Why? I don't know.) Fans responded well to the book when it came out, especially the additions I'd made to the story. I created a minor villain for the opening battle, a rival of Wesker's with an Hispanic surname, and a gentleman from Spain contacted me to request an interview. He was thrilled to see a character of Spanish descent in a *Resident Evil* novel, and most of his questions were about her and why I'd decided to make her Hispanic. Don't ever tell me representation doesn't matter.

I also received an email from a reader who was distraught that her favorite franchise character Jill Valentine died in opening battle. I wrote back and told her the book was simply my interpretation of the script, and that events were only canon if they appeared in one of the films. I was tempted to tell her that I couldn't kill Jill Valentine because she wasn't real, but I decided that would be too cruel, even if I meant it as a joke. For whatever reason, Jill Valentine meant a lot to this reader, and I felt I should respect that. Hell, I've lived most of my life dwelling in my own imagination. I know how important unreal things can be to a person. Sometimes they're all we have, and sometimes they save us when nothing else can.

Seeing the final film was a weird experience. The scenes seemed to fly by at superspeed, and I realized it was because I had gone slow when writing them and I'd expanded them. The actual scenes were much more focused and compressed. It was also bizarre seeing the visuals since I'd imagined the scenes on my own, and the finished result didn't match exactly with what I'd imagined. I found myself thinking, *So that's what that looks like*, more than once. I had to guess at a lot of the action since it wasn't spelled out in the script, and the characters' specific moves were somewhat different in the film. The biggest surprise to me was that the script contained lots of interaction between characters along with the action, and it had a strong emotional core. All of that had been stripped from the film, and I realized it was to make more room for the action. Every script I've novelized had scenes like that which were removed. (Except *Terrifier 2*. Every bit of that script, including important character moments, appears in the finished film.) After this, I've never complained about action films being all plot with little-to-no characterization. The scriptwriters include that material, but it doesn't make it to the screen. (That would drive me insane if I as scriptwriter. Good thing I only like writing prose.)

A couple other things happened to me when I saw the movie. Receiving the script before the film came out was cool. I was one of the few people on Earth who knew what was going to happen in the movie. Fans are desperate to get the scoop on upcoming movies, and they fill social media with speculation and rumor. I felt special, like I had a secret I couldn't share with anyone. But when the film was released, I realized what I'd known hadn't really been special. Eventually, everyone knew what I'd known. The world had caught up to me.

The other thing that happened was that I couldn't enjoy the film as an audience member. Writing the novelization had been the ultimate spoiler. Giving up the normal enjoyment of watching a film in order to write the novelization was totally worth it, though. I got to interact with the film in a way few people ever get to, and that was extremely cool.

Lessons?

- **I taught myself how to turn a script into a novel.** This was huge. Not only did it enhance my skillset as a writer, it opened up new possibilities in my tie-in career.
- **I learned that sometimes you gamble and win.** And many fans appreciated my additions to the story.
- **I no longer complain about action films lacking characterization**. Or any type of film for that matter—and I have a lot more respect and sympathy for screenwriters.
- **No matter what I do, I can never fully recreate a film I haven't seen yet for a novelization.** My job is to write a book *based* on the script, almost as if I was directing my own version of the film. It's not only okay if they don't match completely, it's a good thing. This way, readers get a richer experience of the overall story, kind of like watching the extra features on a DVD.
- **I got a reminder of how important even supporting characters can be to audience members**. Every character is someone's favorite when you write a tie-in, so it's important to write each and every character as well as you can.

xXx: The Return of Xander Cage
Titan Books (2017)

For whatever reason, Titan asked me to do a total of three novelizations in a row, and this one was second. I'd watched the first two *xXx* movies, so I knew the franchise well. I approached the writing of the book the same way I had last time—reading through the script, jotting down ideas for expansion, typing up the dialogue, researching the film on the Internet, looking for pre-release images, and trying to get the details of all the weapons and vehicles in the script correct. This took some work, since no specific details were given about them, and I found myself researching things like powerboats and motorcycles that can ride on water (which I was surprised to discover were a real thing!). The main plot is that bad guys are using super hi-tech to pull satellites from the sky and drop them on specific targets, specifically people they want to kill. The script's opening scene had a satellite in an orbit ten miles above the surface of the Earth. I had a feeling that was way too low, and my research confirmed it. I also needed to research how big a satellite would have to be not to burn up in reentry so there would be enough left to still hit and kill someone. After that, I double-checked all the technical information the script provided, and if it wasn't accurate, I fixed it. (No way in hell I wanted to get emails from readers haranguing me for not knowing how far above Earth satellites orbit.)

I didn't get sent the script. I had to access it on the studio's computer system via a password. Like the previous script, this one contained a number of character-centered scenes and the story had an emotional core, all of which never appeared in the final film. This time when I included such scenes, I knew readers would get something from my novel that they couldn't get from the film. This script spelled out the action scenes in more specific detail, which made them easier to write than the ones in *Resident Evil: The Final Chapter.*

I needed to add material to flesh out the script, of course. This was the third film in the franchise, but Xander Cage didn't appear in the second. That was called *xXx: State of the Union*, and the main character was Darius Stone, played by Ice Cube. Darius made an appearance late in the script, and there was a hint that he and Xander knew each other. So I decided to write a flashback scene showing how the two of them met. I had them dealing with a riot in Detroit caused by a drug that turned its users into homicidally violent maniacs. (Basically, I put them in a zombie apocalypse scenario. Maybe *Resident Evil* was still fresh in my mind.) This was one of the biggest gambles I took when writing the book.

The other gamble—not that I realized it as such at the time—was that when I wrote scenes from Xander's point of view, I depicted him as thinking and strategizing during some action scenes, using a combination of his brain, his instincts, and his reflexes.

But writing this book was different than any other I've ever done. For one thing, it had an *extremely* short deadline. I write fast, but I knew it would be a challenge to finish the book in time. And to make things even more difficult, I was scheduled to be a guest at a convention in Barbados during the time when I was supposed to be writing the book. I was invited to the con because of the *Supernatural* books I'd written, so there's another example of how writing media tie-ins can open doors for you. This was going to be my first trip out of the country (if you don't count one afternoon visiting the Canadian side of Niagara Falls when I was nineteen), and my wife was going to come with me. I wasn't about to cancel the trip and let down the con organizers, nor was I going to bail on the novelization. The deadline was so short my editor might not have been able to find another writer in time.

The plan was to go to Barbados for a week, attend the con, then I would fly home while my wife stayed an extra week to explore the island. Her mother had recently died, and she wanted some alone time to think and grieve. I was worried about leaving her. Not because she would be on her own in another country. She's lived in Australia and New Zealand and is way more experienced as a traveler than I'll ever be. (In general, she's far more competent at everything than I am.) I was worried about how she'd be emotionally while I was gone. My college's fall semester was beginning as well, so I had to return. My wife and I checked in with each other every day, and overall, her extra week in Barbados was a good one for her. She got to swim with sea turtles, which was a highlight for her.

I, on the other hand, had about a week the write my book.

I wrote every free moment I had, I drank copious amounts of coffee around the clock, and I slept as little as I could get away with. Toward the end, I got so loopy that I considered adding an "after-the-credits" scene to the ending where Vin Diesel's SF/action character Riddick lands on Earth in a spaceship to seek Xander Cage's help. Luckily, I recognized this as a gamble that was definitely *not* worth taking. I finished the book right on the deadline, but I needed another day to proofread it. I emailed my editor to ask for a one-day extension, but the deadline to get the book into production was so tight, she told me to send the file to her and she'd proofread it as she edited it. I sent her the book and got some much-needed sleep.

Within a few days, we had the studio's feedback. They wanted me to remove the sequence in Detroit. Sometimes you gamble and lose. They also wanted me to remove every instance where Xander thought anything. "He's a man of action," they said. "He doesn't think."

Remember, license holders are the boss when it comes to tie-ins, so I removed all the material the studio requested. I cut around 10K words in all, and a novel which was supposed to 80K words was now considerably shorter (and, in my opinion, not as good). I wasn't sure Titan would publish the book at that length, but there wasn't much time for me to add anything more, so they put the novel into production, and it came out on time.

As usual, I learned a few things from writing this book:

- **I can write a book in a week, but I probably shouldn't.** Not if I want to stay healthy and sane, anyway.
- **I love Barbados!**
- **Always doublecheck technical info.**
- **Never write a bizarre after-credits scene when you're sleep-deprived.**

Kingsman: The Golden Circle
Titan Books (2017)

The third book in my novelization trifecta was the sequel to *Kingsman*. I'd seen the original film and loved it, so I was really looking forward to writing this book. This time the studio emailed me a copy of the script. The deadline for this novel wasn't so bad, maybe a couple months, and I got to work, following what by now had become my normal novelization process. As with the last two scripts, there were character-based scenes, and I wondered how many of them would eventually be cut from the finished film. (Would you believe all of them?) The writing went smoothly, and I submitted my draft to the editor, feeling pretty good about the job I'd done.

Until the editor emailed me to ask what the hell I'd done to the story. It was vastly different from the script the studio had given her. We realized immediately what had happened—the studio sent each of us a different version of the script. The editor emailed me her version, and I read it, comparing it to mine.

It was *significantly* different. No wonder my editor had a mini freakout when she saw my draft. I had no idea what to do, so I shrugged and decided to add the parts I liked from this new script to my novel and create a combined version.

When I finished this second draft, my editor emailed to tell me that the film's director, Matthew Vaughn, wanted me to come to L. A. and watch a near-final cut of the film so I could make sure the novelization and film matched. I was in shock. The most common question novelization authors get from people is if the studio lets us see an advanced screener of the film. They do not. People also sometimes ask if writers are flown to Hollywood to see the film before it's released. We are not. This is literally the one thing that *never-ever-ever* happens in the process of writing a novelization. But it was happening to me.

Titan Books paid for my flight and an overnight stay at a hotel close to Fox Studios. (This was before Disney gobbled up their TV and film divisions.) I live in southwestern Ohio, and I needed to get up super early to catch my flight, so I got maybe four hours of sleep. It wasn't a direct flight (of course), and by the time I reached the hotel, it was around 2 pm PST but 5pm by my biological clock. I was scheduled to meet the head of licensing at Fox, Steve Tzirlin, in a few hours, so rather than hang out in the hotel room, I grabbed my leather satchel with my notebook and pens, found Fox Studios on MapQuest, and set out. It took me maybe twenty minutes to get there, and I had the sidewalk all to myself. Like a famous 80s song says, no one walks in L.A. When I reached Fox Plaza, I had a big grin on my face. The building had been used as Nakatomi Plaza in *Die Hard* (in exterior shots, anyway), and I could almost imagine seeing Hans Gruber falling off the roof.

I went inside. The lobby was small, just a couple narrow hallways, with a single security guard standing watch over twelve elevators in the middle. I continued past and out the other side to take some pictures, then I went back in and went into the ground-floor café. I got a coffee, took a seat, and watched. I saw a lot of bearded, slightly disheveled men with leather satchels like mine come in, and I guessed they were scriptwriters who'd come to pitch film ideas to a producer. I also saw a lot of young men and women in nice business attire come down to collect orders of coffee and food (often quite large ones), and I guessed they were assistants or interns that had been sent to play fetch for their bosses. I overheard some conversations taking place near me, mostly about film-related stuff. And as I sat there and sipped my coffee, I realized this place—which at first had seemed like something out of a dream—was just a place where people worked. They did very cool work here, of course, but work nonetheless.

I'd called Steve when I got to the building, and after a couple hours, he called me and told me to come up to his office. I headed up and met Steve in person. Since this was the licensing office, they had all kinds of awesome toys, mugs, apparel, and books related to Fox IPs. Steve told me I could have as many goodies to take home as I wanted. I didn't want to be greedy (and I was mindful of carrying a bunch of extra stuff with me on my flight home). I took a *Bob's Burgers* mug, a *Predator* action figure, an *Alien* figure, and a Bart Simpson canvas bag. Then Steve led me onto the studio lot to a small screening room. It was Friday, and no one was around except the projectionist who was going to run the film for us. Steve and I took seats and the movie started.

One thing I haven't told you—I wasn't allowed to bring a computer into the screening room with me. I was only permitted to write in a notebook. The director had also insisted that I get everything down. I mean *everything*. Every. Damn. Detail. Every event, every bit of scenery, every word of dialogue. The projectionist had to stop the film every minute or so (and sometimes rewind and replay stuff if necessary), I would write in my notebook as fast as I possibly could, and then we'd watch another minute of film, wash, rinse, and repeat. It took six hours to get through that movie, and the story was different in many significant ways from either of the two scripts I'd seen. By the time we were finished, I'd been up for twenty hours, and I was exhausted. I'd planned to walk back to my hotel, but Steve gave me a ride. I went to my room, set my alarm for early in the morning so I could catch my flight home, and I crashed hard.

I felt much better in the morning—until I realized I'd left my satchel and notebook in Steve's car last night. I texted him and hoped he'd wake up in time to get the message. I was outside the hotel, waiting for my cab, when Steve pulled up in his car and handed me my satchel. I thanked him profusely, my cab came, and I got the hell out of L. A.

When I returned home, I had a dilemma on my hands. I had three different versions of the movie to work with. What exactly should I put in the damn book? I shrugged, said screw it, and wrote the third draft using my favorite bits from each version of the film. I finished the book, my editor liked it, Steve approved it, and this adventure finally came to an end.

Lessons learned:

- **When you think something will *never* happen in the tie-in business, it still might happen.** Like a surprise trip to a movie studio.
- **Even when you've been writing tie-in fiction for a while, and you think you know how the process works, you should still expect the unexpected.** What's the difference between a beginner and a pro? Beginners don't know shit while pros *know* they don't know shit.
- **You need to use as much creativity in how you manage tie-in projects as you do writing them.** Sometimes more.
- **You've got to go with the flow, baby.** And sometimes this means you end up doing a lot more work on some projects than others—without getting paid extra. C'est la vie.

Alien: Prototype
Titan Books (2019)

I first met editor Steve Saffel at a convention in 2000. I told him I was a creative writing teacher as well as a writer myself, and I asked what he thought my students should know about the current publishing landscape. We had a great conversation, and Steve gave me some good info to pass along to my students. I doubt he remembers our meeting then, but over the years we interacted at various events as well as online and became friends. When Steve started editing tie-in books for Titan, he asked if I'd be interested in writing an *Alien* or *Predator* novel, and of course I said yes. A few years went by, and eventually a slot opened up and we were able to work together on an *Alien* project. Disney was in the process of acquiring Fox by this point, so I have no idea who the exact license holder was at that time. Whoever it was wanted to more closely link the various *Alien* media—games, comics, novels—so my novel would feature a character from the comics, former Colonial Marine Zula Hendricks, and it would link to a novel Keith DeCandido was writing called *Alien: Isolation*, which was based on a video game and featured Ellen Ripley's daughter Amanda. Isn't corporate synergy beautiful?

The situation reminded me of how *Dark Ages: Gangrel* was part of a thirteen-book series, and the project sounded *way* less complicated than that, so I wasn't worried about that aspect.

Steve is an editor who likes to be involved in the creative process, helping writers to generate ideas and coaching them along the way. Not every writer would like such a hands-on editor, but I found the process very useful—especially a tie-in novel that was supposed to connect to other books/comics/games. Steve never said, *Here's what I want you to write.* He worked to help *me* write the best book I *could.* Remember when I talked about self-focused feedback vs writer-focused feedback earlier? All of Steve's guidance was writer-focused.

The big problem with *Alien* media—at least as I see it—is that the xenomorphs are always the same. The embryo-implanter hatches from an egg, injects the embryo into a host, the host dies when the infant xenomorph bursts out of their chest, the xenomorph rapidly reaches adulthood and tries to kill every living thing it comes in contact with. It's hard to avoid repetition with a rigid story structure like that, especially when xenomorphs are more like biological machines than sentient beings.

Zula was a wonderful character to work with. She'd failed her squad on her first mission, suffered a severe back injury, and was discharged from the Colonial Marines. She was disgraced, disabled (although healing slowly), and self-doubting. There was lots of rich territory to explore there. Her companion was a Synth named Davis who at this point was only an artificial consciousness without a body. I liked the dynamic between the two characters, and I thought it would be a fun challenge to find ways for Davis to help Zula without a physical form.

Corporate machinations are a huge part of the *Alien* universe, but I didn't want to write about Weyland-Yutani. I wanted to invent a rival corporation that was trying everything it could to unseat Weyland-Yutani as the greatest power in the galaxy. Plus, if the corporation in the book was my invention, I could do whatever I wanted with it without affecting canon. I decided to call the rival corporation Venture, and I gave them a specialty to avoid the cliché of a shadowy evil corporate entity without a defined purpose. Venture specialized in creating and selling equipment for space colonization. I figured there would be a lot of corporate espionage in the *Alien* universe, so I gave Venture an ulterior motive: to get hold of an ovamorph so they could have their very own xenomorph to study and exploit, hopefully making them more powerful than Weyland-Yutani.

Steve came up with the title *Prototype* because Venture hoped their xenomorph would be the first of many.

I wanted my xenomorph to be different. When writing a tie-in, it's important to find a different slant on the IP, one that doesn't violate canon but which will make your story stand out from others. In the movies, it's established that xenomorphs can take on the genetic characters of the bodies they hatch from, so I wondered what would happen if a xenomorph was born from the body of a person with a deadly disease. This idea became the necromorph—a xenomorph that contracted cellular necrosis (a space disease I made up) from its host. The necromorph had rock-hard lesions over its body which made it more resistant to weapons fire, it could cough a cloud of black disease-spreading gas, and it sprayed liquid that caused immediate cellular breakdown.

I then put these elements together. The necromorph rampages through a domed planetary settlement (a Venture prototype itself), and Zula—unable to find any other work—is head of security for the installation and, along with her staff, must stop the necromorph. And she's determined to do this without losing any people, as she did on her first Marine mission.

Steve worked with me on getting the outline into shape, and when we sent it to the license holder, it was approved. I wrote the book, and because of all the preparation Steve and I did, little revision was required. (The two best words a writer can hear—after *check enclosed*—are *light edit*.)

One of the things I always do, whether I'm writing tie-in or original fiction, is check the Internet to make sure a term I invented hasn't been used before. (I check short story and novel titles on Amazon for the same reason. Titles can't be copyrighted, but I prefer mine to be original, if possible.) I could've sworn I ran *necromorph* through Google without finding anything, but when the book came out, readers pointed out that *necromorph* is the name of a type of monster in the videogame Dead Space. So maybe I only thought I'd checked out the name? If I ever get to write a sequel to *Prototype*, I'll give my necromorph a new name to differentiate it from the ones in Dead Space.

By this point in my career, I was used to keeping fans in mind while at the same time forgetting them, so I didn't feel much pressure working with a beloved property like *Alien*. I was fifteen when the original film came out in 1979, and I remember reading a review of the film in the local newspaper. (Kids, if you don't know what a newspaper is, ask your grandparents.) That kid would never have believed that he'd get to write an *Alien* novel one day.

So what did writing *Alien: Prototype* teach me?

- **Doublecheck your invented terms so you can avoid embarrassing mistakes.** (And the rage that might follow from Dead Space fans).
- **Working with a collaborative, experienced editor is very different than working with a collaborative, inexperienced editor who'd rather be a writer.** I think this one's self-explanatory, don't you?
- **Although the *Alien* franchise is more horror/adventure than science fiction, I wanted to get the science right—without bogging down the story with a lot of extraneous detail.** People read tie-in novels for entertainment, and when it comes to background, history, technical information,

exposition, etc., they should be kept to a minimum and presented only when integral to the story. This is generally true of any fiction with a primary goal of entertaining the reader.

EXERCISES

1. Pick a favorite movie of yours. Watch it and make notes about scenes that could be expanded or places within the story where new scenes could be added. Write some notes about what new scenes you'd create if you were writing the novelization.
2. Use my necromorph to practice inventing terms for tie-in fiction. Let's say you're me, and you received a note from the license holder that you have to change the name because it's used in Dead Space. Come up with five alternatives that communicate the idea of deadly plague-spreading monster.

VOICES FROM THE TRENCHES

BEV VINCENT

How did you get into writing tie-ins? I'm not particularly known for writing tie-ins, but I have written two short stories for tie-in anthologies—one for *Doctor Who* and another for *The X-Files*. In both cases, I responded to calls that required first pitching a story in a few sentences and then, once approved, writing the short story. It was a matter of being in the right place at the right time or knowing the editor so I was aware of the project when it was first announced. These opportunities don't happen often and are usually quite competitive.

What do you like about writing tie-ins? What are the rewards for you? For me, it's all about getting to play in someone else's sandbox for a while. I was a fan of both properties before pitching stories, and the idea that I could contribute something to those universes was quite exciting. I mean, who wouldn't want to write a *Doctor Who* story or relate an unknown adventure featuring Scully and Mulder? I guess you could call this a tie-in, too: I was recently invited to write a story set in the world of Stephen King's *The Stand*. That was another pinch-me gig!

What challenges have you faced in your career as a tie-in writer? The biggest challenge is finding out about the opportunities out there, because I don't always have my ear to the ground. Being a member of IAMTW (International Association of Media Tie-In Writers) helps because there are occasional calls for story pitches on that message board. One downside of writing a tie-in is that you generally don't own the rights to the finished story, so you can never reprint it somewhere else—even in a collection of your short stories.

Does writing tie-ins require a different skill set than other types of writing? If so, what are these skills? Both stories I've published required a significant amount of research. The core ideas for the stories came fairly quickly, but then it was a matter of getting the details right. Unlike a non-tie-in story, you can't just make everything up. I watched many hours of television episodes to nail down the details of the respective universes. You don't want to create discontinuities or go against the canon of the property. Your characters must be in character, or else you have to come up with a reason why they aren't. Especially if you are writing stories set in the middle of an existing series, you can't interfere with the timeline of what happens next.

Do you think it's possible to be pigeonholed as a tie-in writer, making it more difficult to publish your own work? If so, how do you deal with this? I haven't done enough of this kind of work for it to be an issue. I would write more tie-in stories if the opportunity arose, but it hasn't yet.

What advice do you have for writers who want to break into the media tie-in field? I honestly don't know how you break into the field. I think one thing that is helpful is to establish a reputation as someone who can deliver on schedule. Projects like these often run at an accelerated pace and the ability to hit all the benchmarks is important. Editors will remember people who make their lives easier. Equally, they will remember authors who make things difficult!

BEV VINCENT is the author of several nonfiction books, including *The Road to the Dark Tower* and *Stephen King: A Complete Exploration of His Work, Life, and Influences*. He co-edited the anthology *Flight or Fright* with King and has published over 130 stories, with appearances in *Cemetery Dance, Doctor Who: Destination Prague, The Truth is Out There, Ellery Queen's, Alfred Hitchcock's,* and *Black Cat Mystery Magazines*. His work has been published in over twenty languages and nominated for the Stoker (twice), Edgar, Locus, Ignotus, Rondo Hatton Classic Horror, and ITW Thriller Awards. To learn more, visit bevvincent.com.

BOBBY NASH

How did you get into writing tie-ins? After doing a few stories for Moonstone anthologies, I was invited to do a story for *The Green Hornet Casefiles*. That was my first professional attempt at doing a tie-in.

What do you like about writing tie-ins? What are the rewards for you? There's a lot of fun to be had playing with the characters I grew up reading and watching. From a creative standpoint, fun is always a nice bonus. From a business perspective, tie-ins tend to come with a built-in audience. There are readers who might never have read my stuff otherwise. The hope is, if they like what they read, they might pick up some of my other books.

What challenges have you faced in your career as a tie-in writer? I don't have a literary agent. Not from lack of trying. Just haven't connected with the right one. That has limited some of the tie-in options open to me. The other challenge is one I put on myself to make sure I get it right. The characters have to sound right, act right, move right. Tie-in audiences are fans of the property. They will notice if you get it wrong.

Does writing tie-ins require a different skill set than other types of writing? If so what are these skills? In terms of writing the story, not really. I still write like me. The biggest difference is in knowing what stories you can tell. Writing tie-ins is not the same thing as writing fan fiction. There are rules. Usually, a lot of them. Things you can and can't do. I run into people all the time who ask why I don't just (fill in the blank), which is usually a story that we can't tell. You can't cut off Spider-Man's arm unless it can grow back by the end of the story. You can't kill Spock unless he's alive again at the end of the story. Based on experience, I know what type of stories I can and cannot pitch.

Do you think it's possible to be pigeonholed as a tie-in writer, making it more difficult to publish your own work? If so, how do you deal with this? Maybe. I see a lot of writers who do non-tie-in work, but some do nothing but tie-ins. It could be by choice, or you could become pigeonholed. I'm pretty low on the list for that to have impacted me yet.

What advice do you have for writers who want to break into the media tie-in field? As with everything, be professional. Yes, you're wanting to write this character you've loved forever and it's exciting, but it's still a business. Meet your deadlines. Follow the story bible guidelines. Most importantly, have fun. Just be aware that it's not always easy to get into writing tie-ins. Most writers do not start their career doing tie-ins. Do work that gets you noticed.

BOBBY NASH is not a man of action or a hero. He is, however, an award-winning author who pens novels, comic books, short stories, screenplays, audio dramas, and more. Nash is a member of the International Association of Media Tie-in Writers, International Thriller Writers, and Southeastern Writers Association. On occasion, he acts, appearing in movies and TV shows, usually standing behind or beside your favorite actor, but sometimes they even let him speak. Scary. We know. For more information on Nash and his work, please visit him at bobbynash.com

SCOTT SIGLER

How did you get into writing tie-ins? I blame Jonathan Maberry. He knew of my love for the *Alien* franchise and garnered me an invite to write a story in *Aliens: Bug Hunt*, called "Dangerous Prey." It's the first story from the xenomorph point of view. I'm really proud of it and very grateful to Jonathan for connecting me to the world of tie-ins.

What do you like about writing tie-ins? What are the rewards for you? I had the honor of writing a canonical novel in my all-time favorite fictional universe. To see my name on the cover of *Aliens: Phalanx* is a huge honor, a drop in the bucket list I didn't know I had. I've watched *Aliens* well over 100 times and it's my all-time favorite film. I saw the film in the theater when I was 17—my 17-year-old self couldn't have imagined being part of that lore.

What I like about it most is the challenge of directly connecting to the primary property in the franchise. When I write for *Aliens*, I'm obsessed with finding a new story to tell which perfectly matches the biological structures laid down in the first two films. It's not easy, as the property has been revisited many times, and the backstory has changed over and over again. I write love letters to the original fan base, because I'm one of them. Same thing for my work with *Predator*—I want those who adore the first two movies to feel like my work fits in perfectly, before the big changes that, by necessity, come with every multi-decade franchise.

Does writing tie-ins require a different skill set than other types of writing? If so what are these skills? A great story is a great story. The only real difference for me is the in-depth study of someone else's work, and applying my particular style in a way that fits the originator's vision. My work with *Aliens* and *Predator* ties in seamlessly with those properties, and yet at the same time, my particular style is obvious and prevalent. Fans of my scifi/horror work feel right at home even though I didn't create the original properties.

What advice do you have for writers who want to break into the media tie-in field? I have none. After *Aliens: Phalanx*, I'm out of the tie-in biz save for when I'm invited to write a short story.

SCOTT SIGLER is a #1 *New York Times* bestselling author and the creator of eighteen novels, six novellas, dozens of short stories, and thousands of podcast episodes. An inaugural inductee into the Podcasting Hall of Fame, Sigler began his career by narrating his unabridged audiobooks and serializing them in weekly installments. He continues to release free episodes every Sunday. Launched in March of 2005, "Scott Sigler Slices" is the world's longest-running fiction podcast. His rabid fans fervently anticipate their weekly story fix, so much so that they've dubbed themselves "Sigler Junkies" and have downloaded over 50 million episodes. Subscribe to the free podcast at scottsigler.com/subscribe.

CHAPTER SIX
MY PULSE-POUNDING ADVENTURES IN MEDIA TIE-IN LAND
2021-2024

Halloween Kills
Titan Books (2021)

It had been a few years since my last novelization, and I was beginning to wonder if I'd ever get the chance to write another. So when the good people at Titan got in touch to ask if I'd like to write the novelization of *Halloween Kills*, I was doubly excited. Once for having the opportunity to write another novelization, and twice (and more importantly) I was going to get to write about Michael Fucking Myers! The original *Halloween* is one of my favorite movies of all time, and I've probably watched it more times than any other. I was mesmerized when I saw it in the theater during its original run, and aside from *Psycho*, it was the first slasher film I'd ever seen, and forever after I'd measure all others against it. (Plus, I'd already written about Freddy Krueger and *Alien*, and now I'd get to add Michael to the list of horror icons I've been lucky enough to work with.)

I was given access to the script on the studio's computer system via password. What I didn't know was that the password was only good for three days, then I had to request a new one. The first time I couldn't access the script, I almost had a full-blown panic attack! I followed the same basic process I've already established in this book—reading the script, looking for areas where I could expand, coming up with ideas for new scenes I could add, typing the dialogue, looking for promotional photos on the Internet, reading articles in which the director discussed the themes of the film, then beginning to write the book.

I've seen all the *Halloween* films, and some I like better than others. I was lukewarm about *Halloween* 2018 for a number of reasons, but the biggest was that the filmmakers had gotten rid of the idea that Michael and Laurie were siblings. When I first heard of this change, I thought, *Great. Remove the emotional core of the franchise, the one aspect that makes it different from all other slasher films. That's a smart move.* And when I read the script for *Halloween Kills*, I was puzzled, because while Michael and Laurie still weren't siblings, they seemed to have more of a connection in this film. There were also some hints here and there that Michael might be supernatural, at least a little, but they were only hints.

As I did with *Resident Evil: The Final Chapter*, I read the novelization of the previous film (written by John Passarella) so I could make the two books connect as much as possible. That way, readers who read his book and then read mine would (hopefully) have a richer reading experience. If there were details that didn't match—in John's book the Myers house burned down years ago, in mine it had been sold and renovated by a couple—I tried to find ways to reconcile them. In my book, I say there are rumors that the house burned down years ago, but in truth it didn't. Do I have to take this kind of care when writing a novelization? No. I doubt many people noticed what I'd done. But I want my books to be the very best I can make them, whether they're original or tie-ins.

The biggest—and most fun—challenge for me was trying to figure out how to write from Michael's point of view and still preserve the mystery of what goes on in his mind (if anything). I thought of the way I'd written from the necromorph's point of view in *Alien: Protégé*, and I did the same sort of thing for Michael, focusing on the most basic of surface level thoughts and having him act primarily from some unknown instinct. I thought of him as a two-legged land shark—cold, inhuman, implacable, and enigmatic. Based on the reviews, most readers seem to think I did a good job writing from the point of view of a character who appears not to be sentient enough to *have* a point of view.

To further help me capture Michael's character, I snagged a (probably bootleg) PDF of Dennis Etchison's novelization of *Halloween II*. Dennis is one of my absolute favorite writers, and I have his novelizations of *The Fog* and *Videodrome*. But physical copies of *Halloween 2* are very expensive, so while I do not condone pirating media, in this case the artist in me triumphed over the ethicist. When Dennis wrote from Michael's point of view, he referred to him as the Shape, and so had John in his novelization of *Halloween* 2018. I'd never been a fan of this alternate name for Michael, but now I thought it worked well to help make Michael's viewpoint more unusual, distant, and creepy.

I don't usually tinker with the dialogue of a script much when I write a novelization, but some of the dialogue in *Halloween Kills* was repetitive, especially on the page and not spoken by a skilled actor. For example, a good actor can speak a piece of dialogue like, "No, no, no," and give each *no* a different cadence and emotional heft, in ways that are impossible to achieve in pure prose. So I trimmed sentences like this down to one "No," and I thought they worked better in the novel.

Early in the film, Michael escapes a burning house, and I had to research how hot housefires burn, and come up with ways Michael could survive (without protective gear) long enough to actually get outside. The character of Michael Myers exists in a liminal state between real and supernatural. He's at once both and neither. (He's basically Schrödinger's Slasher.) So as unlikely as it is that he could've survived the fire, I found ways to make it (barely) possible.

I wrote the book in March of 2020. COVID-19 was just beginning to really get going, and classes at the college where I teach were cancelled for a month while the administration tried to figure out what the hell to do. My wife and I actually came down with COVID at this time. There were no diagnostic tests yet, but weeks later we both took antibody tests once they were available to see if we really did have COVID, and the tests confirmed it.

The book had a short deadline (as novelizations tend to do), and I was sick as a dog. I usually enjoy good health, and if I get a cold, it's only bad for a day or so. Our doctor told us how to take care of ourselves. My wife has lung issues, and she has a small machine so she can take breathing treatments when she needs them. Our doctor told us both to use the machine as often as we needed, and I think that's what kept our conditions from worsening. Remember that novelizations are timed to come out one week after a film's release, and there was no wiggle room in the deadline. I couldn't ask for an extension because I was sick. Besides, I was miserable and bored. Why not write?

Years ago, I read a book by Brenda Ueland called *If You Want to Write*. In it, she talks about how writers can heal themselves through their work. I figured this was a perfect opportunity to put that principle into action.

I wrote every waking moment when I wasn't taking a breathing treatment. Most of the time I felt feverish and weak, but I kept going. Living inside the story of *Halloween Kills* kept my mind from focusing on my physical condition, and the words poured out of me onto the screen. I honestly don't remember how long it took me to finish the book. One week? Two? Certainly no longer than that. Despite being sick, I had a great time writing the book, especially adding some of my own scenes and adding deeper characterization in existing scenes. Because the script gave a nod to *Halloween III: Season of the Witch*, I thought it would be fun to throw in some other Easter eggs. My two favorites are the delivery guy from White Horse Pizza (a reference to Rob Zombie's *Halloween II*) and giving Tommy Doyle a Cult of Thorn tattoo on his wrist. The Cult of Thorn is a story element in *Halloween* 4, 5, and 6, and fans have mixed feelings about it, to say the least. I thought for sure the studio would make me take out that detail, but they didn't. It was great fun watching fans debate online about what the significance of the tattoo was. (The only significance was that adding it to the story made me laugh maniacally.)

Once the book was finished, the studio reviewed it, and the only significant revision they requested was to restore every line of dialogue I changed to what was in script. As I mentioned before, much of the dialogue was weirdly repetitious, and occasionally it was unclear or didn't make sense, so I fixed it. But—everyone say it with me now—the license holder is boss. I did what they wanted and the book was approved.

Up to this point, the studio hadn't announced there would be a novelization, let alone that I was the author. They finally did announce that there would be a book of *Halloween Kills*, but they still didn't mention I was the author. And then the movie's release got bumped back a year because of COVID. The studio said nothing more about the book, and I had to keep my mouth shut for an entire year about writing it. I did enjoy reading fan theories about the film over the course of that year, though. I was like, *Nope. That's wrong. So's that. That's waaaaay the fuck wrong.*

But the year passed, I was announced as the author, and the movie came out.

Within hours of the first showing, it seemed, people were making fun of "Evil dies tonight!" and there was a lot of negative reaction to the level of violence in the film. It's always weird when you write a novelization and then people don't react as positively to the movie as you hoped. You didn't write the movie, of course, but it feels like people won't give your book a chance if they dislike the film it's based on.

Fortunately, readers in general really liked the book, and because I was able to expand certain parts of the story, some even thought the book was better than the movie, which was a nice compliment.

I asked my editor at Titan if I could write the novelization for *Halloween Ends*, but she said the producers had insisted on a particular writer, and that's who they had to go with. The author in question was Paul Brad Logan, one of the film's screenwriters. At first, I wondered if the studio hated my book so much, they wouldn't let anyone but Paul write it. But once it came out, I understood why Paul had to write it. He wanted to detail what Michael was up to during the interval between *Kills* and *Ends*, and because of that he was the perfect person to write the book.

Evil may die tonight, but the lessons I learned from writing *Halloween Kills* will live forever:

- **Think twice before changing too much dialogue in a script.** Did the screenwriters read my book and were displeased when they saw I altered some of their dialogue? Who knows? But it was a good reminder to respect the original film when writing a novelization.
- **Maybe Brenda Ueland was on to something.** Do I think I was literally healed by work? More likely I healed while I was working, and working kept my mind off how cruddy I felt. But the mind-body connection is a real thing, so maybe it's possible. I don't really care exactly *why* it works, just so long as it *does* work.
- **You shouldn't become emotionally invested in the success of the IP your book is based on.** Whether you're writing a novelization or an original story tie-in, you need to keep your work separate from the source material. You were hired to do a job, you did it to the best of your ability, you're (hopefully) proud of what you produced and there will be people who read and enjoy it. And the check you got for writing the novel cleared. What more could a writer want? And unless you're one of the lucky few who manage to get royalties for your tie-ins, whether the source material is a raging success or a disappointing flop will have no economic consequences for you.
- **NDA's have to be honored.** I knew I couldn't tell anyone (okay, *maybe* I told my immediate family members) that I was writing *Halloween Kills*. All news about the movie—including that I was writing the novelization—was the studio's to announce, and once the movie's release was delayed a year, I had to keep my mouth shut about writing the novelization until such time as the studio decided to reveal that I was the author. If I had told the world about my involvement with the project before COVID hit America, I'd have had to deal with fans constantly emailing to ask me to divulge the movie's plot details. It would've been an absolute nightmare.

Planet Havoc: A Zombicide Invader Novel
Aconyte Books (2022)

Marc Gascoigne was the publisher at Black Library when I wrote my *A Nightmare on Elm Street* novel. He left to form Angry Robot Books, and because we'd worked together on *NOES: Protégé*, he got in touch and asked if I had anything original to submit to his new publishing house. That's how my *Nekropolis* series was born. Marc eventually moved on to create a tie-in publishing company called Aconyte Books. They specialize in tie-ins based on games and Marvel Comics properties. I loved working with Marc, so I reached out and asked him if he had any licenses he'd like me to write for. He did! The first was a zombie game, but after I wrote an outline for a book, the company decided to kill the project. I never found out why. Marc then had me try some proposals for Marvel characters. Aconyte had acquired a license to publish books on Marvel heroes that aren't exactly household names. Midnight Sons was one of those properties, but Marvel withdrew Blade (one of the Midnight Sons) because of the forthcoming Blade movie. Then I got to try Elsa Bloodstone, and the same thing happened, maybe because the character was slated to appear in the *Werewolf by Night* TV special. So then I got the opportunity to come up with an outline for a book featuring Man-Wolf (whose human self is J. Jonah Jameson's astronaut son John Jameson). That didn't work out either. None of this was Aconyte's fault. With so many Marvel movies and TV shows coming out, a lot of characters were being suddenly deemed off limits for tie-ins just in case they might be needed for other media.

My agent started to get concerned at this point. I'd been writing multiple proposals (and revising them) for Aconyte without getting any contracts. I'd done a lot of work over the course of many months with nothing to show for it. But as I said earlier, I loved working with Marc, and Aconyte had the license to some cool properties, and I *really* wanted to write a book for them, so I decided to keep going. Plus, Marc was determined to find a property I'd be right for, but for him, that meant a *horror* property. That's when I realized publishers viewed me as a writer who wrote both original and tie-in horror—but *only* horror. (Or at least they thought my strongest work was in horror.)

Whatever the reason, in the Land of Tie-Ins, I'd become the Horror Guy.

Looking back now, it's blindingly obvious. Thirteen of my twenty-one tie-in books up to that point in my career were horror or horror-related vs seven that weren't. And twenty-three of my original novels were horror/dark fantasy and only three weren't.

In terms of tie-in writing, I'd thought of myself as being able to tackle any type of project, but the vast majority of the tie-ins I'd actually published screamed H-O-R-R-O-R. For some reason, I'd viewed my original and tie-in fiction as parallel but separate aspects of my writing life. But horror is the genre I love the most, so of course that's what naturally comes out of me, regardless of what type of fiction I write. Besides, I kind of liked being the Horror Guy.

Eventually, Acoynte got a license to produce tie-ins based on the Zombicide board game. There were three different settings at the time: medieval fantasy, contemporary Earth, and a future galactic civilization. Marc thought I'd be right for the science fiction game, which was called Zombicide: Invader. I was assigned an editor, and she sent me a number of PDF copies of reference material from the game company, including some *Zombicide: Invader* comics. I read through them, researched the game on the Internet, looked at all the images I could find, watched play-through videos on YouTube, and bought the game. I read the game rules, looked at all the different cards, played with the cool small plastic figures of alien monsters and space-suited humans. I didn't actually play the game myself, though. Like I told you earlier, I don't like to play games. What I do like about them—what I like best about anything—is when they stimulate my imagination.

I was a little concerned. The game was reminiscent of *Alien* in many ways, and the "zombies" in this version were more like inhuman mutants than walking dead. I decided to do my best to make this book different than my *Alien: Prototype* novel. There was some lore about the game setting, but since it wasn't a roleplaying game, it wasn't developed in a great deal of depth. But it was enough to get me going. I decided to set my novel 100 years in the game setting's future, so I would have more freedom to do what I wanted without disturbing the game setting. In the game, there's an alien-zombie outbreak on a planet, so I had my outbreak occur on a neighboring world, again so I'd have the freedom to wreck the planet as much as I wanted.

The basic scenario I came up with was this: faster-than-light engines exist, but they're only good for two or three trips before they basically melt down and need to be replaced. These engines have made intergalactic space travel possible, but it's not easy, convenient, or cheap. Everyone is trying to develop the tech to create engines that last longer. The system where the original invader outbreak occurred has been quarantined for a century, but the galactic government recently sent probes there, and on a neighboring world they discovered strong energy readings. Hoping this energy might be harnessed to create superior warp engines, a research team is dispatched. They're never heard from again,

Word has gotten out about this energy source, and a team of mercenaries have been hired to go to the forbidden system and acquire samples. A galactic patrol ship detects them, gives chase, and both ships end up crashing on the planet. The survivors are forced to work together to find out what happened to the research crew and then survive a new outbreak of invaders. Action and mayhem ensue.

My working title was *The Summoner's Battleground*. The Summoner was the Big Bad invader monster that controlled all the rest—and who was planning to obtain a starship, escape the planet with its minions, and spread its contagion throughout the galaxy. Eventually, my editor renamed the novel *Planet Havoc*. Without consulting me. I thought that was strange, but I wasn't fond of the original title, so I didn't say anything.

The novel outline went through several revisions, but eventually the owners of the game company—who'd also made suggestions along the way—approved it. When I saw a copy of the final outline my editor had sent them, I saw that she'd rewritten portions of the text. Without consulting me or letting me know she intended to do so.

I started to have a bad, but familiar, feeling.

The drafting of the novel went well. I liked the cast of characters I created, and I enjoyed writing about them fighting monsters, killing monsters, being killed by monsters, and being changed into monsters. All great fun. When the draft was finished, I sent it to my editor. It took her a long time to get back to me with comments, but I figured she was busy working on other books. If we got too close to the publication date and weren't ready, maybe Marc would move the pub date back a bit. Once the editor gave me her feedback, I read her accompanying letter and skimmed through her track changes comments. Her many, many, many comments. I was shocked. I had never gotten so many requests for changes before. Some were changes that could've been worked out in the outline stage, such as the suggestion that the two leads needed stronger character arcs. How was I supposed to do that? The novel took place over the course of a few hours, and the characters were all desperately trying to survive during that time. When would the characters have time to have arcs? Besides, I'd already given them arcs. The commander of the galactic ship had been disgraced when she accidently killed a number of innocent aliens on a planet, and she was trying to find redemption. The commander of the mercenaries was a former military man who wasn't totally comfortable in his role and had to face this truth. Both characters need to find a way to accept themselves for who they really were, and working together to survive helped them do that. There was no romance between them, but they clicked well as partners and friends. They were the only two who survived by the time the invaders and the Summoner were defeated, and since they had no ship, they needed to somehow find a way off the planet—together (leaving room for a possible sequel). The editor had wanted me to write a pulp horror/action novel, which I did my best to deliver, but I still gave my characters arcs—all of them—but they could only be so complex given the constraints of their desperate situation. So I was flummoxed. The editor couldn't explain what kind of arcs she wanted. Just stronger ones.

There were a ton of other requested changes, too, most of which were short of specifics. But they added up to the editor wanting me to rewrite large sections of the book—

—and she wanted me to do it in two weeks.

I immediately called my agent.

My agent contacted my editor, explained that given the number of requested revisions, I'd need at least a month to work on the book. The editor agreed, and I gained a little breathing room. I mentioned before that I'm a fast writer, but I can't write fast if I don't know what the hell *to* write. It was almost as if the editor was trying to get me to entirely overhaul the book in the way she … would … write … it.

Oh no.

A quick Google search later, I found the editor's website, and sure enough, she was a writer in addition to being an editor. It had happened again.

Understanding what was going on helped, but I still had to revise the damn book. I wasn't angry at my editor. We'd chatted on Zoom and corresponded via email, and I thought she was a perfectly lovely person. So I took a very deep breath and got started.

I reread her editorial letter, went slowly through her track changes comments, and every time I found myself feeling resistant to a suggestion, I asked myself if my ego was getting in the way, if I was just too lazy to do the work she was asking of me, or I sincerely didn't agree with the comment. It took me two weeks of going over her suggestions again and again to finally figure out how to apply them so I could start revising. During those two weeks, I brainstormed all kinds of different and bigger character arcs for the leads, trying to find ones that I could add to the story without changing the entire book. A huge part of the Zombicide Invader game is how fast and relentless the creatures are. Given that, plus the overall scenario I'd created for my characters, I couldn't find a way to give my two leads enough downtime to even think about their emotional issues, let alone process them, work on them, and ultimately experience character growth. None of the alternative arcs would work unless I scrapped the entire book and rebuilt it from the ground up using those new arcs as the foundation. So I decided to strengthen the leads' existing arcs in bits and pieces throughout the novel, gave them a little time between bouts of terrifying and deadly encounters with monsters to reflect on their issues, etc. I did my best to address every question my editor had and incorporate every change she wanted in the time that I had. But there was simply too much for me to do in a month. Two months, maybe. Three months, yes. But not one.

I sent her the revision, and she sent it to the Zombicide folks as well. They loved it, and my editor approved it without further comment. Maybe the editor and I simply weren't a good combination. It happens. I harbor no ill will toward her or Aconyte, and if I ever do another book with them, hopefully the process will go more smoothly.

Lessons?

- **It's always good (if not fun) to perform an ego check when dealing with edits.** The longer you write and the more you publish, the more tempting it becomes to think that you've obtained a level of skill where you shouldn't need to make a lot of changes to a manuscript. This is a temptation to be avoided.
- **Given the short deadlines tie-in projects often have, developmental edits should, if at all possible, be dealt with at the outline stage.** Since tie-in writers always have to create an outline for editors and license holders, that's an excellent stage to work out important plot and character issues. There often isn't time to do it with a full manuscript, depending on the publisher's production schedule.
- **Sometimes small changes here and there can add up to a big impact on a story.** I didn't get any feedback on the final changes I made to the book, so I don't know if I managed to strengthen the leads' character arcs to my editor's satisfaction. But in general, if an editor has a feeling that something should be stronger, you might be able to fix the problem with a series of smaller changes sprinkled throughout the manuscript at key points. The trick is figuring out where those key points are and what exact changes to make. Sometimes all you can do is give it a try and see what happens.

Terrifier 2
Cinedigm (2024)

The folks at Bloody Disgusting decided to start a book line, and they contacted me about writing the novelization of *Terrifier 2*. I'm not sure why they approached me—maybe because I'd written the novelization of *Halloween Kills*—but I was thrilled that they did. I'd loved *Terrifier*, and my oldest daughter and I made sure to see *Terrifier 2* when it hit theaters. Nothing like seeing Art the Clown and a whole lot of gore on the big screen! I agreed to take the gig and signed an NDA. It took a bit of time to get a contract ironed out as this was Bloody Disgusting's first foray into publishing and they were still learning about the process. But once that was finished, I was ready to go. They emailed me a PDF of the script, and I immediately read it.

This was going to be my fifth novelization, but it was my first time novelizing a film that had already been released and which I'd seen multiple times. There were very few differences between the script and the finished film, and those were extremely minor. And while the four other scripts all had character-oriented scenes left out of their final films, everything in the *Terrifier 2* script showed up on the screen. I mean *everything*. There were no extra scenes for me to include in my book. The novelizations I'd done before this one ran 80K words on average, but the Bloody Disgusting folks wanted 100K. Even though the script was long (the finished film comes in at around two-and-a-half hours), I was still going to need to come up with some material to add and, as usual, I jotted down ideas for cool scenes as I made my way through the script. I then typed all the dialogue.

I decided to do what I'd done for *Kingsman: The Golden Circle*. I'd watch a bit of the movie, then write a bit of the book, then go back to the movie, then return to the book, and I'd keep going like that until I finished. I could replay scenes as often as I needed to, and I turned on closed captioning so I could see the finished dialogue. (I usually have closed captions turned on when I watch anything on TV. As a writer, I want to see how the dialogue looks written out.) The dialogue in the movie tended to be a bit more condensed, so I used the movie version whenever I could in my book.

Being able to see the people and the sets and hear the tone and rhythm of the actor's voices allowed me to write a richer book than if I'd had to rely primarily on my imagination. At times, it was like I was merely reporting what I was seeing and hearing, and that made the writing go even faster for me than it usually does. Art's character posed a bit of problem, though. He's a nightmarish clown figure who never speaks, so he's like Michael Myers in that way, but unlike Michael, his face and body are very expressive. (This is all due to David Howard Thornton's masterful portrayal of Art.) Since Art didn't reveal his thoughts vocally, I decided it wouldn't feel right to depict his thoughts in the book, but David Howard Thornton was always able to make clear what Art was thinking or feeling at any moment in the film, through facial expression or body language, and I tried to do the same thing in my book.

While I loved the first *Terrifier*, the second was a much richer story. Art was given antagonists in the form of Sienna and her younger brother, and he was given a companion in the Little Pale Girl (along with a dead, eviscerated possum who I named Splatty in the book). Because of these relationships, this film had a much deeper and stronger emotional core, and there was a lot of mythic imagery this time as well. I appreciated all that as an audience member, and as a writer it was golden territory to explore.

I had an absolute blast writing this novel, and it took me about four weeks from start to finish. The folks at Bloody Disgusting loved what I'd done, and as of this writing, the book is in production and should be available by the time you read this. If you're thinking of checking it out, be warned. Just like the film itself, the novelization is extreme horror, and while there's lots of characterization and a strong emotional core in the story, there's a ton of blood and guts, too. There's been talk of my novelizing the other two films in the series, but I haven't been given contracts to sign yet. I hope I get to write those books. Art the Clown forever!

Blood-splattered lessons I learned from writing this book:

- **Novelizing a finished film is very different than novelizing just a script.** You have a wealth of detail that you can draw on from a finished film, and it makes for a richer writing—and I hope reading—experience.
- **You can write extreme horror and still have a strong emotional core in your story.** Extreme horror, whether on film or in prose, often doesn't explore characters' emotional relationships. And when it does, it usually feels perfunctory and tacked onto the story. Not so in *Terrifier 2*.
- **Closed captions are your friend.** I appreciate them both as an artist, and as someone who turns sixty in a couple months.
- **David Howard Thornton is a genius.** Art the Clown is *the* iconic horror villain today, and that's due in large part to his performance.
- **You can set stories during holidays without them coming off as cheesy.** For some reason, I've never liked horror that takes place during a holiday. The trappings and rituals of the holiday seem to detract from the horror rather than add to it. *Halloween* is an exception for me because Michael is inextricably bound to that holiday. But the first two Terrifier films take place during Halloween, and the third will take place during Christmas. In *Terrifier* and *Terrifier 2*, Halloween doesn't loom larger than the plot or characters, and it's not constantly referenced visually or in the character's dialogue. These films have shown me how I can set stories during holidays in ways I find satisfying to me as a writer. Now I can finally write that Arbor Day horror novel I've always dreamed about doing!

THE ONES THAT GOT AWAY

Like in any writing career, there are ups and downs throughout the years. I don't want to give you the impression that everything I've tried has always worked, and with tie-ins, there's no guarantee that every project you're offered will make it to completion.

- I love *Star Trek*, and I'd kill to write a *Trek* tie-in. I've tried periodically over the years to land a *Trek* gig, but all of my proposals were rejected by the various editors who read them. "Maybe someday," he said wistfully.

- I've also tried to write books for Warhammer and Warhammer 40K, but each proposal was rejected with the same comment. *You don't understand the setting.* And, of course, the editors didn't explain exactly what that meant so I could fix it. I did finally manage to sell a short story titled "Skin Man" to *Anathemas*, a Warhammer 40K horror anthology. But when I proposed some novel ideas to the editor afterward, crickets.

- Some projects I was approached for but never materialized: an *NCIS: Los Angeles* novel, a *Person of Interest* novel, a *Diablo* novel, a *Tomb Raider* novel, and a *Family Guy* novel.

- I was asked to do the novelization of a science fiction movie with a female protagonist, but the publisher decided a woman author should write it. (I was disappointed to lose the gig, but I understood why the publisher thought a woman would bring a more authentic perspective to the book.)

- There was some interest in me writing a novelization for *Top Gun: Maverick*, but the publisher decided to go with someone with military experience (which makes perfect sense). The book never came out, though.

- Del Rey approached me about writing a *Sleepy Hollow* tie-in. I wrote an outline for a story about an immortal Benedict Arnold who was in possession of the thirty pieces of silver Judas was paid to betray Jesus. The coins gave him dark powers, and the heroes had to stop him. My agent sent the outline to the editor, who came back to us and said they'd decided to go with a different writer. (It turned out to be Keith DeCandido, and Keith is awesome, so if anyone had to get the gig over me, I'm glad it was him.) What I didn't like was being asked to audition for the job without being told that's what was happening. I don't know for sure, but I think these editors figure writers might not write an outline for free if they knew they were only one writer out of a number being considered. I recently had the same thing happen again. I was approached for a novelization and asked to write a sample chapter. Only after I sent the chapter to the editor did my agent discover it was another group audition situation. At least this time I got paid for writing the chapter. As of this writing, I'm still under consideration for the gig. Wish me luck! (Update: I got it!)

- I tried to write adventure fiction for Gold Eagle (which has since gone out of business). They published the popular *Executioner* series, so I submitted a couple sample chapters and an outline for a novel. The editor decided to pass. A few years later, Gold Eagle started a spy series called *Room 59*. I managed to land a two-book contract to write for this series, under the house name Cliff Ryder. I finished the first book and was halfway through the second when Gold Eagle canceled the line. Neither of my books came out.

- I had an opportunity to audition to write kids' books under the Erin Hunter house name. The editor gave me a book outline and asked me to write a sample chapter based on the opening scene. I did, but she decided I wasn't right for the job.

- Insight Editions asked me to write a *Supernatural* travel guide. They told me they wanted a book featuring all the towns Sam and Dean had been to. When I pointed out that Sam and Dean usually went to generic small midwestern towns with nothing special or interesting about them aside from whatever evil they'd gone there to fight, the editors asked me to write the guide having the brothers talk about a case in each town, with me adding lore about urban legends in that state. I wrote an outline, but when the editors saw it, they decided the urban legend angle didn't work and told me to drop it. I then tried writing the travel guide as if Sam and Dean were creating a resource for Hunters who might come after them, discussing what threats the Hunters might face in various places. The editors decided it was too much like another book they published, *Bobbie Singer's Guide to Hunting*, and they decided to scrap the project entirely.
- My agent is friends with a Hollywood producer, and he and his partner were readying a pitch for a TV series. They wanted a tie-in book to accompany their pitch because, so they told us, Hollywood studios found pitches more persuasive if producers also had a book to show. I'd never heard this before, so I don't know how true it is. At any rate, I was given some material about the show and asked to develop an outline. I wrote several outlines, but none of them hit the mark. The producers would've been happy to have me keep working for free, but my agent asked them for some money at this point, and they regretfully parted ways with us. You have to watch out for Hollywood folk. They love to get as much out of you for free as they can. But once you ask to be paid, they'll vanish in a puff of smog.
- Perhaps my strangest tie-in offer came from someone who emailed to ask if I'd be interested in writing *Supernatural* Trivial Pursuit questions. The money wasn't great, and the work itself looked like it would be dry and dull, so I passed.

EXERCISES

1. Watch a movie with the sound off and the captions on. Type up some of the dialogue exchanges between characters to get a feel for how each of them speak. Dialogue in TV shows and movies is usually sharp and concise, unlike how most people speak to each other in real life. Was the dialogue sharp and concise? If so, did you find that effective? Was the dialogue a bit flabby and meandering? If so, try to tighten a few lines and see what effect that has.
2. Pick a scene from a movie and novelize it. How did it turn out? What could you do to make it better?

VOICES FROM THE TRENCHES

DAYTON WARD

How did you get into writing tie-ins? In 1997, I entered the very first *Star Trek: Strange New Worlds* writing contest sponsored by Pocket Books, the Simon & Schuster imprint which at the time was publishing *Star Trek* novels. The contest was for new, unpublished writers and winning entries were paid for their short stories, which were collected into an anthology. My story was one of that first year's 18 winners. For each of the next two annual contests, I sent a story that was selected. At that point, I'd rendered myself ineligible to enter future contests, after which John Ordover, the editor at Pocket overseeing the contest, offered me a contract to write a *Star Trek* novel. That was in 2000, and I've been writing or co-writing (among other things) *Star Trek* novels for Simon & Schuster ever since.

What do you like about writing tie-ins? What are the rewards for you? For me it's a way to play with characters and other "toys" from a universe I already enjoy as a fan. That's particularly true for *Star Trek*, but I've also written stories for other licensed properties (*Planet of the Apes, Predator, 24, Mars Attacks*), each of which was some flavor of "dream job" because of my affection for the property. There are several other TV and film franchises I'd love to take a crack at if such an opportunity ever presented itself.

What challenges have you faced in your career as a tie-in writer? Finding work in this field is always a challenge. Editors of these lines almost always are dealing with production schedules and development life cycles which are even more hectic than seems to be the norm for "regular" books. There's also the added layer of review and approval from the IP owner, who in many cases is very demanding and particular about who writes for their property. Because of this, it's understandable that editors often end up cultivating a stable of writers they've learned are reliable and easy to work with, which does a lot to alleviate some of the chaos. That makes "breaking in" to write for this or that property a tough nut to crack, for experienced writers as well as someone hoping to somehow get their foot in the door somewhere.

Does writing tie-ins require a different skill set than other types of writing? If so what are these skills? The biggest difference I've experienced between writing original fiction and tie-ins is the level of collaboration the latter demands. You have to embrace this notion if you hope to succeed with tie-in writing. There's working with your editor, of course, but also the license owners and their representatives who review and approve outlines and manuscripts to make sure you're doing right by "the brand." That might mean making changes to your story to accommodate requests or decrees from the studio, whether it's to avoid colliding with something being developed for TV or film or just because they don't like the way something's been portrayed using their characters. Depending on the project, you may also be working with other writers to varying degrees. Perhaps there's a shared continuity of the sort that has at times dominated older franchises like *Star Trek, Star Wars, Alien*, or *Predator* just to name a few of the bigger brands. You might end up exchanging emails or text messages or just sitting in a bar somewhere, comparing what you're doing with each other and making any necessary adjustments to ensure everybody remains in step. This sort of ante gets upped when you take part in something like a multi-author miniseries or other "event" that requires you to work out entire storylines across different books and coordinate efforts with the other participants. All of that might sound scary, but I've contributed to several projects of this sort and for me that level of collaboration is honestly one of the most fun and rewarding parts of the job.

Do you think it's possible to be pigeonholed as a tie-in writer, making it more difficult to publish your own work? If so, how do you deal with this? I suppose that's certainly possible, though I can't say I've encountered it myself. Admittedly, a big reason for that is that I enjoy tie-in writing and I end up jumping from project to project without a lot of time left over for striking out on my own. My writing partner, Kevin Dilmore, and I have been playing more and more in the short fiction arena to help scratch that particular itch.

What advice do you have for writers who want to break into the media tie-in field? As I often advise writers who are just starting out, putting all your hopes on landing a tie-in gig without having established any sort of writer "street cred" is—with precious few exceptions—pretty much unheard of. This somewhat dovetails with my earlier comments about the editors of these books and their reliance on writers they know can deliver quality copy on schedule without (too much) fuss. So, I encourage new writers to get some publication credits under their belt in the form of original novels and short fiction; something you can show to an agent or publisher that demonstrates you can finish what you start. This is just one of the reasons I miss those Strange New Worlds writing contests. They proved to be something of a talent scout when it came to adding new voices to the *Star Trek* mix. I can certainly trace my success as a writer back to that first contest, and I'd love to see it or something like it make a return, and for other licensed properties with tie-in lines to offer their own version of such an endeavor. I know there are financial and logistical hurdles to navigate to make such projects viable, but a boy can dream!

DAYTON WARD is a *New York Times* bestselling author or co-author of more than 40 novels and novellas, often working with his best friend, Kevin Dilmore. His short fiction has appeared in more than 30 anthologies, and he's written for magazines such as *NCO Journal, Kansas City Voices, Famous Monsters of Filmland, Star Trek*, and *Star Trek Communicator* as well as the websites Tor.com, StarTrek.com, and Syfy.com. Learn way more about Dayton than might be considered healthy, including where to find him treading water in the various social-media timesinks, at daytonward.com.

ROBERT GREENBERGER

How did you get into writing tie-ins? After working at Starlog Press and the DC Comics, I got to edit the *Star Trek* comic (and later other media tie-ins) which led to a relationship with the editors of the *Star Trek* novels at Pocket Books. That led to an invitation to write some fiction and things sort of grew from there.

What do you like about writing tie-ins? What are the rewards for you? The obvious response is the thrill of getting to write in worlds that touched me as a kid or a reader. Having a chance to play in a favorite sandbox has always been tempting. The fun then becomes finding a character or corner of the franchise that has been overlooked and ripe for exploration.

What challenges have you faced in your career as a tie-in writer? It's a mixed bag. I find myself vying with good friends for the same handful of slots to a franchise or, finding out all the assignments were given out before you even knew there were opportunities. Depending on the license holder, the restrictions can be minimal to incredibly restrictive. When I wrote the novelization to *Hellboy II: The Golden Army*, I was sent the script without restriction and was free to write as I wanted. Then came the daunting news that director Guillermo del Toro himself was going to look at the manuscript. Imagine my relief when it came back with zero changes requested.

Does writing tie-ins require a different skill set than other types of writing? If so what are these skills? Some of the skills involved include being able to research the property with whatever they give you in addition to whatever else you can find. You have to match characterization and speaking patterns for the established characters, then craft characters or worlds that fit that particular universe. Of course, you also need a story that helps deepen our understanding of the established characters without altering their status quo. Or being able to adjust on the fly when the property makes a change on short notice. Producing comics based on a long-running series such as *Star Trek: The Next Generation* forced us to set stories well behind what were being broadcast. We'd be looking for gaps in stardates to set the stories and match whatever the status quo was at the time.

Do you think it's possible to be pigeonholed as a tie-in writer, making it more difficult to publish your own work? If so, how do you deal with this? Writing has always been alongside a day job so I don't think I established myself deeply as a tie-in writer where it became a problem. Others, who wrote exclusively for one franchise, may have found it hard to be thought of as anything but that kind of a writer. And of course, Bookscan has done more to pigeonhole writers than anything else.

What advice do you have for writers who want to break into the media tie-in field? The rule of thumb for writers pitching a publisher still applies: Know your market. Who holds the rights to publish tie-in fiction? Are they open to pitches? Who should you contact to introduce yourself and make that pitch? Being agented helps, but not every publisher requires an agent to be involved. I've used an agent only once and have somehow managed to write tie-ins for decades.

ROBERT GREENBERGER has been a writer, editor, and teacher since 1980, with day jobs at Starlog Press, DC Comics, Gist Communications, *Marvel Comics*, *Weekly World News*, *Famous Monsters of Filmland*, and *ComicMix*. His tie-in work includes writing for *Star Trek*, Hellboy, Green Hornet, *Predator*, Zorro, *After Earth*, Superman, Batman, and others. A cofounder of Crazy 8 Press, he continues to write tie-in and original fiction and nonfiction. He also teaches high school English in Maryland where he makes his home. Website: bobgreenberger.com.

STEPHEN D. SULLIVAN

How did you get into writing tie-ins? I kind of fell into writing tie-ins twice. The first time was when I was working at TSR, Inc.—the original publisher of Dungeons & Dragons—and my friends Bill Willingham, Jeff Dee, and I convinced their advertising department that we could produce a better D&D comic book series than an out-of-house advertising agency. So, they hired us as freelancers, and Bill and I (with Jeff) created an original D&D comic-book-style serial advertisement that ran in Marvel comics during the early nineteen eighties. I did the writing, and Bill (and Jeff) drew it.

About fifteen years later, I decided to move from writing comic books into writing novels, for a variety of reasons. At the time, one of my comic book writer/editor friends was ghost-writing novels for the *Boy Detectives*, a famous, longstanding children's series. I asked him if they might need other writers, and he put me in touch with his editor. I wrote a book in a spin-off series the *Boy Detectives* had going at the time, and then moved onto the main series, where I ended up writing twelve novels, including the final book in the original run.

My work and experience doing those helped me get other tie-in work.

What do you like about writing tie-ins? What are the rewards for you? I've gotten two basic rewards for writing tie-ins. The obvious one is the money. Freelance writers need a constant influx of money to continue being freelance writers. We're like sharks; we have to keep moving, keep the money flowing, or we sink into a soul-killing day job.

The second, and for me often the more important reward, is getting to play in cool worlds that I like and enjoy. I've had a great time writing things like *Dragonlance, Spider Riders, Thunderbirds*, and *Iron Man*. What author wouldn't want to write Tony Stark, Reed Richards, or the Teenage Mutant Ninja Turtles?

Doing tie-ins, and doing them well, is a blast. If the editors hadn't changed, I'd probably still be writing *Boy Detective* books. After a while, the iconic characters start to feel like family.

What challenges have you faced in your career as a tie-in writer? Honestly, securing the work has always been the biggest challenge. Once I've gotten an editor to hand me a tie-in property to work with, I've very seldom had any problems doing the job.

Yes, sometimes you have to do rewrites to meet the requirements of a property, and sometimes those requirements change in the middle of a project. But for the most part, the people I was working with trusted me to do the job, and I trusted them.

When I was writing Marvel movie novelizations, people warned me that they were notoriously hard to work with, but I didn't have any trouble. I think the rewrites on *Iron Man: The Junior Novel* took me less than a day—and a lot of it was changing a word here or there.

Does writing tie-ins require a different skill set than other types of writing? If so, what are these skills? Tie-in writing is different in that you're not your own master. Generally, in a novel, I'm serving my own goals and needs. Characters get to go where my plot takes them and interact in ways that make sense to the story I'm telling.

In tie-in writing, whether you're working from a pre-existing movie script or idea, or creating something out of whole cloth, you're serving entirely different goals.

First of all, you're serving the property and trying to make the work exciting within whatever strictures that property brings. You can't have Johnny Storm, the Human Torch, shooting ice from his hands. If you're working from a movie script, you have to stick to the script and try to use as much of the dialogue as you can. And you better not cut out anything that becomes a memorable line or catch phrase to the movie audience!

Obviously, you're also serving the wants and needs of the people who have given you the assignment—both the editors and the licensors. You don't do that, you're out of a job, quick.

But it's also super important to serve the needs of the fans of that property—not necessarily with "fan service," but by respecting what the fans love about that property, and by making sure that any risks you take within the story pay off for them, as well as for you and the license holders.

Do you think it's possible to be pigeonholed as a tie-in writer, making it more difficult to publish your own work? If so, how do you deal with this? It's absolutely possible to get pigeonholed in any type of work, and writing tie-in properties is no different.

You could get caught writing just *Boy Detective* stories, or just superheroes, or just movie tie-ins, or just horror adaptations, in the same way you as you can get wrapped up in doing just one particular job in one particular way. "Oh yeah, Steve … He's the guy who writes stories about mutant turtles."

If the people giving out jobs start thinking about you one way, it'll limit the kind of jobs you're offered or even the jobs publishers will let you do.

When I was working in comics, I had one editor who came to think of me as the guy who wrote wacky comedy stories, because I'd done some very successful ones with some artist friends. That guy would "keep me in mind" for similar things, but never offered me any writing that involved doing drama or anything with that company's non-comedy characters.

So, if you can work on a lot of different types of properties—comedy, drama, superhero, horror, detective, kid stuff, more adult stuff, etc.—you'll be better off.

And that applies to both tie-in work and the kind of self-owned novels that publishers will buy from you. Moving between tie-ins and things you own is tricky, and I recommend that tie-in authors start working on their own creator-owned properties early.

The only way to break out of the pigeonhole is to try not to get caught in it. Do diverse work both for tie-ins and for yourself.

Happily, today there are a lot more micro-publishing and self-publishing opportunities now than there used to be. So if you get stuck, sometimes you can work your own way out. Just because some editor in New York says "No," it doesn't mean you can't do it nowadays.

What advice do you have for writers who want to break into the media tie-in field? Like all writing, breaking into tie-in writing is hard. It takes hard work and persistence, and the ability to do more cold calling than most writers ever want to do. (Unless you're lucky enough to have a good agent to do it for you.)

You want to develop contacts in the industry, because that's where a lot of your work will spring from. I got many jobs by being recommended by editors who liked working with me and would tell me about other work.

But to get to that point, I had to work on the writing, too. And that I did on my own. I had to write a couple of (still unpublished) novels to have the samples needed to get that first *Boy Detectives* book.

I'd recommend not writing fan fiction, but working on your own stuff in both long and short forms, to develop your skills. Join a writing group that has professional writers as members to get valuable feedback. Keep writing.

Finally, people should make sure to keep writing their own stuff while writing tie-in work. Edgar Rice Burroughs reportedly had a "one for them, one for me" policy, because if it had been up to his publisher, he'd have written nothing but Tarzan books for the rest of his life.

Far too many of us get near the end of a good tie-in career only to have the industry change and our royalty-earning tie-in books (if we're lucky enough to have them) put out of print. You want books that you own and control on the shelves, as well as all the cool stuff for Marvel and other Big Properties.

Writing tie-ins is a lot of fun, but at the end of the day, you don't get to take those characters home and keep them.

STEPHEN D. SULLIVAN is an award-winning author of more than sixty books, among them trilogies for *Legend of the Five Rings*, *Spider Riders*, and *Dragonlance*. Other cool stuff he's worked on are *Dungeons & Dragons* and *Star Wars* (games), *Teenage Mutant Ninja Turtles* and *The Simpsons* (comics), *Iron Man* and *Thunderbirds* (junior novels), and the 2017 film *Theseus and the Minotaur*. His latest projects include *Dr. Cushing's Chamber of Horrors*, *Monster Shark on a Nude Beach*, and *Frost Harrow* (modern-Gothic supernatural), *Atomic Tales* (50s SciFi), and his Scribe Award-winning novelization of the "Worst Film Ever Made," *Manos: The Hands of Fate*.

CHAPTER SEVEN
HOW TO GET TIE-IN WRITING EXPERIENCE

It's the plaintive cry of every new jobseeker:

They say I need experience, but how do I get it if they won't hire me?

As I've mentioned elsewhere in this book, when it comes to handing out tie-in gigs, editors seek writers with a solid list of novel credits in traditional publishing. That could mean you've published original work, of course, but editors like it even more if writers *also* have credits writing tie-in fiction. So how do aspiring tie-in writers get the experience they need?

First, work on becoming the very best writer you can be. Despite what some people think, tie-in novels aren't a lesser type of fiction produced by second-rate writers. You have to be a damn good writer to land a tie-in gig. So the more you do to make yourself the best writer you can be, the greater chance you'll have. Besides, we all should continue striving to improve our craft throughout our careers, shouldn't we?

Write and publish original novels. You need to establish a track record in order to be considered for a tie-in writing job. Writing and publishing original novels with good presses (whether small, medium, or large) is the best way to do this. It *is* possible to get a track record in other ways, such as writing comics or videogames, which show you can work with other people's IP's. But experience in these fields doesn't necessarily show an editor that you can produce quality novel-length prose fiction.

Get an agent. Good agents regularly check with publishers to see what they're looking for. If a publisher is searching for tie-in writers, agents can suggest one or more of their clients. An agent can vouch for your skills and abilities if your publication record is on the thin side, so you might not need as much experience as if you were going it alone. As far as I know, no agents specialize in tie-in fiction, though. It's just one of the types of fiction they handle, and not every agent is interested in it. Make sure to research exactly what sort of writing a literary agent likes before you approach them for possible representation. (This is good advice when trying to land an agent in general.)

Read the Voices from the Trenches interviews in this book. By now, you've surely noticed that the first question I asked the Voices authors was "How did you get into writing tie-ins?" This was so you'd see many different paths to embarking on a tie-writing career—paths you might be able to emulate.

Get Writing. There are several types of writing that are kinda-sorta related to tie-in fiction that can help prepare you for the real thing.

Fan Fiction. Fan fiction is written by fans for fans, and its primary purpose is to have fun. It allows fans to more deeply explore beloved characters and settings from books, games, movies, TV shows, etc. Writers of fan fiction get to inhabit their favorite worlds, go inside the minds of the characters that live there, and tell stories of their own invention—stories that would likely never exist otherwise. Some people (not me) consider fan fiction childish, but these same people likely look down on tie-in fiction as well, and maybe genre fiction as a whole. But fan fiction can be a great way to strengthen your writing skills and get feedback from your peers. Some writers view their fan fiction as a hobby, while others take it very seriously and work hard to improve. In this case, fan fiction can be a good training ground for both tie-in and original fiction, but because you're working with established characters, it's especially good preparation for tie-in fiction.

There are some drawbacks to writing fan fiction. If all you do is write fan fiction, it could delay—or even prevent—the development of your own unique voice as a writer. You can also get into the habit of writing to please your readers, giving them what they want instead of giving them the story *you* want to write. And you might get into the habit of exploring areas in your fan fiction that license holders would never allow in tie-in fiction, such as *My Little Pony* BDSM stories. (Don't laugh; Rule 34 is a real thing.) Writing more, uh, *expansive* fan fiction like this can make it more difficult for you to write characters as they really are instead of how you want them to be.

Another drawback to fan fiction is that you can't sell it. Whatever the IP, it's owned by others, not you, and it's illegal for you to attempt to make monetary profit on it. (Don't look at me like that—I don't make the laws.) You can circulate it for free among your friends and online communities, but you can't publish it on Amazon. Fan fiction *is* considered fair use (meaning it's legal to write it) as long as it's transformative, meaning that you change something significant about the property, including the type of stories that you tell. If you tell a story about the *My Little Pony* characters marooned on another planet, that's transformative. It's not the kind of story that the series would generally present. (Can you tell my wife and daughters are *Pony* fans? I'm not a brony, but I've picked up a lot from them.)

Even if fan fiction is fair use, license holders usually discourage the production of it in order to protect their copyright. If they don't attempt to defend their copyright, it's a tacit agreement that they're surrendering it. So if a license holder sees any fan fiction on the Internet that looks like its violating their copyright, they'll try to get the author to take it down. But if you stick to fair use, you should be fine.

If you want to use fan fiction as a way to build skills depicting media properties in prose, I'd advise sticking as close to the original characters, setting, and premise as possible. But if you want to write a story about King Kong and Godzilla getting married and going on their honeymoon, more power to you.

IDEAS FOR WRITING FAN FICTION

Here are some possible areas to explore in your fan fiction.

- **Another day at the office.** This is a normal day for the characters. So if they're homicide detectives, they're investigating a murder. If they're pirates, they're attacking another ship and stealing its cargo. This is the closest to tie-in fiction.
- **Waiting for the phone to ring.** This is when the detectives or pirates (or whoever) don't have a job to do yet, and they're hanging around, waiting for something to happen. What do they do while they wait?
- **Exploring new ground.** Put the characters into situations they normally would never be in, such as my earlier example of the *My Little Pony* characters going into space and being marooned on another planet. You can also put the characters into a genre they don't normally exist in. What if Sam and Dean Winchester fought in WWII? What if you put an *Alien* xenomorph into a rom-com? The only limits here are your imagination.
- **Behind the scenes.** What goes on with the characters when the camera isn't rolling? How do superheroes get their uniforms repaired after a battle? Who disposes of all the dead bodies in a zombie apocalypse? How does Batman get to sleep—and remain asleep—after a night of crimefighting? How does a Federation starship captain find a moment of peace on their vessel?
- **Meanwhile, somewhere else …** When Godzilla is duking it out with another kaiju, what's happening elsewhere in the world? Are people watching the action live? Are they making bets on which monster will win? In *Lord of the Rings*, is one of the orcs starting to question the whole blindly-following-Sauron-thing they've got going on? In a Lovecraftian universe, what do the ancient gods do while they wait for those idiot humans to finally find a way to open a gateway between dimensions?
- **Filling in the blanks.** Is there any aspect of a property that you're writing about that hasn't been developed? For example, everyone in Klingon society can't be a warrior. What's a Klingon chef like? A Klingon farmer? A Klingon artist? Do Kilingon warriors have fans among the general populace? Are they famous among their people? Tie-in fiction often explores areas like this, at least in part, so writing fan fiction like this could be good preparation.
- **Exploring a character's history (especially a supporting or minor character).** The background of main characters in a property such as *Star Trek* are often well explored, but what about some of the crew on the bridge, the ones who never speak and are never named? We don't know anything about

them. Was there anything in Gaston's past in *Beauty and the Beast* that made him turn out to be such a jerk? How did King Kong survive on Skull Island when he was an orphaned baby?

- **Exploring character's future.** Many years ago, I wrote a story about an unnamed superhero modeled on Superman who was old and living in an assisted living facility. Most of his powers were gone, but he still had x-ray and telescopic vision, and if he saw a crime being committed in town, he called 911 and reported it. I wanted to show that older people can still be useful, and that heroes can stay heroes throughout their lives. What do you think your favorite characters' lives will be like in the future? Will they still be adventuring? Will they have settled into a different role, and are they happy with where they're at?

- **Highlighting other characters.** Does your favorite franchise have any less-popular or minor characters that you feel don't get their due? Well, in fan fiction, you can give them their chance to shine by centering a story around them.

- **A day off.** What does James Bond do on his day off? Where does he go when he takes a vacation? Maybe Batman schedules one day off a year for his mental health. What does he do on that day? Is he able to forget about crimefighting? Does trying to relax drive him nuts?

- **Satires.** *Megamind* is a satire of Lex Luthor and Superman, turning their traditional rivalry on its head to make a point about society telling us who we are instead of letting us find out for ourselves. Satire makes fun of a subject in order to illuminate an aspect of that subject or society itself. It's different from parody, which makes fun of a subject simply for entertainment, without any deeper purpose. Parody is also considered the lowest form of humor. Calling Superman Stupidman and having him wreck everything by trying to use his powers to help people is simplistic and not particularly imaginative. It's fun to write, but you probably won't learn much from doing it.

- **Mash-Ups.** This is a fan fiction favorite. Someone once wrote fan fiction where my zombie detective Matt Richter met the Benedict Cumberbatch version of Sherlock Holmes, and they worked on a case together. That's the kind of story that can only exist in fan fiction. You can write about Moana teaming up with Thor, but even though both characters are owned by Disney, there's no chance in hell they'd ever end up in the same story in real life—unless you write it as fan fiction, of course. Match-ups like this almost never happen in tie-in fiction, so writing fan fiction about them probably isn't the best preparation for writing tie-in fiction.

- **An Event Story.** This is like *Avengers: Infinity War* and *Avengers: Endgame* or *The Flash* movie. Huge stakes, multiple characters teaming up to save all of existence. These can be a lot of fun to write as fan fiction, but tie-in fiction tends to feature a normal adventure of the characters rather than a decidedly abnormal one. Sometimes aspiring tie-in writers will pitch big ideas like God/Chuck returns to the *Supernatural* universe, and in order to defeat him, all the Sams and Deans from throughout the multiverse must team up. A tie-in editor would never go for that kind of story. The idea is too far outside the bounds of a regular *Supernatural* tale. So mash-ups tend not to be good practice for writing tie-in fiction.

- **Create original characters for established worlds.** This is what I did for my *Alien* tie-in, as well as my Wizards of the Coast novels. Because this is what you often need to do in tie-in fiction, this type of fan fiction is excellent preparation for writing tie-ins.
- **Erotica.** If you really want to show the characters from your favorite IP enjoying sexy times, go for it, but unless the IP already deals with sex, you'd probably learn more about writing erotica than writing tie-ins.

A WORD OF CAUTION

Do *not* send a tie-in editor your fan fiction as writing samples. If you've written a piece fan fiction that reads like a regular adventure for the character, then it can make a good sample—just don't tell the editor you originally wrote it as fan fiction. You want the editor to view you as a professional, not as an amateur. You might consider fan fiction to be just as legitimate as any other type, but the reality is that not everyone feels this way, and the editor you send your sample to may be one of those people.

STORY SITUATIONS

At the end of my how-to-write-horror book *Writing in the Dark*, I presented a list of story situations that writers could use to expand their plots beyond the basic predator-prey pattern that often shows up in horror. I'm offering the list here to give you even more ideas to drawn from when writing fan fiction. Of course, you can use the list as inspiration for any type of short story or novel, tie-in or original.

- Missing child/family member/friend
- Lost love, obsessive love
- Robbery
- Salvage
- Hiding from past, trying to forget past
- Childhood boogeyman
- Abusive parent or spouse
- Seeking revenge or justice
- Trying to escape (physical place or situation)
- Murder/assassination
- Seeking boon from a powerful force
- Seeking to end one's life
- Dying of illness, other dying of illness
- Sick, wounded, disabled
- Hiding secret, trying to uncover secret

- Confronting past, escaping past
- Trying to remember, trying to forget
- Seeking to atone, seeking to condemn
- Helping another, hurting another
- Trying to start a business/run a business/save a business
- Trying to save someone physically, mentally, emotionally, spiritually
- Trying to have a child
- Seeking peace, seeking war
- Trying to find something, trying to get rid of something
- Trying to find identity, a community, a home, a place
- Seeking to understand
- Seeking to deceive
- Seeking to overcome evil, seeking to spread evil
- Seeking power, domination, control
- Creating chaos/establishing order/reestablishing order
- Seeking riches
- Serving a higher power, seeking a higher power to serve
- Seeking truth, concealing truth
- Protecting a secret, uncovering a secret
- Addiction
- Illness: seeking health or relief, causing illness
- Exploring
- Establishing law, abolishing law, destroying law
- Preserving culture/tradition, changing it, disrupting it, destroying it
- Quest
- Protecting others, harming others
- Survival, self-preservation
- Settling a new place/taming environment
- Enslaving, freeing
- Reconciliation
- Seeking advancement, growth, evolution, enlightenment, apotheosis
- Seeking to remember, seeking to forget
- Seeking to obtain, seeking to get rid of
- Creating, destroying
- Seeking knowledge, forbidden knowledge, imparting knowledge
- Seeking artistic expression, censoring
- Persecuting others

- Earning a living
- Being an outcast, wanting to join a group, wanting to get out of a group
- Protesting, supporting
- Practicing religion, escaping religion
- Colonizing, repelling colonizers
- Seeking to entertain, seeking to repel or repulse, seeking to shock
- Seeking approval
- Seeking allies
- Establishing/destabilizing/abolishing government
- Preserving the past, breaking with the past
- Revelation of something wonderful, revelation of something awful, realization of a profound or terrible insight
- Trying to get home, leaving home
- Facing the end of the world
- Invasion
- Espionage/intelligence gathering
- Celebration, ceremony, memorial, anniversary
- Entrapment, imprisonment, escape, seeking freedom for self or others
- Making things the way they once were/keeping things from returning to the way they once were
- Fulfilling an obligation, escaping obligation
- Trying to determine what's real
- Seeking to overcome fear
- Testing one's self
- Raising children, establishing a family
- Feud, estrangement, reconciliation
- Seeking love
- Seeking sexual fulfillment
- Facing the end of life
- Facing disgrace, reestablishing honor
- Exile, isolation, lost, stranded
- Rescue
- Hunting
- Competition
- Disease: contracting it, fighting it, one person or group
- Becoming leader, conspiring against leader, overthrowing leader, killing leader
- Dealing with disaster, dealing with death
- Death of loved one

- Seeking renewal
- Seeking fame, seeking power
- Manipulating individual or group
- Seeking sanity, seeking to drive someone mad
- Starting relationship, ending relationship
- Getting married, getting divorced
- Starting school, graduating, leaving before graduating
- Entering military, leaving military
- Moving, changing locations, changing homes, changing jobs
- Seeking a job, losing a job
- Building, tearing down
- Leave-taking, reunion
- Transformation
- Changing history, preserving history, concealing history
- Finding one's purpose
- Seeking meaning
- Rejecting civilization, living in the wild, back to nature
- Going into hiding
- Becoming involved in a scandal, being disgraced
- Delivering something of vital importance

THEME ANTHOLOGIES

Theme anthologies are book-length collections of short fiction (although sometimes poetry is included as well) centered around a particular concept. Each piece is written by a different author who tries to find an effective, interesting approach to the theme.

Among the anthologies I've had stories published in are such diverse titles—and themes—as *Dead Detectives, Shakespeare Unleashed, Attack From the 80's, Human for a Day, Imaginary Friends, Vengeance Fantastic, Villains Victorious, Guardian Angels, Prom Night, Civil War Fantastic*, and (perhaps the weirdest of all) *Alien Pets*. The idea is that the theme will be an effective marketing hook, and for this reason, many writers are cynical about these anthologies, feeling that the themes constrain creativity and don't lead to a writer's best work. But in a very real sense, the plethora of "Year's Best" anthologies center around a theme as well: the best work (stories, essays, poems, etc.) published in a given year. And let's be honest; how many readers are going to plunk down anywhere from six to twenty-five dollars for an anthology called *Really Good Stories by Really Good Writers About Whatever They Felt Like Writing*?

Besides being a good business tool, a theme can be a lot of fun for writers to work with. It can provide structure and spark ideas, in the same way that a poet might be challenged by attempting to write a sonnet or sestina. And writing for theme anthologies can be good preparation for writing tie-in fiction. You learn to write with a set of given elements and within specific parameters, and once you start publishing your stories, you'll have writing samples to show tie-in editors.

Whenever I start a story for a new anthology, I always ask myself the same question: How in the hell am I going to write a story about *that*? (Remember *Alien Pets*?) I find the challenge invigorating, and sometimes frustrating, but always fun.

TO MARKET, TO MARKET

So you want to try your hand at writing a story for a theme anthology. How do you find markets to submit to?

It's not always easy; some anthologies are invitation-only, meaning the editor contacts specific writers and asks them to submit stories. But there are anthologies that are open to any writers, and you can find their submission information listed in writers' magazines, like *Writer's Digest*. Various writers' organizations supply market information to their members, but even if you don't yet have the credentials to join, you can often subscribe to their newsletters or market publications. Often, various writing-related websites, sometimes affiliated with professional writers' organizations, sometimes not, will have message boards where people post market information. (There's a list of such organizations at the end of this book in the Resources section.) Publishers post anthology guidelines on their websites or on social media platforms.

Even if an anthology is by invitation only, you might still be able to submit to it. Read and research published anthologies and compile a list of editors' names. These editors attend a number of writers' conferences throughout the year. If you find yourself at the same conference, go up and introduce yourself and ask if the editor has any open anthology projects that you might be able to submit to. If you can't attend such conferences, you might be able to track down editors' e-mail addresses—especially if you are a member of a writers' organization with access to other members' contact information. Send a short, polite e-mail inquiring if the editor has any open projects you can submit to. You'll be surprised how often an editor is willing to look at a story for a supposedly "closed" anthology.

AN IDEA IS WORTH SEVERAL THOUSAND WORDS

So, after diligent research and perhaps a little networking, you've discovered an anthology you'd like to submit to. How do you come up with a story idea?

First, remember that your story has to center on the anthology's theme. Sometimes these themes can be broad—Love, Friendship, Revenge, etc.—and sometimes they can be very specific. I've done stories for anthologies based on TV shows like *Xena: Warrior Princess* and role-playing games like *Dark Tyrants* where the guidelines are very clear on what the editors expect and what writers can and can't do with the characters and concepts. Whatever the theme, broad or narrow, your story needs to add to the anthology's exploration of it while at the same time avoiding covering the same ground as all the other stories. And if the anthology is also genre-specific—horror, science fiction, mystery, romance, etc.—you have whole host of other concerns to attend to as well.

I always begin by mulling over what personal experience I've had with the theme. For example, the cross-genre anthology *A Dangerous Magic* was built on a theme of fantasy stories dealing with romance. After thinking back on my own romantic experiences over the years, I came up with the idea of how our view of romance evolves (or doesn't) as we mature, from putting the object of our affections on a pedestal to, hopefully, achieving a more balanced and realistic view of our loved one. Thus my story "The Man of Her Dreams" was born, a tale about a woman whose literal (and absolutely perfect) dream lover comes to life one day. At first, she's thrilled but she soon realizes that it's possible to have too much perfection.

I had a harder time coming up with an idea for the anthology *Vengeance Fantastic*. I guess I'm not a very vindictive person because I couldn't think of any time that I wished to get revenge on someone. But then I turned the question around: was there a time when someone might have wished to get revenge on me? Years ago, when I worked as a reporter for a small weekly newspaper, I did some theater reviews, and I always felt uncomfortable criticizing actors' performances. What if one of those actors had wished to get back at me for a negative review? "Exits and Entrances" became a story about a theater critic with a poison pen (or more accurately, a poison keyboard) and the ghost of an actress he'd once devastated with a mean-spirited review. But to keep this story from being a cliché, I had my critic character believe the ghost has come back solely for revenge when, in reality, like Marley's ghost, she's returned to help save the critic's soul.

AVOID CLICHÉS LIKE THE PLAGUE

And that brings me to one of the most important considerations when writing a story for a theme anthology: avoiding the obvious and the cliché. Since an anthology might contain stories by a dozen or so different writers, you want to avoid writing the same kind of story as everyone else. To do this, try to find an aspect of the theme that isn't apparent at first glance. For *A Dangerous Magic*, I chose not to write a fantasy story that merely had elements of romance in it. I wrote about a central issue regarding the concept of romance itself: the difference between the ideal and the real. For *Vengeance Fantastic*, I wrote a story that at first seemed to be about revenge, but turned out to be about redemption (though my character certainly does get what's coming to him in the end).

Don't go with your first, second, or even third idea. Keep pushing yourself to explore the theme until you come up with an idea that's more original, and perhaps more offbeat than any of the others the editor is going to see. That way, your story will stand an even greater chance of being accepted for publication.

While getting a story published (and receiving a check to cash) is nice, the main reward of writing for theme anthologies for me is that I've written stories I never would have otherwise, and they've often turned out to be some of the best work I've done. The themes have not only sparked ideas, they've taken me in directions I never would have explored otherwise and helped me grow as a writer.

And they can do the same for you.

PUBLIC DOMAIN CHARACTERS

Copyright laws in the United States last for the creator's life plus seventy years. After that, their work falls into the public domain, which means it belongs to everyone on Earth forever. Recently Winnie-the-Pooh and the earliest depiction of Micky Mouse have entered the public domain (which I'm sure chaps Disney's ass to no end), and there are hundreds upon hundreds of characters other people created that are available for you to use in your writing, free of charge. You can find a long list of public domain characters here: https://comicvine.gamespot.com/in-the-public-domain/4010-2526/characters.

Since no one owns public domain characters, writing about them technically doesn't count as tie-in fiction. As I've said before, tie-in fiction is licensed by whoever owns the IP. Public domain characters are free for anyone to use. Artistically, writing about public domain characters is almost the same as writing tie-in fiction, but the difference is there's no one to stop you from writing about *your* version of the characters and their world. And writing about public domain characters can count as original fiction, too. *The Wizard of Oz* became public domain in 1956. Gregory Maguire wrote the Oz-based novel *Wicked* in 1995, which became the smash-hit musical.

The International Association of Media Tie-in Writers have put out two anthologies where writers use public domain characters in their stories: *Tied In* and *Two-Fisted Team Ups*. I have a story in the first volume, and you can find it in Appendix One at the back of this book.

If you want to use your public domain-based fiction as samples to present to a tie-in editor, I suggest sticking as closely to the original property as possible. But if you want to go the Gregory Maguire route and use public domain works as the basis for original fiction, I'd suggest creating your own unique version of the work as he did with his *Oz* novels.

PASTICHE

This is another fictional form that can give you experience writing about characters you didn't create. Pastiche is when you write fiction about recognizable characters, but you change just enough about them not to get sued (if they're not in the public domain yet) or you change things about them for artistic reasons. For example, Philip Jose Farmer's legendary novel *A Feast Unknown*, which features Lord Grandith (based on Tarzan) and Doc Caliban (based on Doc Savage). The story features a lot of sex and violence (and sometimes combinations of the two), which is likely why Farmer opted to go the pastiche route, that, and the freedom it gave him to shape the characters for his artistic purposes. If you're looking to write pastiche and sell it to a publisher, I think you'll have a hard time, since it'll be obvious your story is a knockoff of *Star Trek* or *Bridgerton*. Lovecraftian pastiches seem to be an exception. If elements of your pastiche are exaggerated and played for laughs, it can slip into parody, and while there's nothing wrong with parody in general, it probably won't serve you well as a writing sample when trying to land a tie-in job (unless the IP you hope to write is a parody itself).

SELF-PUBLISHING WRITERS AND TIE-INS

Self-publishing writers can't write licensed tie-ins on their own. Even if you had the money to pay a studio or game company the licensing fee they require, since they want to control and protect their IP, they prefer to go with an experienced, traditionally published author. But self-publishers can do the next best thing to writing a tie-in. They can write stories with public domain characters or write pastiche or parody of an IP (as long as they change some details, such as character names, place names, etc.).

BOOK PACKAGERS

Book packagers are publishers who develop book lines "written" by house names, write outlines for the individual volumes, then hire writers to turn the outline into a prose novel. These are work-for-hire gigs (see the next chapter for more info on work for hire), and writers get no byline on the books. They're all credited to the house name. They're not exactly media tie-ins, but they share some similarities, and if you've written novels for a book packager, you'll have some writing credits and experience that will put you ahead of other writers who hope to land a tie-in writing job. I've listed the website addresses of a couple book packagers—Working Partners and Relay Publishing—on the Resources page at the end of this book.

EXERCISES

1. What public domain characters would you most like to use in stories? (Check out the list at the web address I provided earlier if you're not sure which characters are in the public domain.) Make a list.
2. Pick your favorite character from the list, and jot down ideas for stories you could tell about that character. You can use the Story Situation list I gave you for help coming up with story ideas.

VOICES FROM THE TRENCHES

AMANDA BRIDGEMAN

How did you get into writing tie-ins? I was approached by a publisher who had worked with me previously on an original novel for a different publishing house. They were obviously familiar with my work, knew I was reliable, and liked working with me, and I with them. I'd always wanted to do tie-in writing, so it was an awesome opportunity and I jumped at the chance!

What do you like about writing tie-ins? What are the rewards for you? Being able to create stories in the iconic worlds I love so much, is a reward in itself. Also having the opportunity to learn more about each world is amazing. For example, I was a massive fan of the *X-Men* cinematic universe, so being invited to pitch in that world was incredibly exciting. However, all the stories needed to be based on the comics, which I wasn't as familiar with—but having the chance to delve into and spend a lot of time with the comics was an absolute treat!

What challenges have you faced in your career as a tie-in writer? The biggest challenge is getting up to speed quickly on worlds you're not 100 percent familiar with. Many of the big IPs like *X-Men* and *Warhammer* have decades upon decades of lore and universe to get your head around. Thankfully, between the Internet fan pages/wikis and knowledgeable editors, you can get up to speed pretty quickly.

Does writing tie-ins require a different skill set than other types of writing? If so what are these skills? Yes, in terms of being able to "paint inside the lines" and release control. With original stories you are the boss, you make the rules (of the universe), and you have control (over the characters). With tie-in fiction you must adhere to the set rules of the universe, and character use can be limited. Certain characters will be off limits, etc., so you can't bring them into your story. With some, you also can't really introduce new (main) characters or elements to the world. Therefore, you need to come up with an interesting story that fits the existing and unbreakable parameters. Your proposed ideas might be discarded or steered in another direction. As you are a "writer for hire," you must respect the fact that the characters and the world don't belong to you. So, if you like to have full control (make final decisions) over what you write, then avoid tie-in writing.

Do you think it's possible to be pigeonholed as a tie-in writer, making it more difficult to publish your own work? If so, how do you deal with this? I think you can be. Once you have a good relationship with the publisher, they'll often let you continue to pitch on whatever properties they've licensed. That can be a very tempting thing to do, as writing for these amazing IPs is so much fun, not to mention an honour—they're great brands to be associated with. However, you can fast get stuck in an endless rotation of commissioned stories that you run out of time to work on any original ideas—and it's the original work that will generally bring a writer long-term royalties (and you own the IP, which could be sold on for development in other formats such as film/TV, comics, plays, etc.). Career-wise, it's up to the writer as to what they want to do and what their goals are. For me, I want a healthy balance of both original and tie-in fiction.

What advice do you have for writers who want to break into the media tie-in field? From my experience and from what I've seen, relationships are key. First you need to prove that you can write a good story, whether short story or novel. Once you've proven your writing standard (through being traditionally published, or winning/shortlisting for awards, or perhaps mega-selling as a self-published author), it's about finding who is publishing the tie-in fiction you want to break into and see if you can get an introduction. It's not easy, as there are only so many writing gigs every year, and many tie-in writers are already embedded with those publishers. The publishers will generally go with who they know, and who they trust will deliver (to a particular standard, and on time). That said, the smart publishers stay on the lookout for new talent. Just keep trying and don't give up. Most importantly, keep an eye out for any Open Submission/Pitching opportunities (whether short fiction or novels). Occasionally they'll pop up and that may be a chance to break in.

AMANDA BRIDGEMAN is a two-time Scribe Award winner, an Aurealis and Ditmar Awards finalist, and author of several novels and short stories. Her original fiction includes the sci-fi crime thriller *The Subjugate*, which is being developed for TV by Anonymous Content and Aquarius Films. Bridgeman's media tie-in fiction includes work for Marvel (*X-Men*), Black Library (*Warhammer 40k*), and Z-Man Games (*Pandemic*).

WILL MCDERMOTT

How did you get into writing tie-ins? I was working at Wizards of the Coast in the magazine department, which was right next to the TSR book department (that had recently arrived after the acquisition). I began working with the book department on game guides for Magic: The Gathering, and when they asked for story synopses for the backstory of the sets, I pitched the idea of turning the synopses into short stories set in the world. These were my first forays into shared-world writing. Based on the strength of those stories, I was invited to submit to anthologies and then contracted to write two Magic: The Gathering novels.

What do you like about writing tie-ins? What are the rewards for you? I love playing in someone else's sandbox and adding to the continuity of a larger story. I have added very much beloved characters to universes I have written in, such as Balthor in Magic: The Gathering, and Seek and Destroy in the Necromunda universe.

I also love doing the research for tie-ins, which often involves watching TV shows I have loved (again) or binging new shows or movies. For my first Kal Jerico novel, I had to read through all of the Necromunda graphic novels for my research, which was a blast and gave me a great sense of the flair of the main character.

What challenges have you faced in your career as a tie-in writer? Honestly, the biggest challenge is always finding new work. Writing stories is not just about doing the research and the writing. You also have to get that initial conversation with the licensor and publisher. There is a lot of legwork and networking involved in writing (in any medium or form), which has never been my strong suit.

Does writing tie-ins require a different skill set than other types of writing? If so what are these skills? You still need to write a compelling story with compelling characters, just like any other type of fiction. But, you have to remain true to the characters and the worldbuilding that has come before. So, generally speaking, you cannot make major changes. The main characters can grow a little, but not in any significant way that will impact other stories that come after by other authors. The same goes for the world itself.

This can constrain your choices as a writer. But to tell a compelling story, you must find a way for the story to have an impact or your readers just won't care. You can't kill off a main character, so putting them in any type of danger is often hollow because readers will know they will survive. So, one thing you can do is place other characters around the main characters, make the main characters (and the readers) care for those characters, and then put those characters in danger.

Do you think it's possible to be pigeonholed as a tie-in writer, making it more difficult to publish your own work? If so, how do you deal with this? I have found it hard to break out of tie-in writing. But I have also found it hard to get the attention of publishers of larger tie-in properties, so the fault may lie with me. I find it much easier to publish short stories set in my own worlds than longform stories in my own settings. Anthologies are where I shine. If you can get the attention of a few anthology editors, this can open up the field a little more to writing in your own worlds and breaking out of tie-ins. Again, the networking required to get the attention of larger publishers is an issue I have always struggled with in this business.

What advice do you have for writers who want to break into the media tie-in field? As with any other form of fiction writing, you must hone your craft and the only way to do that is to write (a lot)! Also, read (a lot). Read good fiction by strong authors. My favorites include Terry Pratchett, Robert J. Sawyer, and Tim Powers. And when you read, read critically. Watch how the authors build their characters (with actions, deeds, and dialog). See how they construct their sentences to add impact to a scene. Think critically about how they weave plot, character development, world building, and action into their stories. See what they do to pull readers into the story and keep them interested in what is happening to the characters.

Then, if you truly want to write tie-in fiction, immerse yourself in both the main media outlets for those universes, but also read the stories that other authors have written in that universe. This is your research. You need to know how the characters are handled, how the stories are built. Not just because this is what the audience wants, but because this is what the licensor and publisher are likely to be looking for. Remember you always have more than one audience. You have the readers and your editors, but also their publishers and stakeholders they must work with.

WILL MCDERMOTT turned a love of science fiction and games into a writing career. He has published nine novels, more than 20 short stories, and helped create innumerous worlds, characters, and stories for card, board, and video games. His fiction is often set in gaming universes, including *Magic: The Gathering*, *Warhammer 40K*, *Renegade Legion*, and *Mage Wars*. He is known for bringing larger-than-life characters alive, including *Warhammer*'s Kal Jerico and Mad D'onne, *Magic*'s Balthor the Stout, and more recently, *Night Stalker*'s Carl Kolchak. McDemott's most recent *Night Stalker* novel, *Hotel of Horror*, was published in 2023. For more information, check out willmcdermott.com.

CHAPTER EIGHT
THE BUSINESS OF TIE-INS

I'm placing the chapter on the business of tie-ins before the chapter on how to write them not because business is more important, but because you have to land a tie-in gig with a publisher before you can start writing. So if you don't tend to business matters first, you won't get a chance to write tie-in novels. Okay?

Moving on …

When I teach classes on novel writing, we start out by discussing the students' goals. I show them a PowerPoint slide with two different quotes:

"Sir, nobody but a blockhead ever wrote except for money."—Samuel Johnson

"There's no money in poetry, but then there's no poetry in money either."—Robert Graves

Before we proceed further, I tell the students that no one goes into the arts to make money. If people wanted to make money, they'd become doctors or lawyers. Writers may want to make money from their art so they can eat, pay bills, and make *more* art, but their writing comes from a creative need, not a financial one. At a convention, you might hear someone say, "She just wrote that tie-in for the money," and that might very well be true. But she *wrote* in the first place to fulfill herself creatively. I didn't become a writer and teacher to make tons of money. I did it to feed my soul (and make enough money to survive along the way). Don't get me wrong; I'll take as much money as the world is stupid enough to give me, but I don't seek it.

And no creative should ever look down at another for making money with their art. You think it's easy to get someone to pay for the privilege of experiencing your dreams? It's hard as hell, and when it happens, it's like a goddamned miracle.

I tell my students to think of a continuum, with money at one end and artistic satisfaction at the other. Wherever they find themselves on the continuum at any time in their career, for any given project, is fine. And now I'm telling you the same.

That said, tie-in fiction is published primarily for entertainment, so if you're a prose stylist or like to experiment with form and subject matter in your work, a career writing tie-in fiction would be artistic starvation for you. But if you do want to write tie-in fiction, it's inevitable that you'll need to deal with various business concerns, some of which any fiction writer must contend with, and some which are geared more specifically to tie-in writers.

Like work-for-hire contracts.

WORK FOR HIRE

I've mentioned work for hire elsewhere in this book, but we need to discuss it in more detail, as it's one of the defining features of tie-in writing.

Work for hire means that you are contracted by a publisher—usually on the basis of an outline and sample chapters—to write a novel using pre-established characters and settings. These projects are often called *tie-in, media-related*, or *licensed* novels because they relate to an existing product, such as a roleplaying game, TV show, movie, or comic book. Authors sometimes receive advances and royalties on these projects, but more often they're paid a flat flee with no royalties. The creators of the original properties—usually movie, TV, and game companies—own the copyright to the finished work.

Work-for-hire projects are sometimes looked down upon in the publishing industry because they're perceived as "pre-fab" creations. After all, if the characters and settings already exist, how much work does the writer have to do? Another reason is, since the writer doesn't retain rights to the book once it's finished, work-for-hire is seen as exploiting authors.

I would never sign a work-for-hire contract for my original fiction—that would be like selling my car or my house. Once it's gone, it's gone. But I have no problem signing a work-for-hire contract for a tie-in project. When I wrote my *Supernatural* novels, I knew I didn't create Sam and Dean and their world, and I didn't own them. I'd been hired to write *about* them and their world, but they weren't mine and never could be. That was okay. I knew the deal going in.

So the first part of the tie-in business you need to make peace with is that contracts in the field are almost always work for hire. If you're not comfortable with that, maybe tie-in writing isn't for you. I suppose you or your agent could attempt to negotiate better contract terms than work for hire, but the key word here is *attempt*. These companies are called license *holders*, not license *letting-goers*.

The rest of the clauses in tie-in contracts are basically the same as contracts for original work. The Science Fiction and Fantasy Writers Association has a ton of resources at their website to help authors, and you can learn everything you need to know about book contracts here: www.sfwa.org/other-resources/for-authors/information-center.

FINDING TIE-IN WORK

As hard as it is to get starting writing tie-in fiction, it can be just as hard—if not harder—to keep finding tie-in gigs. Once you've written a few for a publisher, they might start coming to you with projects. If you build up a reputation as a skilled, professional tie-in writer, editors you've never worked with before might contact you about a gig, or other writers might recommend you to editors. But editors don't stay with a publishing house forever, and some publishers stop putting out tie-ins altogether, leaving you hustling for work once more.

So whether you're looking to score you first tie-in writing job or your one hundredth, here are some tactics you can try.

START SMALL

Don't try to land a gig writing *Star Trek* novels right away. You'll need an agent, and even then, you'll have a hell of a lot of competition. Try writing short stories first. Some publishers and game companies use tie-in short stories on their websites or in magazines devoted to their IPs. Some have open calls for anthologies based on their IPs. If you want to write novels, a smaller publisher or game company might be more open to working with a newer tie-in writer than Titan Books or Simon & Schuster.

YOU EVER THINK ABOUT PUBLISHING A TIE-IN NOVEL?

If there's a smaller game company you know or a small indie film company, you could approach them at an event or send them email or a message on social media to ask if they've ever thought about putting out a tie-in based on one of their IPs, and that you'd love to do it. You can offer to write it for a small fee, say $100 to $500 dollars, or you can write the first one for free so you'll have a credit to your name. If the company doesn't already publish books, you can offer to help them self-publish it via Amazon. Sure, this tactic is a gamble, but you never know when you'll contact someone at just the right time." You know, we've been thinking about doing a tie-in, but we just haven't gotten around to it yet."

FOLLOW GUIDELINES ON PUBLISHER WEBSITES

Some tie-in publishers have guidelines on their websites for all writers, including non-agented ones, to follow. Others have a brief statement saying they don't accept submissions from unagented authors. Either way, you should find some submission or contact info on their site.

MAKE COLD CALLS

Speaking of contact info …

If you're the assertive type—and you have some publications under your belt—you can probably find a phone number or email address on a publisher's website so you can contact them about writing tie-in fiction for them. Internet searches often reveal phone numbers that aren't listed on a publisher's website.

I only tried this twice, and both times it worked out, but I had a list of writing credits already. (And I probably got lucky.)

NETWORK AT CONVENTIONS

First, know that networking will not, repeat NOT, replace having writing experience and publishing credits. No one is going to give you a tie-in job just because you're good at schmoozing.

Second, I believe it's better to think of what you're doing as getting to know people as opposed to networking. That phrase implies you're only using them to further a goal, and not only is that skeevy, the person you talk to can sense what you're doing. So much of what happens in publishing is based on human relationships, and if you're a genuine person when you talk to someone, that'll go a long way to helping you connect to them.

Those things said, if you're at the same convention as editors and game publishers, you can find an opportunity to chat with them, maybe after a panel they've been on or maybe in the dealers' room/exhibitors' hall when they're at their company's table. Prepare by reading some of the tie-ins they've published before you get to the con, so you can let them know you're familiar with their line. Talk a bit about how the con is going, how are their sales, have they done anything fun or heard any surprising news? *Then* talk about the tie-ins they have coming up and ask if they have a need for new writers. If they're super busy when you first get there, come back later. If during your conversation, they need to speak with someone else, let them. As soon as you can, write down what you talked about so you don't forget it. Don't record your conversation while you're having it. That's creepy.

Some people suggest (and I agree) that going to conventions is a form of privilege, that the cost of the con, travel, hotels, and food—not to mention the time away from work and family—means that cons are not accessible to many people. Many cons have a virtual component, although that still costs money, and it's almost impossible to network during a con's virtual component. If you can afford to go to a con, maybe by sharing costs with a friend or two, it's worth it, not just for the networking opportunities but for the chance to be around other writers and make connections with them. If you can't afford large cons or aren't willing to spend the money to go to one yet, you can see if there are any cons within easy driving distance from where you live. There will be fewer writers and editors there (maybe no editors at all), but it's a way for you to see if you like going to cons and find them useful before spending the cash to go to larger ones.

I've listed the websites of some of the largest cons where you might encounter tie-in editors on the Resources page at the end of the book.

NETWORK ONLINE

Follow tie-in writers, editors, and publishers on social media. Interact with them and get to know them a bit before you start asking questions about the tie-in business and if editors have any open slots for new tie-in writers. Following publishers on social media is a great way to hear about open tie-in anthologies or any other opportunities. If a publisher has a message board at their site, and they're active on it, so much the better.

NETWORK WITH OTHER WRITERS

Networking with experienced tie-in writers can teach you a lot about the craft and business, and they might be able to give you leads on which publishers you should approach (and perhaps share contact information with you, too).

RESPOND TO OPEN CALLS

Submit to every open call that comes up. If the submission call is for short stories set in a weird west game scenario, and you hate weird west fiction, write a goddamned weird west story and submit it anyway. If you want to establish a career for yourself writing tie-in fiction, you need to take advantage of every opportunity you can find.

GET AN AGENT

Getting an agent isn't easy, but once you have one that can approach tie-in publishers on your behalf, the more receptive editors will be to hiring you to write a tie-in for them. There's no guarantee, of course—there never is in the world of publishing—but having an agent can get you to the front of the line, and that's a major advantage.

THE THREE MOST IMPORTANT TOOLS FOR GETTING MEDIA TIE-IN WORK

If you've read the chapters detailing my adventures writing tie-ins (and if you haven't, why the hell not?), you already know the basic process for submitting to tie-in editors. They give you a property to write for, you develop several short pitches, the editor and the license holder select one for you to expand into an outline, and once the editor and license holder are satisfied with it, you get a contract and can start writing. Sometimes you may be asked to write a sample chapter or two before you get the gig, but that hasn't happened very often to me. Let's talk about each of these tools in more detail.

PITCHES

In the tie-in world, a pitch is a short description of a story that you are proposing to write. The story does not exist yet, and won't exist unless the editor and license holder approve the pitch. One of the great things about pitches is that you don't need to spend a lot of time and effort writing an original novel, only to have it rejected. You only write the book when you know an editor wants to publish it. Pitches are written in simple, plain language. You're not trying to dazzle anyone with your literary prowess. You just need to get your idea across quickly and simply so the editor and license holder can assess it and make a decision on it (and perhaps suggest revisions).

To write a pitch, start with a sentence that summarizes the basic premise: *A military black ops captain stumbles into a nightmare world where dreams can kill you, ruled over by the demonic serial killer Freddy Krueger.* Then give a brief summary of the plot, detailing the hero's ups and downs in the story, any major subplots, and how they finally win.

I've included four pitches I came up with for a *Supernatural* tie-in in Appendix 2. The pitch for *Children of Anubis* was the one that was ultimately chosen by the editor and license holder.

PROPOSALS

A proposal is like a combination of a pitch and an outline. I guess you could think of it as a long pitch or a short outline. The nice thing about a proposal is that the editor may also consider it an outline, so you've already taken care of that step. I've included my proposal for a *Sleepy Hollow* novel (which was ultimately rejected by the editor) in Appendix 3.

OUTLINES

Outlines, like pitches, should be written in plain, easier-to-read language. Some writers like to jazz them up a bit, infuse them with energy and a sense of style, but since the editor has requested this outline, I don't think you need to sell it to them by making it entertaining to read. But you do you. Outlines are written in present tense and cover the events of the novel from beginning to finish, including the ending. Only the major plot points have to be covered. The editor doesn't expect you to know every single thing that's going to happen in the novel until you've actually completed it.

There's no set length for an outline unless the editor gives you one. My outlines can run anywhere from five to ten pages (although my agent says five is better because editors are busy and like to read short documents when they can).

If you're normally a discovery writer and hate planning, that's too bad. An outline is a must for landing a tie-in gig. And while the editor and license holder expect you to make some changes to it as you draft, they generally expect the manuscript you turn in to be more or less the same as the story you originally presented in your outline.

I've included the outline submitted for my novel *Supernatural: The Children of Anubis* in Appendix 4. This outline is just over twelve pages, which makes it a long one. I'd submitted a shorter one to the editor originally, but she asked me to revise it and put in more detail. The outline in Appendix 4 is the revision.

SAMPLE CHAPTERS

As I said earlier, it's rare that I've had to write sample chapters for an editor, but I've done it. I've included the sample chapters I wrote in my (failed) attempt to try and land an *Executioner* novel gig in Appendix 5.

HOW TO MEET INSANE DEADLINES

As I've mentioned numerous times throughout this book, short deadlines are a common aspect of a tie-in writer's career, and if you expect to keep that career once it's going, you *have* to meet those deadlines. It's one of the hallmarks of a professional tie-in writer. So, let's talk about how to get more writing done, faster.

- Make a commitment to being productive.
- Make sure others know about, understand, and respect your commitment to being productive.
- Closed office door while writing. Do Not Disturb Sign on door of home office.
- Stay away from email, social media, the Internet, videogames, etc., during writing time. Turn your devices off, throw them out of the window, sell them on Ebay.
- Set short-term goals: How much to you want to accomplish during today's writing session?
- Set long-term goals: How much do want to accomplish in a day, a week, a month, a year?
- You can make these goals general: I want one hour of uninterrupted writing time a day for a week.
- You can make these goals specific: By the end of the month, I want to produce a polished, ready-to-submit short story (or whatever).
- Setting goals makes it easier to explain to others what you're doing. Instead of saying, "I'm trying to write," say, "Today I'm working on my main character's backstory."
- Cut back on some activities and time-wasters: Who needs TV? A clean house? Clean clothes? Sleep? Food?
- Write first thing in the morning before the day starts making demands on you.
- Go to bed an hour earlier and wake up an hour earlier to carve out some writing time.
- Write before going to bed. You may lack some energy, but the day's other work is done, everyone else is asleep, and you can finally do what you've been looking forward to all day.
- Write during breaks. Even small increments of writing time add up.
- Schedule your writing time, perhaps at the same time every day or on the weekends.
- Make a writing date, an appointment with another writer who also wants to be more productive. You work next to each other, support each other, and keep each other accountable.
- Set a quota for how much writing you want to produce—a day, a week, a month, etc. Always strive to make your quota, but don't beat yourself up if you miss it. Try to hit your quota next time.

- Get away from home. Write at a coffee shop, a restaurant, a bar, a park, a monastery, wherever.
- Take a weekend getaway for just you and your writing.

EXERCISES

1. Read a published tie-in novel, then write a pitch and an outline for it. How did it go? Was it easier than you expected? More difficult?
2. Now come up with an original tie-in idea for an IP you love. Write a pitch for this idea, then develop that pitch into an outline. Was this easier or harder than writing a pitch and outline for an already-existing story? Why?

VOICES FROM THE TRENCHES

KEITH R.A. DECANDIDO

How did you get into writing tie-ins? I started out as an editor of tie-ins. From 1993-1999, I worked as an editor for the late book packager Byron Preiss, and part of my job was to edit tie-ins, most notably an extensive series of prose novels and anthologies based on Marvel superheroes, which were co-published by Byron and Berkley Books from 1994-2000, and which I was in charge of for most of its run. Being the editor of that line gave me pitching opportunities, and I also did some writing for the series itself (with other editors on staff editing my work), including a Spider-Man novel, two Spider-Man short stories, and short stories featuring the X-Men, the Hulk, and the Silver Surfer. Most notably, several authors I hired to write tie-ins were also editing other projects. As an example, Andrew Lane co-wrote an X-Men short story for me, and he hired me to write a Doctor Who short story shortly after that.

What do you like about writing tie-ins? What are the rewards for you? Well, besides the obvious reward in that they pay me, there's also the fact that virtually every tie-in I've written has been for a property that I either was a huge fan of going in (*Star Trek, Farscape, Supernatural, Leverage*), or became a big fan of when I did research for the project (*Resident Evil, Gene Roddenberry's Andromeda, World of Warcraft, StarCraft*). I've gotten to write characters I've always loved and admired and enjoyed, from Spock to John Crichton to Spider-Man to Ellen Ripley to Kato to Samantha Carter to Worf.

What challenges have you faced in your career as a tie-in writer? Oh, lots. There's the two-and-a-half weeks I had to write the *Serenity* novelization. There's having to completely rewrite the B-plot of my *Command & Conquer* novel because of a change to one line of a game script. But the biggest challenge is probably every time I've had to come in at the beginning of a license when people are still feeling their way around and figuring out what they want. It's a lot easier to do the fourth book in a license than the first one.

Does writing tie-ins require a different skill set than other types of writing? If so what are these skills? In general, it's the same skill set. You still have to tell a compelling story with a beginning, a middle, and an end with interesting things happening to characters you care about. The only real difference is that, in tie-in fiction, you have to capture the character voices. If your Jean-Luc Picard doesn't sound like Sir Patrick Stewart, if your Leia Organa doesn't sound like Carrie Fisher, your readers will reject you.

Do you think it's possible to be pigeonholed as a tie-in writer, making it more difficult to publish your own work? If so, how do you deal with this? I don't think it's anywhere near the same issue as it used to be, mainly because the publishing world has gotten so much more varied and complex. When I first started thirty years ago and the only real options were to go with one of the big New York publishers, that was more of a concern. Now, though, with so many presses of different sizes, not to mention self-publishing options, it's significantly less of a problem. I certainly haven't had any problems putting my original work out, though, of course, it doesn't get anywhere near the same sales as the tie-in fiction …

What advice do you have for writers who want to break into the media tie-in field? You should at the very least have a strong familiarity with the property in question. Readers can absolutely tell when you only have a passing familiarity with the property, and can also tell when you don't have any real enthusiasm for it. It's not necessarily a requirement, but at the very least, even if it's something you're not a huge fan of, you should at least find something in the milieu to focus on that excites you.

KEITH R.A. DECANDIDO is the author of 60+ novels, 100+ short stories, and 50+ comic books over the course of a 30-year fiction-writing career. He was favored in 2009 with a Faust Award for Lifetime Achievement in the tie-in field by the International Association of Media Tie-in Writers. He has written in more than 30 licensed universes, from *Alien* to Zorro, including TV shows (*Star Trek* and *Supernatural*), movies (*Kung Fu Panda* and *Cars),* games (*Resident Evil* and *World of Warcraft*), and comics (*Spider-Man* and *Thor*); and he has created multiple universes of his own, most recently the Supernatural Crimes Unit series that will debut soon from the Weird Tales Presents imprint of Blackstone Publishing. DeCandido also writes about pop culture for a variety of sources, primarily the award-winning *Reactor Magazine* (formerly *Tor.com*), and he is a longtime fiction editor (including curating multiple anthologies, among them *Double Trouble* and *The Four ???? of the Apocalypse*), a fourth-degree black belt, a musician, and possibly some other stuff he can't recall due to lack of sleep. Website: decandido.net.

TEEL JAMES GLEN

How did you get into writing tie-ins? I was offered the opportunity by one of my regular publishers of my own fiction who had acquired licensing for a classic property. He liked what I did and four other opportunities came from them. Since then I've been fortunate to write IPs for other publishers and properties.

What do you like about writing tie-ins? What are the rewards for you? Well, in a sense, depending how established the IP is, most of the work has been done for the writer in that the world, general style and dynamic of the characters exists. (This is a two-edged sword, of course if you have a lot of history to work your tale into). The rewards are generally (aside from the fee) working with a recognizable property that will attract more readers.

What challenges have you faced in your career as a tie-in writer? Just getting known is the biggest challenge. Doing a good job on IP X does not necessarily mean the IP owners of Z will see that you can do that particular property. And when you write for an IP write it as if you have loved it all along—not just respect it.

Does writing tie-ins require a different skill set than other types of writing? If so what are these skills? As I mentioned, if the IP is "deep"—with a lot of stories already written/filmed, you have to fit your story in and can have a lot of history to be in line with. Also, a good idea—even one you love can be changed or even torpedoed completely at any stage in the process because you are there to serve the larger world of the IP as it may have to pass through many levels for full approval. For this reason, you have to A: not be too precious with an idea and B: plan and outline well enough for the various editor in the chain of command to know what is to come when you write the finished story. This leaves less room for "improvisation" in writing the tale but can actually force you to find deeper levels to your work.

Do you think it's possible to be pigeonholed as a tie-in writer, making it more difficult to publish your own work? If so, how do you deal with this? I've only done a dozen or so different IP and none of them have made enough noise so far to get me typecast. Check back with me in a bit.

What advice do you have for writers who want to break into the media tie-in field? Just write the best stories you can regardless what you write. If you want to do a particular area of IP writing—Games, SF, Detective etc.—write stories in that genre that respect the genre and network. Eventually good work gets noticed.

TEEL JAMES GLENN has killed hundreds and been killed more times—on stage and screen, as he has traveled the world for forty-plus years as a stuntman, swordmaster, storyteller, bodyguard, actor, and haunted-house barker. He is proud to have studied swordsmanship under Errol Flynn's last stunt double and been beaten up by Hawk on the *Spenser for Hire* TV show. He did over 200 episodic appearances on Soap operas, seventy feature films, and sixty Renaissance festivals all over the country. Glenn has dozens of published novels, and his poetry and stories have been printed in over two hundred magazines, including *Weird Tales, Mystery, Pulp Adventures, Space & Time, Mad, Cirsova, Silverblade, Heroic Fantasy, Blazing Adventures,* and *Sherlock Holmes Mystery*. His novel *A Cowboy in Carpathia: A Bob Howard Adventure* won the Pulp Factory Award for Best Novel in 2021. Additionally, he won the 2012 Pulp Ark Award for Best Author and was a finalist for the Derringer Short Mystery Award in 2022. His novel *Callback for a Corpse* was a second-place winner in the CWR Poll as Best Mystery. His website is TheUrbanSwashbuckler.com.

CHAPTER NINE

WRITING TIE-INS: SHORT STORIES, NOVELS, AND NOVELLAS

Before we dive into this chapter, I need to make something clear.

While this book is about writing tie-in fiction, it's not a book about writing fiction in general. If you want to learn how to better handle character, plot, description, dialogue, conflict, point of view, setting, exposition, theme, etc., there are a million books, websites, and YouTube videos that will hook you up. And you do need to be skilled at all the elements of fiction writing, because it doesn't matter if you're writing original fiction or tie-in fiction. You're writing *fiction*, and you need to be damn good at it either way. Plus, if the IP you're writing about belongs to a specific genre—such as horror, science fiction, mystery, etc.—you need to at least be familiar enough with those genres to do a good job. Got it? Then let's get started.

READ TIE-INS

"But you shouldn't *have* to read books in order to write them."

I occasionally hear this from a student or sometimes see it posted on social media. It's true. It's not necessary to read in order to write. But it is if you want to write *well*. More than that, you need to read if you want your writing to be competitive. If you're self-publishing you can do anything you please. You can self-publish a book even if you can't spell *dog* or write a single coherent sentence. I believe the vast majority of self-published writers started out as readers and still are readers, just like traditionally published writers are. But if you want to write tie-ins, then you should read tie-ins—especially those written about the specific property you want to write for. You need to see how different writers take a non-prose form—like film, TV, animated cartoons, games—and transform it into prose. If you want to write *Star Wars* novels, it's not enough to have watched all the movies and TV shows (but you should do that, too). You need to read *Star Wars* books, especially current ones, so you not only see how *Star Wars* works in novel form, but you can get an idea of the kind of stories the current editor of *Stars Wars* fiction is buying.

In Lawrence Block's classic how-to-write book *Writing the Novel from Plot to Print*, he suggests a technique writers can use to more fully and deeply understand the way novels in their chosen genre are put together. Choose five novels of the type you want to write. In our case, that would be tie-in novels, and perhaps even ones based on a specific property, like *Star Wars*. Read all five to become familiar with the stories. Then go back and reread all five, this time outlining the scenes. (All you need to do is write down what happens.) If you want to get more detailed, you can note how much dialogue and description are in scenes, how much exposition and action, etc. You can color code your outlines to make them easier to read, choosing different colors to highlight information about dialogue, description, etc. If you do this, you will level up as a novelist, guaranteed. (And of course, you can use this technique to help you learn how to write any kind of novel.)

MEDIA AND THE WRITTEN WORD

Movies and TV series use images, colors, movement, sound, light, shadows, camera angles, special effects, and music to provide what their creators hope is an enthralling experience. A huge part of the fun of roleplaying games is being able to talk and laugh with your friends. It's the same with videogames, which also can provide an immersive experience like film but with the added factor of agency. You can control your avatar's movements, make choices, interact with other characters and the environment. No matter how hard you try, you cannot replicate any of these experiences in prose. When you write tie-ins, you use the original media as a *basis* for a prose story. You translate the property from one medium—one artistic language—to another. And since you're writing prose, you to need to …

RESPECT THE PROPERTY

If tie-in fiction has a Prime Directive (beyond telling a great story), it's this. If I ever did write a *My Little Pony* tie-in, I would respect the characters, their world, the kind of stories told in the series, and the fans. I would never approach a tie-gig with contempt for the property, nor would write it with a wink at the audience to let them know I think this property is really crap. I also wouldn't kill characters that aren't mine to kill, destroy settings that aren't mine to destroy, and alter history or lore that isn't mine to alter. Tie-in writers describe this attitude as if you've been invited over to someone's house to play with their toys. You should make sure you're careful when you play with them, that you don't damage them, and that you return them in as good a condition as you found them.

TAKE ADVANTAGE OF WHAT PROSE CAN DO

Maybe you can't replicate the sound of a phaser firing or a transporter activating on the page, but you can let readers know what's going on inside the head of the Starfleet officer firing the phaser or the transporter operator desperately trying to safely rematerialize crewmembers during a heated space battle with Romulans. Prose allows you to let readers know what characters are thinking and feeling, both emotionally and physically in ways no other medium can do. That's its great strength. Focus on the characters, what they're doing, what they think, and how they react as they're doing it.

REPLICATE THE *FEEL* OF THE PROPERTY

Star Wars has a lot of fast action and movement between settings. Indiana Jones movies have more action, faster action, and moves between more (earthbound) settings even faster. Both properties hail back to the golden age of pulp fiction, both focus on adventure, both are action-packed and fast-paced, but they *feel* different. *The Lord of the Rings* is high fantasy, while *A Game of Thrones* is grimdark fantasy. The characters in *Supernatural* and *Buffy the Vampire Slayer* battle unearthly forces that prey on humans, but the tone of the two series couldn't be more different. You should do your best to recreate what makes the property unique, what makes *Star Trek* feel like *Star Trek*, what makes *CSI* feel like *CSI*. This is one of the most important things a tie-in writer can do in their stories.

BE ORIGINAL (WHILE STILL RESPECTING THE PROPERTY)

You want to avoid telling the same kind of stories that the property you're writing about is known for. Jason returns to the camp where he died every Friday the 13th to kill whoever is around—usually a bunch of horny teens. *Alien* stories usually deal with another xenomorph outbreak, either a lone xenomorph or a group of them. Superman usually fights villains that can provide a suitable challenge for him, either in strength (Bizarro) or in intellect and deviousness (Luthor). What if Jason was captured by a billionaire and brought to a compound where the billionaire could hunt him? What if the military wants to weaponize xenomorphs, and they use tech to join the minds of soldiers to the creatures so the soldiers can direct them in battle? And what if the link goes both ways, and the soldiers start to exhibit xenomorph-like behavior? What if Superman loses control of his powers, becomes a danger to everyone around him, and must find a way to stop a super villain without using his powers?

A big part of the fun of writing tie-ins is that you can explore different types of stories that the audience doesn't usually get to experience, so try to think outside the box when coming up with plots for your tie-in fiction. But not *too* far out of the box. You still have to make sure to respect the property. You can't have Superman say to hell with it and use his out-of-control powers to stop the super villain, but at the cost of several thousand human lives. Superman would never willingly sacrifice a single life (despite what Zack Snyder might think).

DEVELOPING IDEAS FOR TIE-IN FICTION

In one of My Pulse-Pounding Adventures in Tie-In Land chapters, I talked about how I like to create my own settings and characters in addition to using pre-existing characters such as Sam and Dean in *Supernatural*. This gives me the freedom to break some toys if I want because they're *my* toys. Often the main plot of the story can revolve around these characters. That's how episodic TV series work. The main characters face a new problem for each episode, and often a new character is part of the problem somehow. Maybe they're the cause of it, maybe they're affected by it, but the series leads must deal with the problem and help this character (or stop them if they're a threat).

Are there any pre-existing characters in the property that you feel are underused? Develop your story around them. That's why I used Garth in *Children of Anubis* and Jonas in *Stargate SG-1: Valhalla*. Garth was working the same case as Sam and Dean, and Jonas was dealing with a problem in a separate storyline from O'Neill, Carter, Daniel, and Teal'c, and the two storylines eventually joined.

Is there an aspect of the property's setting that's never been covered or even established that you might like to explore? Do Hunters have fans or even groupies in *Supernatural*? The *Enterprise* has a night-shift crew. What happens if they're on duty when a crisis occurs, and the day crew are unable to help for some reason?

What if there's some kind of reversal to the property's premise? Sam and Dean are being hunted by a pair of monsters whose job it is to slay Hunters. Some force has altered the timeline, and Jean Luc Picard and his crew are now pirates who plunder starships instead of flying them. What if someone found a way to tame xenomorphs?

You can borrow from other genres. What if a disgraced Klingon warrior began working as a private detective? What if a Predator crash-landed outside of a town in the Old West? Wounded and without weapons, it's hunted by a sheriff's posse and also by a gang of outlaws. *Quantum Leap* excels at this kind of story, since Donald P. Bellisario originally envisioned it as an anthology series telling a different story every week.

THE PROBLEM OF EXPOSITION

It can be tempting to include a lot of the property's lore in your tie-in fiction, especially if you want to make sure readers unfamiliar or only slightly familiar with the property are up to speed. But too much exposition bogs a story down and turns it into a dull Wikipedia entry. In general, use only the absolutely necessary exposition, only when you absolutely need it, and keep it to a minimum. One way to do this is to use a trick I learned from my mentor and friend, Dennis L. McKiernan. Dennis wrote high fantasy, and sometimes as he was writing a scene, he would start relating the history of the castle his characters were in, the great battles that were fought around it. etc. Dennis always had two files open on his computer. One was the story he was writing. The other was for writing exposition. So when his mind turned to writing information that wasn't necessary for the scene he was writing, he'd switch to the exposition file, write it there, then return to the story file and continue the scene. Later, he'd read over all the information in the exposition file and decide whether to keep any of it, and if so, where to put it in the book so it wouldn't interfere with the story.

I was on a panel at a con with Mike Stackpole when he gave this tip for handling exposition in Battletech fiction (which can apply to any tie-in fiction or any type of fiction, for that matter.). He said you need to let your reader know three things about the Battletech setting: the galaxy is ruled by royal families, people fight in mechs, and mechs are deposited onto a planet by dropships. He said if you can introduce these three things within the first one hundred pages of your novel, you're good.

WRITING DIALOGUE FOR PRE-EXISTING CHARACTERS

If you're writing a tie-in novel with pre-existing characters, there's a lot about them that you need to get right—their personality, mannerisms, ways of thinking … and ways of speaking. If the property you're adapting is a visual medium, such as a TV show or movie, watch video with the closed captions on. Mute the volume so you can't hear how the actors invest the dialogue with emotion—you can't replicate that on the page—but you can create the dialogue as written words, just like the captions do. Make notes about the dialogue. How long are the sentences? Does the character speak in short phrases, full sentences, short sentences, long sentences, one sentence at a time, several sentences in a row? What kind of vocabulary do they use? Common, everyday words? Less common words? Technical jargon? Elevated speech? Swear words? Make character dialogue profiles—short paragraphs describing their speech with a few lines of dialogue copied from the property as examples—to serve as reference while you draft.

TIPS FOR WRITING SHORT STORIES

Short stories tend to run between 1500 to 7500 words. Stories shorter than this are called flash fiction or short-short stories. Longer stories are called novellas. If you're writing a tie-in short story, there's only so much of the original property that you can include. Think of the property as a large tapestry. Now focus in on one small portion of the whole. That portion is what you're going to write about, and you're going to, for the most part, ignore the rest of the tapestry. So if you're writing a short story about Iron Man, maybe you'll tell the tale of the first invention young Tony Stark built that actually impressed his father. Maybe you'll write a story about Tony struggling to decide whether to share his tech with the world. He wants to make the world a better place, but he's also afraid his tech might be horribly misused by some people. Short stories are great opportunities to tell smaller stories that normally don't get covered in novels—peeks behind the scenes, investigations into the unseen corners of a character's life, unrevealed portions of their background, personal dilemmas … In some ways, short tie-in stories are more satisfying than novels because you can give readers glimpses into characters and their world that they wouldn't get otherwise.

Following are some tips for writing effective short stories. There are exceptions to everything on the below list, of course, but they're solid pieces of general advice, especially if you're new to writing short fiction.

- **Start as close to the end as possible.** If you imagine a short story as a piece of art, it would be single painting of a scene that encapsulates the entire story. (Think of a novel as a series of paintings that depict key moments of the overall story.) Try to focus on that scene and tell its story, presenting the bare minimum of material to set it up.
- **Use a short time frame: minutes, hours, maybe a day or two.** It's certainly possible to cover a time period of years, centuries, millennia, etc. But the more time you try to cover in a short story, the more focus and immediacy it lacks. If your story, at least in terms of dramatized action, takes place over the course of minutes or hours, the story will more focused, impactful, and likely have a faster pace.
- **Use an organizational pattern that fits the story idea and/or the property—unless you purposefully want to mix things up.** Conan's adventures tend to be straightforward narratives (after all, he's a straightforward guy). So chronological order might be best for a Conan tale. But maybe you want to do something a little different, so you have parallel storylines—one set in Conan's present, one in his past—and alternate scenes between them. (The present and past scenes would relate to each other somehow, of course.) Or maybe you want to have a long flashback in the middle. Or maybe you'll start at the climax, then the rest of the story is a flashback of how Conan came to be in such a precarious position until the narrative catches up to the beginning and the opening scene finishes. If you're not sure what kind of organizational pattern to use, start writing and see what comes out. You can always revise later.
- **Two or three main characters.** Short stories are short. There's not a lot of room in them, which means you can only develop two or three main characters sufficiently. So maybe you write a *Star Trek* story about shuttlecraft crew taking a criminal to a rehabilitation colony. The shuttle crashes on a planet, and only one crew member and the criminal survive. They have to work together if they're going to stay alive long enough for rescue to come—but of course the criminal doesn't *want* to be rescued. I tell students to think of short stories as one-act plays with two or three actors on a relatively small stage.
- **Don't add too many supporting characters.** This is the flip side of the advice above. The surviving crewmember and the criminal should get the majority of the "stage time" in our *Star Trek* short story. There will be other crewmembers on the shuttlecraft who die in the crash, and someone on their starship who's searching for the lost shuttlecraft, but that's all. And these supporting characters will get very little stage time (especially the ones who die early on).
- **One primary setting.** Just like keeping the characters to a minimum in a short story, it helps to keep the settings to a minimum—one primary setting, maybe one or two minor ones. If your short story

takes place on a lake, you might need to (briefly) show your characters driving there, but your best bet is to start the story with the characters in a boat in the middle of the lake, and fill in any *needed* exposition as the story progresses. Remember, start a short story as close to the end as possible.

- **One point of view.** Are you starting to sense a pattern here? Readers don't have time to identify closely with multiple characters during the course of a short story. Choose one character to be the viewpoint character in the story, the one readers follow throughout your tale. It doesn't matter what voice you use—first person, second person, third person—stay in that one character's perspective from the beginning to the end.

- **One main story problem.** Don't try to squeeze an entire quest into your fantasy short story. Begin your story at the moment your hero sees the magic sword for the first time and needs to find a way past all the wards and traps. If your story features a space battle between two different galactic powers, don't write a blow-by-blow account of the fight. Write about the commander of a damaged starship that's stuck in a rapidly decaying orbit around a planet while the battle continues to rage all around them. One story problem: How do I get the sword? One story problem: How can I save my crew?

- **Include an inner conflict along with an outer one.** If you're writing adventure fiction, and a lot of tie-ins fall into the category, make sure to give your main character an inner conflict to go along with the outer one. Maybe the two are directly connected, maybe not. Maybe they're only connected thematically. For our fantasy quester above, maybe his father attempted to obtain the sword years ago, failed, and came away severely wounded. Disabled for the rest of his life, he sank into a deep depression and drank himself to death. Our hero is determined to get the sword to fulfill his father's quest, no matter what it takes. For our starship commander, maybe she hesitated during the battle—believing this war is unjust and foolish—which allowed the ship to be fired upon. Now her crew doesn't trust her judgment, and some may view her as a traitor. How can she still function as their commander and get them all to work together so they can survive? Inner and outer conflicts work great in novels, too, but there's more room in a novel, so you can take your time working out these conflicts.

- **Two or three scenes (in general).** You don't need much more. For our fantasy hero: one scene trying to get the sword and failing. One scene that's a flashback of the hero as a child with his bitterly depressed father. One scene in the present where the hero tries to get the sword again. This time he manages to get hold of it, but its dark power will destroy him, just as it did his father—unless he agrees to serve the evil god that forged the weapon. (His father resisted evil's lure and was cursed to the end of his days because of it.) Our hero will not give up, so he accepts the offer and becomes a servant of the god, but he *did* get the sword. So … a happy ending, right?

- **Avoid having too many obstacles.** There just isn't room enough in a short story for more than a few. Our space commander's obstacles: The damaged ship, the decaying orbit, the battle still going on (which could result in the ship's immediate destruction if they get hit by a stray shot), and worst of all, her crew now mistrusting and even hating her. I'd prioritize the conflict with the crew as the most important obstacle because conflict between people is always more dramatically interesting. And I'd embody the entire crew's emotions in just a couple people—maybe the first officer and the crewmember who'd been working the weapons console. (Remember, only two or three main characters in a short story.)

TIPS FOR WRITING NOVELS

How long *is* a novel? In general, traditional publishers consider a novel to be at least 50,000 words, but tie-in editors often want lengths between 80,000 to 100,000, with 80-90K words being the sweet spot. Young adult novels tend to run between 25K to 50K words, and middle-grade novels from 10K to 30K.

For new novelists (and sometimes for experienced ones, too) writing an entire novel can be a struggle. So here are some tips to help you make your novels long enough and help them across the finish line.

Aim for the Bare Minimum. If you're having trouble reaching novel length (for your original fiction when you start out), I'd advise you to aim for the shorter end of the spectrum. This is one of the reasons the goal for National Novel Writing Month is 50K words. It's the shortest novel length you can write that isn't YA or MG. Fifty thousand words isn't a marketable length in terms of traditional publishing, but some small press publishers might be okay with it, and if you're self-publishing, shorter novels tend to work better anyway. (Shorter but more frequent releases seems to be the most successful business model for self-publishing.) Breaking 50K on a manuscript for the first time can help you overcome the psychological hurdle of writing a novel. For a lot of beginning novelists, the novel form can seem too intimidating. But once you've hit 50K, you've gotten over the first big psychological hurdle, and you can try to write a longer novel next time. And with some practice, you'll be ready to write the 80-100K word novels tie-in editors are looking for.

A short story is an event; a novel is a series of events that add up to a much larger journey. If the length of a novel seems intimidating, don't think of your story as a novel, but rather a series of connected short stories. For example, if you're writing a novel about a haunting, one scene might be the story of the first time your main character suspects there's a ghost. Another scene might be the story of how the ghost came to be in the first place. Another scene might be the story of the ghost's first attempt to kill your main character or perhaps possess them. You can write these stories in any order you want and combine them later. Using this technique, your novel is almost like a short story collection where all the stories are linked and they add up to a plot progression from beginning to end. And if you need to write some connecting scenes so the stories fit together better, so be it. And if you've already got a novel draft finished but it's too short, ask yourself if there are any other small stories related to the overall story that you haven't told yet, then tell them. For example, maybe the haunting in your novel has been going on for two centuries. This means other people beside your main character have encountered the ghost. Why not tell their stories in your book?

Add more characters. One of the ways I get length into my novels is to use an ensemble cast. This means I can write scenes from different characters' viewpoints, and it allows me to show different aspects of the story. I try to keep the number of characters in the ensemble manageable, around ten or less, with three to five main ones. If I'm writing a tie-in with pre-existing characters, I have to make sure I don't create too many new ones so the main characters get their full time on the stage. Sometimes I'll fall in a love with a character who was originally supposed to have only a few scenes or who was even supposed to die. But I see possibilities for expanding the story with them, so I keep them around. Sometimes I'll introduce a character later in the narrative who's only going to stick around for a while (maybe they're going to be killed by the antagonist) but I'll write a scene of two from their point of view. I want to give them their moment on the stage, give them their dignity, before they have to bow out.

Add more obstacles. One of the easiest ways to make a novel longer is to give your characters more hurdles to overcome. Once, I was listening to an audiobook on the drive home from the college where I teach. It was a fantasy adventure story, and in the current scene, the characters were traveling on foot attempting to sneak past an enemy army at night. Now they could've gotten past without incident, but what fun is that for readers? They got noticed by the army, were chased, and got separated. Two had to jump off a cliff into a river, and two others had to disguise themselves and attempt to pass through the army to get to a castle of potential allies under siege. It wasn't easy, but they all managed to eventually meet back up inside the castle, relatively safe (one of them caught an arrow in the shoulder). The author could've simply had the characters all get from point A to point B without trouble, but by making it harder for them, not only did the author make that part of the story more interesting, he made it longer.

Use the Triangle Technique. Many writers try to create novels using only two points of conflict. Let's use the movie *Jaws* as an example. Two points of conflict: Sheriff vs Shark. But now consider three points of conflict: Sheriff vs Shark and Mayor who wants to keep the beach open during 4th of July holiday weekend at all costs. The novel *Jaws* has a fourth point of conflict. The oceanographer Hooper dated the Sheriff's wife in college and they begin an affair. Adding extra points of conflict not only makes your story richer and gives it more depth, it allows you to regulate the pace of your novel by switching back forth between the points of conflict, and it allows you to make your story—you guessed it!—longer.

Employ Murphy's Law. A lot of beginning writers have almost everything go right for their characters. The characters may have some kind of obstacle to overcome to get from point A to point B, but they will get to Point B, usually unscathed (more or less). For example, say you have a scene where a character needs to get to a job interview, and they're running late. Maybe they almost get involved in a car accident but manage to get there at last. But what if they don't get to the interview? What if something occurs that completely sidetracks them? They get into an accident. Or someone runs up to them at a stoplight and begs for their help. Having something go truly wrong in a scene can send the story off into interesting and unexpected directions—and lengthen your novel in the process. Some books on novel plotting call this a Disaster, as in scenes should always end with something going wrong, whether large or small. I think that approach is too mechanical and could quickly become repetitive, but the basic concept is sound.

Combine story types to develop your novel further. There are many different story motifs, and one way to make a story larger is to combine them. Stereotypical action movies do this well (because the action in and of itself isn't enough to carry an entire film). Let's say the main thing our action-adventure hero needs to do is stop vampires from releasing a genetically-modified virus that will lower humanity's collective IQ to the point where they're no smarter than cattle (thus making it easier to control them and use them as a food source). If our hero knew all this, though, it would make it too easy to locate the vampires and stop them. So we add a Mystery element. Why are formerly brilliant people turning up on the street with low IQ's? Why are there mysterious murders where the victims die of blood-loss? And so on. That's still not enough, though, so let's add a Love story. A scientist who's looking into the mysterious low IQs gets threatened by an equally mysterious assailant (who we'll later learn is a vampire) and our hero ends up saving the scientist and starts for fall for her. Maybe we'll add a Chase too. The vampires are desperate to get their hands on the scientist. They manage to abduct her and the hero goes after them. Now we've got a Rescue, too! So if your novel is too short, add in one or more story types. Following are a few different story types to choose from. I'm sure you can think of many more.

- Chase
- Love
- Rescue
- Revenge
- Coming of age
- Discovery
- Quest for object
- Quest for truth
- Survival
- Escape
- Defense/protection

Stories within stories. Earlier, I talked about how you can think of a novel as a series of stories, and how you can expand your novel by adding more stories. Here are a few specific types to choose from.

- **Flashbacks.** You can show a great deal about characters and setting by adding dramatized flashbacks. Just don't overdo it and have every other scene be a flashback. And if you have more than one, space them out. And try different techniques. One flashback could be a memory, one could essentially be a monologue as a character tells their story to another character, one could be a separate dramatized scene that you insert without any explanation where it came from (readers will understand you're simply showing them something from the past), or you could present it as a dream (which means you can add surreal touches to it here and there, maybe combine it with another memory, or turn it into a nightmare). And speaking of dreams …

- **Dreams.** Other ways dreams can be used are as a portent of the future (if the character's dream is magic or psychic in nature) or as a reaching into the past (again, via magic or science). You can also have bits and pieces of these dreams—or psychic episodes—occur periodically throughout the book, keeping the mystery of what it all means until later, when all the puzzle pieces are in place. You can have characters communicate in dreams. This could be two living people or it could be a living person and a dead person, or people connecting across time or dimensions. It all depends on the kind of story you're telling.

- **Imaginings.** This is the Walter Mitty technique. One of your characters can imagine a dramatized scenario—maybe one they've been dreading or one they hope will happen. They can try to imagine something that happened in the past. These scenes may be short—anywhere from a few paragraphs to pages—but when you're trying to expand your novel, every little bit helps.

- **Hallucinations.** Your character might be under the influence of some supernatural force or they might be sick, injured, drugged or suffering from some sort of mental illness. Any of these could cause your character to experience a dramatized scene that may not be real, but it'll show more about them and, depending on how you write the hallucination, even advance the plot. And if your character (or characters) experience periodic hallucinations, so much the better.

- **Origin stories.** Say you have a character that has a deathly fear of drowning. Instead of telling readers about it in a short summary paragraph, you could write a dramatized flashback showing the origin of this fear. Maybe you're writing a science fiction novel in which a space colony has for some mysterious reason become deserted. You can alternate between scenes of the current investigation into the disappearances with past scenes of the colonists experiencing the events that lead to their eventual disappearance. (This alternating between past and present storylines can work well for short fiction too.) You can tell the origin of a people, a civilization, a technology, a curse … anything, really, just so long as it's pertinent to the story and above all, interesting to the reader.

- **A supporting character's story.** Have an important supporting character? Tell their story, either all at once or in bits and pieces, but tell it in dramatized scenes.

- **Use epistolary techniques.** Epistolary techniques—making a novel be a collage of documents written by the characters—used to be a common storytelling technique. It's still around today, but most people probably know it as found-footage movies. You can use diary/journal entries, excerpts from a fictional book in your world, letters, emails, new articles, web articles, TV news, recorded videos, security footage, records of scientific experiments, etc. Putting excerpts from these things in your novel can enrich it by adding some narrative variety, as well as additional length.

Here are some additional expansion tips.

- **Have your characters work at cross purposes.** Too many writers have all of their characters working well together the entire time, with perhaps a token argument here and there, but nothing so serious that it disrupts the group's forward progress. But you lengthen your story (and add additional conflict and character development) by having your characters argue about the best way to deal with a problem, or having them go their own way to address the problem separately because they can't agree on strategy. Maybe your characters have different goals (and maybe they're concealing their true motives). Having your characters work at cross purposes also complicates your plot, which … yep, makes the story longer.
- **Twist in the middle.** A lot of writers save a plot twist for the end of the story, but what good does it do then? The story's over. But if you include a twist in the middle, it can send your story off in some interesting directions, and make your story longer, especially if the twist is something that plays itself out after a while. What if one of your characters is revealed to have stolen someone else's identity and in reality, they're a criminal? Your other characters will no longer trust them once they discover this secret, and additional complications might ensue, such as the police coming to arrest the character or maybe some of their former criminal associates showing up to collect an unpaid debt. These complications are eventually dealt with, the other characters get over their distrust of the deceptive character (maybe by learning their backstory, as I mentioned earlier) and then everyone gets back to the regularly scheduled plot and the story moves on from there.
- **Sidetracks.** Do you remember back when I talked about writing *The Temple of the Dragonslayer*, and after I was finished with the book, I was told I needed to expand it by 10K words, so I had goblins kidnap one of the characters? That was a sidetrack, and they work *great*.
- **Wrong turns.** Even if characters encounter obstacles on the way toward meeting their goals, beginning writers still have their characters make right choices along the way. (Often *only* right choices.) But you can add length to a novel, and make the story more interesting, if your character makes a mistake that sends them off in a wrong direction, especially if they don't know they're headed in the wrong direction. Ever seen a movie in which characters are searching for a treasure, and after deciphering a series of clues, get to what they think is the location of the treasure, only to find it's not there, and in reality it's located at the place where they started their search? The entire damn story is a wrong turn, sending the characters on an absolutely unnecessary journey. Unnecessary for them, but maybe quite entertaining to an audience. Characters should make mistakes, operate under false assumptions, follow bad (or deceitful) advice on how to proceed, etc.

- **Ask yourself, "What couldn't possibly happen next?" then make it happen.** This is a piece of advice I share with aspiring writers all the time. Too often our plots are simple, contrived things, a subconscious recycling of stories we've read or viewed before. Let's say one of your characters is going to confront their spouse about having an affair, and you imagine them having a huge argument that ends with them deciding to divorce. Nothing especially interesting about that, plus it's not that long. So ask yourself what couldn't possibly—at least in the way you currently envision the story—happen next, then make it happen. Maybe your character walks into the house and finds their spouse dead. Maybe they find the spouse being held hostage by someone they've never seen before. Maybe the spouse isn't there, and there's nothing to indicate where they went. Maybe the spouse's mother has dropped by for a visit and they can't have a discussion about the affair. Or maybe they do have it with the mother present, and maybe she's the one that unexpectedly starts it. Maybe that's the moment when an alien race invades Earth. Whatever. This technique works better in the outline stage if you're a plotter, but you can try it anytime in the drafting process if you're a pantser. I'm a little of both, but I'm never hesitant to make a sudden swerve in my story if a good change occurs to me, and I need to make my novel larger.

Remember what I said several times above: Anything you add should be pertinent to the story and interesting to the reader, not just random words crammed into your novel only to make it longer. You want your novel to be both bigger *and* better.

NOVELLAS

Novels are the most common form of tie-in, with short stories being second, and novellas a distant third. Sometimes editors do seek tie-in novellas, though. Maybe for a collection featuring three different authors, or perhaps for publication as an eBook only. Novellas can be defined as either long short stories or short novels (depending on who you ask), and both definitions are correct. Novellas inhabit a gray zone between short stories and novels, and in some ways, this makes them perfect for media tie-ins, especially ones based on TV shows. The average length of a novella corresponds nicely to the length of an hour-long TV series episode (more or less). But in print form, novellas are such slim volumes that often readers don't feel like they're worth the money to buy, and so publishers generally tend to avoid publishing them. But novella-length tie-ins do happen (I've written some), so I want to make sure you at least have a basic idea how to approach writing them.

The length of a novella is a bit fuzzy, and different publishers might define its length differently. Here's how various writers' organizations define the category for their awards:

- **The Bram Stoker Award for Long Fiction:** 7,500 words in length but no more than 39,999 words in length.

- **The Hugo Award and Nebula Awards:** Novelette: at least 7,500 words but less than 17,500 words; Novella: at least 17,500 words but less than 40,000 words.
- **Shirley Jackson Awards:** Long Fiction (Novella): fiction between 17,500 and 39,999 words in length. Mid-Length Fiction (Novelette): fiction between 7,500 and 17,499 words in length.

In order to write novellas, you need to use both short story techniques and novel techniques. I generally follow the basic techniques for short fiction, although I also follow one of two of the novel-expansion techniques I mentioned earlier. For example, I might have more than one main character, and I'll provide more obstacles to lengthen the story. I may also go deeper into the characters' history. There is no specific formula for which techniques you use when or how many to use when writing a novella. You'll need to experiment to find your way, and you may use a different "recipe" for different novellas.

EXERCISES

1. Choose a scene from a movie or TV show then novelize it. Don't just copy the dialogue and give brief stage directions. Try to flesh the scene out into a fully dramatized piece of fiction. When you're finished, have a friend or family member read it (especially if they're a fan of the original property). Ask for their feedback. Did what you wrote read like fiction to them? Read it over yourself. How do you think you did? What could you have done better?

2. To practice characterization, come up with a threat of some kind, then write brief scenes (one to three pages) of three different media characters responding to it. For example, a group of giant dinosaurian predators is attacking. How would Captain Kirk react? Darth Vader? Wonder Woman? Ben from *Quantum Leap*? Dracula? Try to pick characters that are all very different from each other. When you're finished writing the scenes, ask yourself how they changed from one character to another. What did you find challenging about this exercise? Were any particular characters harder for you to write than others?

VOICES FROM THE TRENCHES

JONATHAN MABERRY

How did you get into writing tie-ins? It came out of the blue. I'd been home, sick with the flu, and started a conversation on Facebook about werewolf movies. I'm a huge fan of that sub-genre and often do werewolf movie marathons when I'm sick. Next day I get a call from someone claiming to be the vice-president of licensing at Universal Pictures. At first I thought it was a joke because I have prankish writer friends, but it turned out to be legit. Her assistant had been following the previous day's werewolf movie chat and mentioned my name to the VP, who was looking for someone to do the novelization of the 2010 Benicio del Toro, Anthony Hopkins, Emily Blunt, Hugo Weaving remake of the *Wolfman*.

I'd assumed that someone doing a novelization would actually get to see the film. Turns out ... no. They gave me a script—an older one that no longer matched the current cut of the film, and let me see three production drawings. And then told me they needed the book in five weeks. This was going to have my name on it, and I wanted to do a good job, so I did a ton of research on the era in which the film was set, the clothing, food, transportation, etc., and then wrote a straight Gothic novel. What astonished me was it became a *New York Times* bestseller and won a Scribe Award.

That put me on the radar of other editors and publishers looking to hire a tie-in writer. Since then I've worked extensively in tie-in work, as writer and editor. I've worked on *X-Files*, Sookie Stackhouse/*True Blood, John Carter of Mars, Hellboy, C.H.U.D., Wizard of Oz*, Sherlock Holmes, C. Auguste Dupin, *GI Joe, Night of the Living Dead, Alien, Predator*, Solomon Kane, Diablo IV, World of Warcraft, Godzilla, *Book of Eli/World of Eli, Deadlands*, Carl Kolchak, *Island of Dr. Moreau, War of the Worlds*, many Marvel superhero characters, and a bunch of others. And I now have some active licenses of my own—the Joe Ledger thrillers, *V-Wars*, and *Rot & Ruin*.

What do you like about writing tie-ins? What are the rewards for you? It's fun to play with other people's toys. Just as it's fun to have writers have some fun with my characters. I've always been a pop culture nerd, and—like so many of my friends—I did a bit of fan fiction when I was younger. Mostly *Blake's 7*, Marvel, and *Star Trek* stuff ... and long before I became a professional writer. If you fall in love with a fictional world, be it *Star Trek* or *Spider-Man* or whatever, the inner writer wants to tell more stories involving those characters and situations. Even now I have a bucket list of licenses I'd enjoy writing.

I love the creative challenge of taking someone else's world and characters and crafting new tales to tell. Being original while honoring the creator and the fanbase. I'm neither fickle nor selfish when it comes to these projects—I don't need the ego-stroke of being the license creator; and I accept that tie-ins are often collaborative with editors and, in comics, with the entire art team.

One of the most enjoyable rewards is editing tie-in anthologies and being able to invite my writer friends in to play. I edited three *X-Files* anthologies, and that was a bucket list right there—for me and for many of the contributors. My shared-world anthology series, *V-Wars*, became a Netflix show, and that showcased some characters created by other writers working in my license. Same with *Aliens: Bug Hunt* and *Aliens vs Predator: Ultimate Prey* (co-edited with Bryan Thomas Schmidt).

As president of the International Association of Media Tie-in Writers, I often have editors and publishers reach out to me about projects, and often I can pass those along to other media tie-in writers, and that feels really damn good.

Another great reward, and one I had not anticipated when I got into this field, is that some active licenses are in the process of expanding, and the writer of tie-ins occasionally gets invited to be more deeply involved. Kevin J. Anderson, who has been co-writing the *Dune* novels since the original author passed, is now a producer on the *Dune* movies and an upcoming *Dune* TV series. I wrote a couple of prequel novels tied to a popular science fiction movie that is now getting a prequel TV series. Some of my characters will be folded into that show, and I am likely to wind up as an executive producer.

What challenges have you faced in your career as a tie-in writer? The two biggest challenges are time and licensor interference. The time thing is an issue when a project comes along and suddenly—for whatever reason—the publisher needs the thing right away. I had five weeks to write *The Wolfman* and only four to write *X-Files Origins: Devil's Advocate*. That's hardly any time at all, but if that's the deal point, then that's the deal point.

Most license holders are pretty chill and don't micromanage. Some, on the other hand, nitpick a project beyond what is reasonable. Often that's when writing for a very large license—video games, ongoing series, etc. They withhold a lot of details that they feel you don't need to know, but which would actually make the process flow more smoothly. And sometimes a work is passed from editor up the line to various executives, each of whom feel it's in their own career best interest to put their two cents in. While I can understand them wanting to protect the integrity of their license, sometimes the notes that come down are wildly off-base or even directly contradictory. Then you have to play politics to get to the heart of what best serves the contract. It's always doable, but there are some dance steps involved. Part of the game.

Does writing tie-ins require a different skill set than other types of writing? If so what are these skills? One of the first and most important things in media tie-in writing is dialing back one's ego. It's not my license, these are not my characters, and it's not my audience. You need to respect the creators and the other writers whose work has helped build the license. Quarrelling with editors over edits is tempting but never fruitful, and so a great deal of tact is involved. I've found that when one accepts that they are painting the walls in someone else's house, it lets you stop complaining about the color choices. They're hiring us to tell a good story, not tell them how to run their license.

Also, there is an audience of fans whose understanding of the license is often far greater than the writer's. While one should never pander to them by giving cliché story points, a wise writer keeps them in mind. In terms of the actual writing, one of the most important points is to get a sense of the verbiage, pace, background details, characterizations, and settings so that the story actually fits—even deserves—to be in the canon rather than a piece of work with familiar character names but no deep connection to the license.

Patience, a deep understanding of each tool in our literary toolchest, enthusiasm, and a sense of fun are all useful when crafting tie-in fiction.

Do you think it's possible to be pigeonholed as a tie-in writer, making it more difficult to publish your own work? If so, how do you deal with this? There's always been a danger of being defined as a tie-in writer, as opposed to a writer who occasionally does tie-in. The advances for tie-in fiction are typically lower than with original fiction, and royalties are uncommon. It's tough to make a living off of it, and there's a trap in that—because editors often go back to certain tie-in writers, those writers take the gigs because they're right there on offer, which keeps them in a loop of doing only, or mostly, tie-in fiction … and that pay level is tough to live on.

With all of my friends and colleagues doing tie-in, or contemplating it, I advise to make sure they get as much original fiction out into the market as they can. This is a policy advocated by a lot of agents who rep tie-in writers. The higher visibility tie-in projects are useful to agents, but being able to say that the tie-in work is a side gig to original fiction is very helpful.

On the other hand, some writers—many (in my acquaintance) who have day jobs—approach tie-in as supplemental income rather than primary money. For them, there's not as much of a desire to go totally original. My personal choice is to bracket a media tie-in project with original works that are in different genres or sub-genres, demonstrating the writer's range across genre lines.

What advice do you have for writers who want to break into the media tie-in field? Anthologies are a great start, and sometimes that means signing on for anthologies built on "expired" licenses (like Sherlock Holmes, Cthulhu, Dracula, etc.) By writing for such an anthology, the up-and-coming writer is in a book with many other writers, and usually a few marquee names. That establishes visibility to readers, and to that anthology's editor—and we editors often curate some or all of our books based on writers' talent and grasp of the basics of business. Equally as important is that many anthology and magazine editors—and I'm both—often read anthologies edited by our colleagues as a way of scouting for talent. The short story market is excellent for this—and it's potentially beneficial to everyone involved.

JONATHAN MABERRY is a *New York Times* bestselling author, five-time Bram Stoker Award-winner, four-time Scribe Award winner, Inkpot Award winner, anthology editor, writing teacher, and comic-book writer. His vampire apocalypse books, *V-WARS*, became a Netflix original series starring Ian Somerhalder. He writes in multiple genres (suspense, thriller, horror, science fiction, epic fantasy, and action); and he writes for adults, teens, and children. His works include the Joe Ledger thrillers, *Kagen the Damned*, *Ink*, *Glimpse*, the *Rot & Ruin* series, the *Dead of Night* series, *The Wolfman*, *X-Files Origins: Devil's Advocate*, *The Sleepers War* (with Weston Ochse), *NecroTek*, *Mars One*, and many others. Several of his works are in development for film and TV. He is the editor of high-profile anthologies such as *Weird Tales: 100 Years of Weird*, *The X-Files*, *Aliens: Bug Hunt*, *Out of Tune*, *Don't Turn Out the Lights: A Tribute to Scary Stories to Tell in the Dark*, *Baker Street Irregulars*, and *Nights of the Living Dead*. Some of his comics are *Black Panther: DoomWar*, *The Punisher: Naked Kills*, and *Bad Blood*. His *Rot & Ruin* YA novel was adapted into the #1 horror comic on Webtoon and is being developed for film by Alcon Entertainment. Maberry is the president of the International Association of Media Tie-In Writers and the editor of *Weird Tales Magazine*. He lives in San Diego, California. Find him online at jonathanmaberry.com.

ANDREA CARLO CAPPI

How did you get into writing tie-ins? Italian-made tie-ins are uncommon, but I found myself working on two ongoing Italian comics properties with their own previous tie-in tradition. It all started in the late '90s, when Alfredo Castelli, creator of the comics series *Martin Mystère*, was editing a short story collection by various writers featuring his character, and suggested a team-up with a non-comics serial character of mine. This would later help me become the writer of original *Martin Mystère* novels, eleven so far, and one of the very few tie-in writers in Italy. Through Castelli I had contacts with Mario Gomboli, publisher of the *Diabolik* comics series, on which tie-in novels were based in the late '60s-early '70s. I suggested a reprise and offered myself for the job. After four original novels, I also got myself hired for the novelizations of the three recent *Diabolik* movies.

What do you like about writing tie-ins? What are the rewards for you? I have the chance of working on characters I already loved as a reader and had influenced me as a writer, particularly the ones in *Diabolik*, which I discovered when I was six years old. Now I'm a fan who is allowed to write their stories with my own style and structures, so they still are my books, though based on characters created by someone else.

What challenges have you faced in your career as a tie-in writer? The first challenge is keeping my identity as a writer, while remaining faithful to long-established characters and to what readers expect from them. When I wrote my first *Diabolik* novel in 2002, readers were extremely suspicious, since there hadn't been *Diabolik* tie-in novels for 30 years. More challenges appear when writing a novelization: last year I had to turn something purely cinematic in the third *Diabolik* movie—I can't explain what, it would be a spoiler—into something that readers wouldn't find deceiving. But I love challenges in writing.

Does writing tie-ins require a different skill set than other types of writing? If so what are these skills? When I write about my own characters … I know them, since they are my projections in a fictional world I create. Writing for a franchise requires studying previously established characters, learning how they interact with their world and, of course, knowing how they have been treated in the original media (comics, in my case). So I must start thinking and reacting like them, till they become as familiar as my own characters … or rather I become them. It's somehow the Stanislavski method applied to writing.

Do you think it's possible to be pigeonholed as a tie-in writer, making it more difficult to publish your own work? If so, how do you deal with this? I thought it might be a risk, but it wasn't. When I started, I had already been writing my own stories in different genres for a few years, mostly thrillers; but only a few mystery writers in Italy are acknowledged as "real" writers and I was already (and still am) typecasted as some kind of "paperback writer." Since tie-ins are not so common in Italy, adding them to my résumé didn't change my position. It helped me reach more readers, anyway, and in 2018 one of my *Martin Mystère* novels won the Italcon award as Best Italian Fantasy Novel.

What advice do you have for writers who want to break into the media tie-in field? Don't let your ego get in the way, because you are working for people with expectations about characters they're already familiar with. You must remain faithful to the characters' psychology and behaviour, and to the flavour of the series. But at the same time, if you have been chosen for writing a tie-in, it means your personal skills as a writer are required, so you have to employ them at the service of the franchise. But, whatever you write, you do it for the readers and, if they like it, you might have a chance to do it again.

ANDREA CARLO CAPPI (born 1964 in Milan, Italy) is an author of thrillers and speculative fiction. He's known mostly for his spy stories, some of them under the penname François Torrent. Since 1991, he's published over seventy titles, including novels, short-story collections, and nonfiction. An editor and translator, Cappi has also written for comics, radio, and TV. Blog: europulpcappi.blogspot.com.

CHAPTER TEN
WRITING NOVELIZATIONS

WHAT'S A NOVELIZATION?

A novelization is when a writer dramatizes a movie script in novel form. The script is the basis for a novel, just as a script is the basis for a film, but the book and movie are two different creative works that grow out of the same source. A script is a blueprint for a performance, but a tie-in author uses it as the jumping-off point for a more expansive story, complete with all the strengths of fiction—immersive characterization, rich description, language used to create images in readers' minds, etc. The writer may lengthen scenes from the script, add more detail to them, or create entirely new scenes that expand the story or our understanding of the characters. It's like taking a two-dimensional image and making it three-dimensional. Tie-in writers—just like a director and actors—breathe life into scripts, using their skill with the written word.

Here's what you need to know about novelizations, should you ever get the opportunity to write one. (I covered some of this information earlier when I talked about My Adventures in Tie-In Land, but I've repeated it here so you'll have it all in one easy-to-refer-to place.)

HOW A NOVELIZATION BEGINS

- A book publisher approaches a movie studio and requests a license to publish a novelization based on one of the studio's films. Sometimes studios contact a publisher and initiate the novelization process.
- The studio gets money for granting the license and it gets a different avenue of promotion for its film.
- Once the publisher obtains the license, the publisher contacts an established author, often someone who has experience writing media tie-in fiction—whether novelizations or original tie-ins.
- If the author is interested in writing the novelization, the publisher checks to see if the studio will approve the author.

- If the studio approves, the author then signs a non-disclosure agreement with the studio.
- The author is then offered a work-for-hire contract (usually without royalties).
- Advances vary, from between $10-$20K in my experience (and usually closer to the low side).
- The author is then granted access to the script (often an earlier version than the final shooting script).
- The script might be sent as hardcopy, via email, or via access to the studio's intranet.
- You do not need to get an outline approved, as with original tie-in fiction. In a sense, the script functions as the outline. You just start writing.
- The deadline might be tight, maybe only a few weeks.
- The studio has final say over what is and isn't included in the published novel.
- The publication date is determined by the movie's release date. The book usually comes out one week after the movie does.
- You can promote the novel all you want, but remember, often there are no royalties. No royalties means that no matter how much promoting you do, no matter how much book sales rise, you won't see another penny from the novelization. For some writers, that means the project isn't worth their time to promote. I've never had a novelization editor expect me to promote a book, but I do it anyway. As I said much earlier in this volume, if my name goes on a book, it's *my* book, tie-in or original fiction.
- The novel's physical shelf life likely will be limited, but the eBook may remain available for years.

THE AUTHOR'S ROLE IN THE PROCESS

- It's much the same as with any tie-in project. You're a hired hand, not the boss.
- Hierarchy: Studio, Publisher, You.
- Your name is still on the book, though, so it's still yours.
- Novelizations are essentially collaborations with people you'll never meet.
- In regard to the novel, you're an additional screenwriter, the director, the actors, the cinematographer, the set designer, the costume designer, the special effects department, etc. You use your imagination to mount a more in-depth "production" of the story.
- Your job *is* to dramatize the existing script, to flesh it out, to bring it to life.
- Your job *isn't* to rewrite the movie, "improve" it, or make significant changes to the story and characters.
- There's not enough material in a script to fill even a short novel. You will need to add a significant amount of material, but you try to add material that complements the script, rather than reinventing it.
- Average movie script length: 7,500-20,000 words (90-130 manuscript pages).
- Average novelization length: 70,000-80,000 words (240-280 manuscript pages).
- The studio *will not* give you any footage to view. (Although Fox did show me the film when I wrote *Kingsman: The Golden Circle*, which was an exception that proves the rule.)

- The studio *will not* give you a trailer to view before the rest of the world sees it. If you're lucky, a trailer will come out before you finish the book, allowing you to at least catch glimpses of the main characters, important settings, etc. This will help you describe them better in your novel.
- The studio *may* give you some production photos for reference, but probably not—especially if those photos haven't been released to the public yet. You might be forced to look for some on the Internet.
- You *will not* get to talk with anyone involved with making the film.
- You get whichever version of the script they send you, and that's it.
- It very likely *will not* be the final shooting script, but we work with what we're given.

ADDING MATERIAL

- Obviously, you'll add more description, character's internal thoughts and feelings, etc. throughout the novel.
- You might extend/deepen conversations.
- You might fill any plot holes you find in the script.
- You might add additional background of characters, setting, history, technology, etc.
- You might add a prologue and/or epilogue
- You might write some scenes before the script's beginning to better set up the story.
- You'll insert additional scenes throughout the novel that further the plot or explore characterization in more depth.
- You can add a side mission.
- You can expand the roles of existing minor characters and give them more to do.
- You can create some new minor/background characters and give them a B-story that runs parallel to the main story. Make sure it doesn't overshadow the main story, though.
- You can create your own minor subplot involving one of the characters or even the setting.

THINGS TO KEEP IN MIND WHEN WRITING A NOVELIZATION

- You can change things, but keep your changes as minor as possible.
- Make changes that will strengthen the novel without altering the script too much.
- Try to capture the tone of the script in your novel, just as you want to capture the original tone of any property you base a novel on.
- You'll use the screenwriter's dialogue, but consider using his or her descriptions/narration sometimes as well. You don't have to do this, but it can add to the collaborative nature of the project and help in capturing tone. You can rewrite the descriptions, but I try to use some of the scriptwriter's original wording when I can. This isn't plagiarism because you've been hired by the studio to novelize the script.

- There's a lot of details you'll have to create: characters' clothing, what the setting for a scene looks like (both indoors and outdoors), what specific props characters use (what type of gun they shoot or what type of car they drive, etc.).
- Until you see the finished film along with the rest of the world, there are a million details you'll have to guess at or make up whole cloth. Make your peace with this or else you'll be mired in indecision when you try to write.
- Don't worry about trying to get your novel "right" in terms of what the finished film will be. Your job is only to novelize the script you received.

WRITING THE NOVELIZATION

I'm going to relate my process learned from writing five novelizations. This is far from the only way to do it.

- First, I read the script.
- As I read, I make notes about material and scenes I can add.
- Screenwriters think in terms of image. Film is ultimately a visual medium. So I try to visualize as much as possible when I read.
- I like to type up all the dialogue first. I'm going to include it in the novel anyway, and this way I know how many words I'm starting with and how many I'll have to add.
- The dialogue in the scripts I've novelized ranged from 8,000 to 12,000 words.
- Four of the five scripts I novelized were sequels to films I'd already seen, but I watched the films again, making notes about the ways actors portrayed the characters—the way they moved and spoke, their facial expressions, etc.
- I search the Internet for any images related to the film that might have been released by the studio and images/raw footage that might have been leaked. I copy those images to my computer for later use as I write. I continue to search for new images every day until the book is finished.
- I search for news stories, interviews with directors, screenwriters, cast, and crew, etc., looking for any insight into the film.
- I hope a trailer will be released before the book is finished. I got lucky three out of four times. (I'm not counting *Terrifier 2* here, since the film had been released in theaters before Cindigm decided to start a book line.)
- I watch the trailers numerous times, sometimes pausing them to capture still images. But still images from the trailers often appear on the Internet very soon after the trailer's release, and I access most of the images that way.
- I sometimes make changes to my novel based on the images when it's clear some details changed during filming. I usually have to make my best guess what those changes are, though.

- I double-check technical and scientific details in the script. If they're incorrect, I fix them. If the plot makes it impossible for me to fix such errors, I try to find a way to make them seem believable, gloss over them, or I ignore them and hope readers won't notice.
- I research settings, clothing, architecture, furniture, technical information etc. as I write, and I add only the information I need.
- I need to choose who the viewpoint character will be in any given scene since scripts don't do viewpoint the same way prose fiction does.
- I connect dots the screenwriters didn't, like how a character gets from Point A to B. The script often skips over those details. These incidents can also make for good additional material, especially if the character experiences difficulties along the way.
- For my third novelization, I decided to write the first draft without chapter breaks. Then once the draft was finished and I knew how many more words I needed to add, I added a couple new scenes, and then I broke the text into separate chapters. I did the same for my fourth one. I included chapter breaks for my fifth as I wrote it. Do whatever works for you.

HOW TO LAND NOVELIZATION GIGS

Like I've said multiple times in this book, tie-in projects overall aren't gigs for beginners, so you need to develop your own original work and reputation as a writer first. Having previous tie-writing experience is a big help in landing novelization assignments. Otherwise, most of the following steps are the same as finding any kind of tie-in gig.

- Check out recent novelizations and who's written and published them. This way, you can get an idea of which publishers to approach, or ask your agent to reach out to.
- See if specific editors are thanked in the acknowledgements of novelizations. Those are editors you or your agent can approach.
- Networking with writers who've done novelizations will help you learn about the industry, who's publishing what, etc.
- Meet tie-in editors at conferences.
- Get editor recommendations from other writers.
- Send an email introducing yourself to editors and give your credentials.

EXERCISES

1. Read novelizations of movies that have been out for a while. Read ones where you haven't seen the movie, then watch the movie. Read ones where you have seen the movie.

Compare the books to the films, see what you liked and disliked about how the writer interpreted the script and translated it into prose form. Make notes about techniques you liked so you can try them later.

2. Pick one of your favorite films. Watch it and make notes about scenes you could extend or new scenes you could add if you were to novelize it. Write one of those scenes. How did it turn out? Are you satisfied with it? If you were to revise it, what would you change?

VOICES FROM THE TRENCHES

KATE HEARTFIELD

How did you get into writing tie-ins? I had published a couple of novels of historical fantasy, as well as some novellas, short fiction and interactive fiction before I started writing tie-ins. My agent, Jennie Goloboy, learned that Aconyte Books was looking for a writer for a particular project, which turned out to be an *Assassin's Creed* novel. It was a great fit for a couple of reasons: I was already very familiar with that videogame universe, and I was already very comfortable researching and writing historical settings. I pitched Aconyte a couple of ideas within the parameters of what they were looking for. We went back and forth a few times to refine them, then got the green light from Ubisoft, the company that makes *Assassin's Creed* games. That was the first of the two *Assassin's Creed* tie-in novels I have written for Aconyte: *The Magus Conspiracy* and *The Resurrection Plot*.

What do you like about writing tie-ins? What are the rewards for you? I love collaborating with a community of people building the same universe, most of whom I'll never meet—and in a way, it feels like collaborating with the fans of the franchise, too. It freshens up my ideas and forces me to think in different ways. I really enjoyed getting to talk to those fans, who were extremely welcoming. And I know that it has brought new readers to my other work.

What challenges have you faced in your career as a tie-in writer? I'm sure I won't be the only writer to mention the timelines, which tend to be relatively short. My deadlines were not that onerous, especially compared to some, but it did require being very efficient. My writing process typically involves some fairly substantial revision, so I had to leave myself some time for that. I was fortunate to work with great editors.

Does writing tie-ins require a different skill set than other types of writing? If so what are these skills? Writing efficiently to deadline is definitely part of the job. My background as a journalist served me well there, I think. There's also a certain tension between having enthusiasm and love for one's creation and having the necessary humility to work within a canon, and to let go when letting go is required.

Do you think it's possible to be pigeonholed as a tie-in writer, making it more difficult to publish your own work? If so, how do you deal with this? Maybe it's because I had already published quite a bit of my own work before I wrote tie-in novels, but I haven't encountered any pigeon-holing. Sometimes people are a little surprised by my *Assassin's Creed* work, since my historical fantasy novels have a literary bent and people may not necessarily associate tie-in novels with the literary side of the market, especially people who don't read tie-in novels. But there's really no difference, to me, when I sit down to write. I'm just telling the story in the best way I know how, in the best prose I can muster to suit the task. And some of my favourite writers have written both tie-in novels and their own work.

What advice do you have for writers who want to break into the media tie-in field? My advice would be to work with properties that you find fun or fascinating and that mesh with your own interests as a writer in some way. I found it a real joy to write *Assassin's Creed* stories, and there are other universes I would love to write in, but I suspect that writing something I didn't care about or find interesting would make me miserable.

KATE HEARTFIELD's latest novel is *The Valkyrie*, a retelling of old legends. Her 2022 novel *The Embroidered Book* was a *Sunday Times* bestseller. She has written two novels set in the *Assassin's Creed* universe: *The Magus Conspiracy* (2022) and *The Resurrection Plot* (2023). Her books, novellas, stories, and games have been shortlisted for multiple awards, including the Ottawa Book Award and the Nebula, World Fantasy, and Aurora Awards. A former journalist, Heartfield lives in Canada. Her website is kateheartfield.com.

SERITA STEVENS

How did you get into writing tie-ins? I was working on a project with a public relations office when they had an assignment to write a novel that showed the beginning of *Cagney and Lacey*- how Lacey met husband Harvey and why Cagney refused to attend her mom's funeral. So I sat down and binge-watched four seasons of the show, taking copious notes before I could produce an outline that the studio approved of and wrote the book that Dell published.

What do you like about writing tie-ins? What are the rewards for you? I like writing tie-ins because you have the characters already established for you, and yet it is a challenge to create a new story with these characters that the viewers will not have seen but will fit in with their sense of these people. It also brings your name more before the public and the publishers.

What challenges have you faced in your career as a tie-in writer? Depending on the tie-in I am writing, sometimes I have to deal with multiple notes from the publishers, or the series actor who might have a reason to chime in with their ideas for the story. And often the deadlines for these books are tight.

Does writing tie-ins require a different skill set than other types of writing? If so what are these skills? Writing a tie-in is much like being in the writer's room on a series that someone else created. You have to get into the head of the creator and the characters that they have created and you have to understand things about their created characters that might not be so obvious. Often you must spend time watching back episodes of the series to get little hints of their past that are not pushed in front of the audience but that you can make use of in the creation of your story.

Do you think it's possible to be pigeonholed as a tie-in writer, making it more difficult to publish your own work? If so, how do you deal with this? While I was a fan of *Cagney and Lacey* before I wrote that tie-in, I have been asked to write books for series that I have not watched every episode of. I have also done tie-ins for features that were coming out where the production company felt it would be helpful to have an IP released at the same time as the movie. In all, I prefer creating my own characters and worlds, though I do love making history come alive. My forthcoming stories, *In His Name* and *Color of Love*, are both historicals based on real events with some fictionalized characters that I created to bring the events to life.

What advice do you have for writers who want to break into the media tie-in field? For someone who wants to do tie-in books, I suggest they study the series, and if there are already tie-in books out there (e.g., for *Murder She Wrote*) to become familiar with them before you query the publisher along with a sample of your writing and several possible loglines for new books. If there are no books yet on the series, you might query the production office doing the series.

A lot depends on who created the series and who now owns the characters. Check them out on IMDb.com and other social media sites. Is the original creator a novelist, as well? If so they might want to do the tie-ins themselves. Even if they are, they might welcome your wanting to help, but all is up to the publisher.

SERITA STEVENS, a registered nurse born in Chicago, came out to Los Angeles when offered a teaching job at USC. With her master's in writing (with honors) from Antioch University in London, she went on to become well-known in the romance and mystery field.

Her first published book, *This Bitter Ecstasy*, a historical romance from Pocket Books, was her introduction to the film industry when she was asked if she could write a treatment of the book for possible adaptation. She continued writing historical romances, including *Tame the Wild Heart*, *Daughters of Desire*, and *Lightning and Fire*.

Turning her attention to mystery and suspense, Stevens wrote historical suspense as *The Bloodstone Inheritance* (young adult mystery), *Unholy Alliance* (nominated for Best Book for the Reluctant Reader from the American Library Association), *Deceptive Desire* (a Western female-driven suspense now in script form as *Logan's Land* and optioned several times), *Red Sea, Dead Sea, and Bagels for Tea* (the Fanny Zindel novels—a Jewish *Murder She Wrote*), and many more, including ghosting and adaptations. She was hired by the studio to write the prequel of the TV series *Cagney and Lacey*. Her website is seritastevens.com.

OUTRO

I really enjoy writing tie-in fiction, and I'm always up for doing more. I find writing it just as rewarding as writing my original work. All writing—including composing a nonfiction book like this one—broadens our experience, sharpens our existing skills, and allows us to gain new ones. In that sense, tie-in writing is the same as any other kind. And have I mentioned it's *fun?* (I believe I have, once or twice.)

In closing, I'll repeat what Mike Stackpole told me so many years ago. I wish you luck finding gigs in the subsidiary book market.

RESOURCES

KEY SOURCES

The International Association of Media Tie-In Writers
iamtw.org

Tied In: The Business, History, Craft of Media Tie-In Writing
iamtw.org/coming-soon/tied-in-the-business-history-and-craft-of-media-tie-in-writing

Turning the Tied
Stories about public domain characters.
iamtw.org/coming-soon/turning-the-tied

Double Trouble: An Anthology of Two-Fisted Team-Ups
Stories about public domain characters teaming up.
iamtw.org/coming-soon/double-trouble-an-anthology-of-two-fisted-team-ups

Murder HE Wrote
Donald Bain details his long career writing popular tie-in novels and novels written under house names.
amazon.com/Murder-HE-Wrote-Donald-Bain-ebook/dp/B007IWW8MQ

The Novelizers:
An Affectionate History of Media Adaptations & Originals
David Spencer's comprehensive history of media tie-in fiction
amazon.com/Novelizers-Affectionate-Adaptations-Originals-Astonishing/dp/B0CLTLKDZL

OTHER WRITERS' ORGANIZATIONS

There are many resources for writers, including market information, at these sites.

The Science Fiction and Fantasy Writers of America: sfwa.org
The Horror Writers Association: horror.org
The Romance Writers of America: rwa.org
The Society for Children's Book Writers and Illustrators: scbwi.org
The Mystery Writers of America: mysterywriters.org
The Western Writers of America: westernwriters.org
The International Thriller Writers, Inc.: internationalthrillerwriters.com
The Association of Writers and Writing Programs: awpwriter.org
The American Society for Journalists and Authors: asja.org/index9.php
The Authors Guild: authorsguild.org
Association of Ghostwriters: associationofghostwriters.org

AGENTS

Association of Author Representatives: aaronline.org

TIE-IN PUBLISHERS

Note: Some of these publishers require you to submit through an agent.

Titan Books: titanbooks.com/help/page/submissions
Simon & Schuster Star Trek: simonandschuster.com/p/startrekbooks
Simon & Schuster Halo: simonandschuster.com/p/halobooks
Simon & Schuster Submissions: simonandschuster.biz/c/biz-manuscript-submissions
Black Library: blacklibrary.com
Aconyte Books: aconytebooks.com
Moonstone Books: moonstonebooks.com
Edgar Rice Burroughs, Inc.: edgarriceburroughs.com
Catalyst Game Labs: catalystgamelabs.com/brands/fiction

BOOK PACKAGERS

Working Partners: coolabi.com/books/#books-working-partners
Relay Publishing: recruitment.relaypub.com/current-job-positions

CONVENTIONS

World Science Fiction Convention (Worldcon): worldcon.org
World Fantasy Convention: worldfantasy.org
StokerCon: thebramstokerawards.com/uncategorized/bram-stoker-award-presentations
DragonCon: dragoncon.org
Gencon: gencon.com
Origins: originsgamefair.com

BIOGRAPHY

TIM WAGGONER has published over sixty novels and eight collections of short stories. He writes original dark fantasy and horror, as well as media tie-ins, and his articles on writing have appeared in numerous publications. He's a four-time winner of the Bram Stoker Award, a one-time winner of the Scribe Award, and he's been a finalist for the Shirley Jackson and Splatterpunk Awards. He's also a fulltime tenured professor who teaches creative writing and composition at Sinclair College in Dayton, Ohio. His papers are collected by the University of Pittsburgh's Horror Studies Program.

APPENDIX ONE
SAMPLE STORY

In 2021, the International Association of Media Tie-In Writers decided to publish an anthology to raise money for charity. Since writers couldn't use media properties owned by others, they used the next best thing—public domain characters. We were given a large list of characters to choose from, and I selected Herne the Hunter. In legend, Herne was a forest-dwelling deity who appeared as a man with the horns of a stag and was associated with the Wild Hunt. I decided to pretend that I was making a modern TV series based on the legend, and I created characters and lore using *Supernatural* and *Grimm* as my inspirations. Once I'd created my "show," I then imagined I'd been hired to write a tie-in story featuring my hero and his companion, and I wrote it as if it was an episode of my imaginary series. The result was "Children of the Wild." It isn't technically tie-in fiction as the rights to the Herne of legend aren't owned by anyone, but I wrote it as if it *was* tie-in fiction. Developing a—I'll call it a mock tie-in for lack of a better term—like this can give you a good writing sample to show tie-in editors. And who knows? If you like what you came up with well enough, you'll have a piece of original fiction that you own and which you can use for more stories and novels in the future.

Children of the Wild: A Herne the Hunter Story
Tim Waggoner
Originally published in *Turning the Tied* (2021)

"I count five," Herne said.

Max tilted his head upward, sniffed the air.

"Seven. Two are hiding—one behind the Chevy off to our right, one beneath the school bus behind us."

Herne accepted Max's assessment without question and didn't look at either vehicle. If Max said there were seven, there were seven. About average size for a pack, although that was the only thing normal about these creatures. Their general shape was canine, but they were significantly larger than regular dogs, almost the size of small ponies. Their teeth were longer and sharper, their heavily muscled bodies covered with thick brown fur. They stood with front legs apart, heads lowered, feral yellow eyes—a sure sign they'd been touched by the Wild—fixed on Herne and Max, growling deep in their throats, muzzles dripping saliva. Although it was midafternoon and the sun hung bright in a cloudless sky, the early April air had a cold bite to it, and a chill rippled down Herne's back. That was the reason he shivered, *not* because Max and he were facing seven snarling killing machines eager to tear the flesh from their bones. That's what he told himself anyway.

They stood in a junkyard, surrounded by old vehicles, metal dented and rusted, windows cracked or missing altogether. A cemetery for machines, cast aside and forgotten. The ground beneath their feet was muddy from last night's rain, and there wasn't much space between the cars to maneuver in. Not the best circumstances for a fight, but there wasn't much to be done about it. Herne gripped a 9mm Glock in his right hand. A crudely formed stone blade hung sheathed at his side, but he wouldn't touch it unless he had to. Sunder was for emergencies only. Max was unarmed, but he didn't need to carry a weapon. He was one.

Herne expected the monster dogs to attack right away, but they held their position, and a moment later he understood why. A huge wolf came loping into view, larger than the others, its brown fur streaked with gray. It was silent, its yellow eyes glimmering with sharp intelligence and deadly calm. When it came within ten yards of Herne and Max's position it stopped. It regarded them for a moment, and then its form blurred, flowed upward like liquid, and when it became solid again, it was human. Well, human*ish*.

"You are not welcome here, Warder."

The creature was seven feet tall, covered with fur, its hand and feet savage-looking claws. Its head retained its lupine shape—protruding muzzle, large pointed ears—but its features were more expressive now, like a human's. Its mouth was capable of speech, though its sharp teeth were a clear reminder that despite its transformation, this creature remained a beast at its core.

"We get that a lot," Max said.

The creature focused its gaze on Max. It sniffed the air, then its eyes narrowed.

"Be silent, *hound*."

Max feigned a wounded look then turned to Herne.

"Did you hear what he called me?"

Herne shrugged. "Better than mongrel. Or cur. Or flea bag. Or—"

"You can stop now, thanks."

"Bow-wow," Herne finished.

Max scowled at him. "Really? Did you have to go there?"

Herne smiled. "Yes. Yes, I did."

The manwolf growled low in its throat.

"You are fools." His mouth stretched into an expression that was half snarl, half smile. "In more ways than one."

He turned away from them and gestured with one of his clawed hands. A moment later, a woman appeared, walking between a pair of smashed vehicles—a petite brunette with long straight hair bound in a ponytail, dressed in a white blouse, black suit jacket, matching slacks, and black open-toed shoes.

Herne was dismayed to see her, but not surprised.

"What are you doing here, Elena? I told you it was too dangerous to follow us."

Elena's expression remained impassive as she looked at Herne, then she blinked and her brown eyes became yellow.

"Oh shit," Max said.

Elena smiled, revealing a mouthful of extremely sharp teeth.

Max looked to Herne.

"This is bad," he said.

"Very," Herne agreed.

Elena snarled, raised hands that had become claws, and rushed toward them.

Earlier.

"Feeling nostalgic yet?"

Max sat in the red SUV's passenger seat, window down, face turned toward the breeze coming in, nostrils flaring as he drank in whatever scents were carried on the morning wind. He liked to ride with the window down, regardless of the weather, and Herne enjoyed teasing him about it, saying things like, *If you see a squirrel, let me know if you want me to stop so you can chase it.* But he wasn't in a teasing mood today.

"Mixed feelings," he said. "How about you?"

Max kept his face pointed toward the window as he answered. "It's different for me. We may have met in Bridgewater, but it was never my hometown. I didn't grow up here."

"Did you grow up anywhere?"

Max frowned. "That's a good question. I must've been a pup once, but I don't remember anything about it."

"Maybe you sprung full blown into existence, like Athena from the brow of Zeus."

"Maybe." The notion seemed to disturb Max, and he fell silent.

Herne wished he hadn't said anything. As conflicted as his feelings about his childhood were, at least he had one.

They made an odd pair, the two of them. Herne was in his early thirties, tall, broad-shouldered, well-muscled, with hard features and hair cut so short his scalp was nearly bald. He usually wore flannel shirts—today's choice was brown and green—along with jeans and hiking boots. His eyes were an icy bright blue, cold and intimidating. In contrast, Max was shorter, thinner, and appeared at least ten years older than Herne. He had a scraggly mop of brown hair and several days' worth of stubble on his face. His features were softer than Herne's, but his eyes—brown with flecks of yellow—hinted at a hidden fierceness. He wore a black hoodie, a T-shirt with the words *Who Let the Dogs Out?* on the front, jeans, and running shoes.

They remained silent for the next several minutes until they drew near a small *Welcome to Bridgewater* sign posted on the side of the road. A couple seconds later, they were past the sign, and for the first time in over a decade, Herne was home. As they drove toward the center of town, he wasn't surprised to see that Bridgewater hadn't changed significantly during his absence. It was much the same as any other small Southwestern Ohio town—old houses situated on tiny plots of land, gas stations, convenience stores, churches, fast food restaurants, bars … Everything seemed shabbier than Herne remembered, grimier, as if time's passage had left a residue that no rain could wash away.

Herne drove toward the center of town. Courthouse Square was the location for Bridgewater's administrative offices, along with the police and fire departments, but there were some small shops as well—a pharmacy, a liquor store, a pizza joint, and a coffee house called Java Nice Day. The last time Herne had been in town, a funky candle and soap shop called Scentsability had occupied the latter's space. His mom used to stop in and buy weird-smelling candles which she'd light up as soon as she got home. His dad always complained about the smell, but he never asked her to blow out the candles.

"I miss your parents too," Max said. "And before you say anything, no, I haven't suddenly developed an ability to read minds. I just know you."

Herne didn't reply. He found a space on the street not too far from Java Nice Day, parked the SUV, and he and Max got out. As they walked to the shop, Max said, "Nervous?"

"Why should I be?"

Max smiled but said no more.

From the outside, Java Nice Day retained the ambience of the candle store—red brick walls, window with fliers for local businesses and missing pets taped to the glass, a wooden front door with peeling paint and a tarnished metal knob. Inside, though, it looked no different than any generic chain coffee store. Sleek plastic tables and chairs, soft classical music playing over speakers mounted on the walls, a chrome and glass counter behind which young men and women with dyed hair and tattoos operated hissing and grinding machines that looked and sounded like they belonged in a mad scientist's laboratory. It was between the morning rush and lunch, and the shop was only half full. People sat talking, typing on laptops, and staring at their phones, except for one woman sitting alone at a table near the far wall. She was looking at Herne and Max and smiling.

Herne hadn't known what he might feel when he saw Elena Benson for the first time in nearly fifteen years. Sad? Happy? Melancholy? Nervous? Self-conscious? Hopeful? He felt all of these things and more.

He walked to her table, Max following a step behind. Elena rose as they approached, and—maybe because she was dressed professionally in jacket and slacks—Herne expected her to offer her hand for him to shake. Instead, she stepped forward and hugged him. He was so startled that for a moment he just stood there, arms at his sides. But then he reached up and hugged her back.

When she pulled away, her smile was tinged with sadness. For what might have been? Maybe.

"It's good to see you," Elena said. She looked at Max. "And your uncle."

Max wasn't a blood relation to Herne, but his parents had pretended he was Herne's maternal uncle in public in order to explain his constant presence to the people of Bridgewater. Some of them had undoubtedly assumed Max was an "uncle," the third member of a polyamorous relationship. The truth was far different.

Elena cocked her head slightly and examined Max more closely.

"You look like you haven't aged a day since the last time I saw you," she said.

"That's because I haven't."

Elena laughed, but Max only smiled. That smile didn't reach his eyes, though. They narrowed as if he were examining her closely. If Max's scrutiny bothered her, she showed no sign of it.

She turned to Herne. "Do you want to get something to drink before we talk?"

A tall white cardboard cup with a white plastic lid sat on the table, next to the remains of a lemon poppyseed muffin on a ceramic plate.

"We're fine," Herne said.

Max looked disappointed, but he didn't say anything.

The three of them sat down, and Elena took a long sip of her drink before speaking. Herne had the sense that she was stalling. That was okay with him. He wasn't sure what to say either.

Max sniffed the air.

"This place still smells like candles. You wouldn't think that scent would pair well with coffee, but it's actually not that bad."

If Elena found the comment odd, she made no mention of it. They spent the next several minutes catching up, talking about what they'd done since parting all those years ago, how mutual acquaintances and their families were doing. Elena spoke for the most part, as Herne didn't keep in touch with many people from the old days, and both of his parents were dead. Eventually the small talk wound down, and Elena took another long sip of her drink, as if she needed the caffeine for what was to come next.

"So," she began, gaze focused on Herne, "you're some kind of paranormal investigator these days?"

"*Some kind* is a good description," Max said.

Herne ignored him. "And you're a famous TV news reporter."

She laughed. "I work for a local station in Cincy. Not exactly the big time. Don't get me wrong—I like my job, but I'm not asked for my autograph everywhere I go. According to your website, you also work as bounty hunters."

"From time to time," Herne said. "It pays the bills."

"Hunting is hunting," Max said. "Only the quarry changes."

Herne thought Max was starting to sound a little too much like a serial killer, so he changed the subject. "How did you find our site?"

"By luck. I was searching for people in your, ah, line of work, and I came across your business: *Wild Things Investigations*. The name intrigued me, and I clicked on the About tab, and up came your picture and biography. To say I was surprised would be an understatement."

"*I* was surprised when we got your email."

Her smile broadened. "I hope it was a pleasant surprise."

"It was," Max said. "Aside from all the stuff about mutilation killings, that is."

Several people close by caught his words and turned to stare.

"In your email, you said three people have been killed by what authorities are assuming was a pack of wild dogs," Herne said. "And that all the victims worked for the town's animal control department."

Elena nodded. "Over the last few years, Bridgewater's had a problem with feral dogs. You know how it is. People's pets run off and never come back, or they come out to the country to dump animals they don't want any longer. The dogs get together in groups and turn wild in order to survive. Several small packs have been spotted in the area, and they've been preying on farmers' livestock—mostly small animals like chickens, but they've brought down some sheep and even a couple calves. The town decided to do something about the situation and hired several new people to work animal control to bolster their numbers. Their mandate was to capture the dogs alive if possible, but rumor has it that they've mostly been shooting them."

Max's eyes flashed with anger and he growled softly. Herne put a hand on his shoulder, and Max quieted. Elena looked back and forth between them, but she didn't comment.

"I'm not sure what the paranormal aspect is here," Herne said.

"There might not be one," Elena admitted. "But lately there have been reports of large, savage-looking dogs roaming the area, things that seem more like wolves, but real big. And they're supposed to have yellow eyes that almost glow."

Herne and Max exchanged a look. Yellow eyes like that were often a sign of the Wild.

"As I said, the three people who were killed were working to get rid of the feral dogs." She glanced around then lowered her voice. "Their bodies were ripped to shreds, but the medical examiner said there was no sign of predation. The animals didn't feed on them. It's like the dogs killed them for revenge. But dogs don't do that kind of thing, do they?"

"You'd be surprised," Max said grimly.

Herne ignored him.

"So you think there's some kind of otherworldly cause to these killings."

"Honestly, I don't know what I think," Elena said. "My station assigned me to do a story on the killings since I grew up in Bridgewater, but the more I look into it, the stranger it all seems. I go with my gut, Artie, and my guts tells me something is seriously wrong here."

Herne smiled. No one had called him Artie since … well, since the last time he'd seen Elena.

"What do you think?" she asked him.

Herne looked at Max then back to her.

"Can you take us to the scene of the most recent killing?"

Elena led the way in her blue Prius, and Herne and Max followed in their SUV. As they headed across town, Herne found his thoughts drifting back to his last days living in Bridgewater.

He'd been a teenager, an only child, and he'd lived with his parents in a cabin in the woods not far from town. Ben and Laurie Herne were nature writers and photographers, primarily doing articles for various magazines. But that was just their day job. In reality, they were Warders, guardians of the balance between what humans thought of as the civilized world and the Wild, the ancient magic that had existed since before the first primates had evolved. The Warders were an old order, their sacred calling passed down from parent to child over uncountable generations. Their patron was the Horned King, a powerful nature spirit that manifested as a great stag and who, it was said, appeared to Warders from time to time to aid and guide them. Max had been given to his parents by the Horned King to assist them in performing their duties, and he had been a good a loyal friend. His mother and father had trained Herne his entire life to one day take on the mantle of Warder himself, but then one day they didn't return from a mission. At first, Herne wasn't worried. His parents could be gone for days, even weeks at a time when they were dealing with a threat from—or to—the Wild. But when nearly a month had gone by, he knew something was wrong. He prepared to go in search of them when Max came home, severely wounded and close to death. Max told him a powerful entity calling itself Jack Sharp had killed his parents and nearly killed him, too. Herne, grief-stricken and filled with rage, vowed to hunt down Jack Sharp, whatever he was, and make him pay for what he'd done.

That night, the Horned King came to him in his dreams and gave him Sunder, a stone weapon carved by the first Warder and imbued with the power of the Wild itself. When Herne woke, he found Sunder on top of his dresser. When he touched the blade, he felt the power of the Wild flow through him, threatening to overwhelm him, and he immediately dropped the weapom. A voice whispered in his mind then. *Touch it only when you need it. And do not hold it a moment longer than necessary, else you will be lost to the Wild.* Herne had heeded the Horned King's warning, and he'd been extremely cautious when handling Sunder ever since.

Before leaving on his quest to track down Jack Sharp, he'd spoken to Elena. They'd been together for almost two years by that point. They'd met in school, in second year Algebra class, and they'd been inseparable ever since. There'd been a distance between them, though, as Herne couldn't tell her the truth about what his parents really did and what they were training him to do. And he couldn't tell her who Max really was, either. When he told her he had to leave town and that he didn't know how long he'd be gone, he hadn't been able to tell her why. She'd been hurt and angry, and they hadn't parted on the best terms. That had been almost fifteen years ago, and despite all his encounters with the Wild since, Herne had never so much as discovered a hint of who or what Jack Sharp might be and how to find him. He would keep searching, no matter how long it took, and in the meantime, he and Max continued to protect the balance between the world of humans and the Wild, working at bounty hunters whenever they needed money. All in all, it wasn't a bad life, but it could get lonely sometimes. Max was a good friend and partner, but sometimes Herne wondered what his life would've been like if he hadn't left Bridgewater. Would he and Elena have gotten married? Had kids? Would he have lived a normal life? Could he have been satisfied with such a mundane existence, or would he have always felt the call of the hunt, reminding him that he had been born for a different, higher purpose? There was no way to know, of course, but he wondered, and he supposed he always would.

He pulled himself out of his thoughts and turned to Max.

"What did you think of Elena's story?"

"She was always intelligent and sensible, and she seems even more so as an adult. She's not the type to let her imagination run away with her. And as for relying on her gut, she spent a lot of time around you when you were kids. Some of your ability to sense the presence of the Wild might've rubbed off on her. Your mother didn't become a Warder until after she married your father. Being a Warder isn't a matter of genetics, at least not entirely. More to the point, what does *your* gut say about this situation?"

"It tells me that I shouldn't have had that second breakfast burrito this morning."

So far, Herne didn't feel anything either way about Elena's story. Still, her description of those dogs—savage, large, yellow eyes …

"How about you?" he asked. "I saw the way you looked at her when we first got to the coffee house. Did you sense anything wrong about her?"

The passenger side window was down, and Max gazed at the passing buildings for several moments before answering.

"Something's not right with all this, but I'll know more when we get to the scene of the most recent killing. Still, I'm inclined to believe her."

So was Herne.

"A junkyard? Seriously?"

Castillo's Salvage and Recycling was located on Bridgewater's eastside, near several small used-car lots, which to Herne's mind was more than a little ironic.

"What's wrong with it being a junkyard?" Herne asked.

"The whole mean junkyard dog thing is a racial stereotype," Max said. "I find it offensive."

"I guess you'll have to take that up with whoever's behind all this."

"It indicates a complete lack of imagination, too." Max shook his head. "Very disappointing."

Elena drove through the junkyard's entrance and Herne followed. There was a chain link gate, but it had been torn halfway off its hinges and was bent and twisted. Elena pulled up to a small white building with a black roof with a sign reading *Main Office* mounted next to an open doorway. Two strips of yellow crime scene tape covered the doorway in an X, and Herne knew the last killing had taken place there. The spaces in front of the building were empty, and Elena parked in one. Herne parked next to her. They all got out and stood in front of the door.

"The first two killings happened next to a dumpster outside a greasy spoon," Elena said. "The second took place behind a grocery store. The victims were both animal control officers searching for feral dogs. The third one happened here. The gate had already been damaged—by those monster dogs wanting to get in, people assumed—and an animal control officer was sent to investigate. He searched the junkyard for dogs, and when he didn't find any, he returned to the office to talk to the manager. One of those things broke down the door and killed the animal control officer. It ignored the office manager, and he was able to escape unharmed."

"Another reason you suspect the dogs are specifically targeting the animal control people," Herne said. She nodded.

Herne reached toward the crime scene tape, intending to remove it so they could step inside, but Max raised a hand to stop him.

"There's no need. I can smell what I need to know from here."

Elena gave Herne a puzzled look, but he didn't explain. Max closed his eyes and inhaled deeply several times. When he opened them, Herne saw the amber flecks in his irises had become more pronounced.

"We're definitely dealing with Wild creatures here. Can you sense it?"

Herne felt a warm tingling on the back of his neck, and he knew Max was right.

"I do."

Herne returned to the SUV, got his gun belt out of the back, and buckled it on. He holstered his 9 mm on his right side, Sunder on his left. When he returned to the others, he looked at Elena.

"It would be best if you got in your car and stayed there until we're finished," Herne said.

"But—"

"It could be dangerous," he said. "We're prepared for this sort of thing. It's what we do."

She frowned. "And I'm *not* prepared?"

Max smiled, displaying a mouthful of sharp white canine teeth.

"Not like we are."

Fur sprouted on Elena's face and hands as she came at them, and her teeth and claws grew longer, sharper. Herne wasn't sure how it had happened, but somehow the manwolf—the creature he was certain was behind the killings in Bridgewater—had infused Elena with some of his own power, transforming her. Had he gotten to her after they'd left to search the junkyard? Or even earlier, when she'd been investigating the deaths on her own? After she emailed him to ask for their help but before they arrived? Had she brought them here at the manwolf's command so that he could ambush them? He remembered the way Max had stared at Elena when they'd first arrived at the coffee shop. He must've sensed something was wrong with her, although he hadn't been able to determine exactly what.

Herne didn't want to harm Elena, but he couldn't simply stand there and let her tear his throat out. Not only did he prefer to live, he knew that Elena would be devastated by what she'd done once she returned to her right mind. His hand was a blur as he drew his Glock, switched off the safety, and got a bead on the half-human, half-wolf creature Elena had become. He wasn't going to kill her, just shoot her in the shoulder, hopefully get her to break off her attack. But before he could fire, Max started running toward her.

He wanted to shout for Max to stop, but before he could speak, his friend's form darkened, as if he were suddenly cloaked in shadow. His shape bent, twisted, reformed, and when the change was complete, he'd become a large black hound, something like a rottweiler but bigger and shaggier. He had become the Black Dog, companion and ally of the Herne family for generations. Elena snarled, lips flecked with foam, and leaped forward as she drew near. Max launched himself into the air to meet her attack, head lowered, and he slammed into her stomach. Air whooshed out of her as she fell to the ground, and she lay there, stunned.

If she had been a true creature of the Wild instead of a victim of it, Max would've gone straight for her throat now that she was down. Instead he turned to meet the charge of two of the manwolf's fully canine servants. Herne guessed they were dogs, likely feral ones, that the manwolf had transformed, just as he had Elena, in order to carry out his attacks on the animal control officers. Max was barking and snarling as he fought with the monster dogs, each of which was as large as he was. Herne saw a flash of movement off to his left and saw two dogs coming at him from that direction. A flash off to his right, and a quick glance in that direction revealed that two more dogs were attacking from that side. Herne was a fast shot, but he knew he wasn't fast enough to take all four of the beasts before they reached him. Besides, they'd been innocent animals before the manwolf had got at them, and he'd prefer not to kill them if he could avoid it. That meant there was only one thing he could do.

Still holding onto the Glock with his right hand, he reached down with his left and drew Sunder.

The instant his flesh came in contact with the stone blade, he felt it—the power of the Wild. It rushed into him like blazing fire, causing every nerve in his body to shriek with equal amounts of pain and pleasure. The sheer strength of Sunder's power threatened to overwhelm him, and he felt his thoughts becoming disjointed, tangled, fragmented. His emotions were amplified a thousand times, and chief among these feelings was anger. The idea that these four animals thought they could stop *him*—a god-damned *Warder*—with something as simple as teeth and claws made him laugh like a lunatic. Sunder would slice through their throats like a red-hot knife through butter, and he would bathe in the dogs' blood as they perished.

He dropped the Glock, transferred Sunder to his right hand, and almost ran toward the closest dog, one on his left. But with an effort of will, he managed to stop himself—barely. He was a Warder, and it was his duty to maintain the Balance. The Wild had no more claim on him than the civilized world. He was his own man and always would be.

His emotions receded as he returned to himself, and he could think clearly again. He held Sunder out in front of him, point first, and turned from side to side, displaying the blade to the oncoming monster dogs. When they drew close enough to sense Sunder's power, they stopped, ears back, heads lowered, yellow-eyes fixed on the ancient weapon. They whined softly and shuffled from side to side, as if unsure what to do. Sunder's mere presence was often enough to terrify the lower-level creatures of the Wild, sometimes even repelling them the way crucifixes repelled vampires in the movies.

"Forget the blade!" the manwolf roared. "Kill him! Tear open his belly, feast on his entrails!"

Herne rolled his eyes. The older a creature of the Wild was, the cornier its dialogue. He risked a glance in Max's direction and saw that his friend was still contending with the two dogs that had attacked him.

He was bleeding from several wounds, none of which looked severe, as were his opponents. Max was taking it easy on them, more or less, because they couldn't help what they'd become. But he knew it was only a matter of time before Max had to go for the jugular. He couldn't keep playing around like this all day. He checked on Elena. She had gotten to her feet, but she was hunched over and cradling her stomach. He hated to see her hurt like that, but it was far preferable to gazing upon her corpse. Hopefully, she'd remained incapacitated until the fight was over, one way or another.

"Tell your pack to back off!" Herne called out to the manwolf, still turning right then left and back again, making sure to keep the dogs' eyes on Sunder. "We don't want to hurt them if we don't have to."

The manwolf released a literal bark of a laugh. "You're a Warder. Killing is all you know."

"Really? Then how come I'm not cutting your dogs' throats right now? And look at Max. He could do a hell of a lot more damage if he wanted to."

The manwolf's yellow eyes narrowed in thought, but he did not reply.

An ear-splitting shriek cut the air, and Herne turned to see Elena coming toward him once again, fangs bared, claws raised. She staggered a little, her abdomen still hurting her, but she'd recovered enough to start moving again. He brandished Sunder at her, and she stopped, raised an arm to shield her eyes, looked away. But when he did that, the other four monster dogs took advantage of his distraction to run several feet closer. He went back to holding the blade out to all of them, facing right, then left, then toward Elena, and back again. But each time he switched positions, the dogs and Elena managed to close the gap between them by several more feet. He knew he wasn't going to be able to keep this up for long. Soon one of the dogs would reach him, or maybe it would be Elena, and he would have to defend himself. There was no guarantee he could do so without harming them, especially when using Sunder.

He heard growling coming from behind him then, and he felt a sick cold sensation in his own gut. Max had said there were seven monster dogs in all. Max was fighting two, and he was holding four at bay. That left one dog unaccounted for. He spun around and saw it coming at him. He shoved Sunder toward it, and the beast came to an abrupt stop, half snarling in frustration, half whining in fear. Now Herne had to defend himself on four fronts, facing each group of dogs and Elena in turn. He did his best to hold them all back, but he was failing. Whenever Sunder was turned away from them, they were able to close the distance a bit more. He knew he could keep this up only a few more seconds until they converged upon him. Max was too busy fighting a battle of his own, and Herne knew he couldn't count on his friend to come to his rescue.

He released his grip on Sunder and let the blade fall to the ground.

Elena and the dogs snarled in triumph and dashed toward him. He curled his hands into fists and raised them, knowing that it would do no good but determined to go down fighting if he had to.

"Halt!" the manwolf shouted.

Elena and the dogs—including the two Max battled—froze. They turned to look at the manwolf, muscles still taut, bodies shivering, desperate to spill blood but unwilling to disobey their master. They remained like this as the manwolf strode over to Herne. Just before the creature reached him, Max—in human form once more and bleeding from a dozen bites and scratches—stepped to his side.

The manwolf regarded them for a moment then said, "You spoke true. You do not wish to kill my children. You cast aside your weapon rather than harm them."

Herne didn't reply. He'd taken an enormous gamble dropping Sunder, and all they could do now was wait to see what the manwolf would do next.

The yellow fire in the creature's eyes dimmed.

"Let us talk."

The manwolf's name was Bloodtooth, and he had come to Bridgewater to protect his those who he saw as his children.

"Your kind bred them from wolf stock, created them to be obedient companions. And then instead of taking care of them, you cast them out to fend for themselves. And when they begin to rely on their ancient instincts to help them survive, what do you do? Hunt them down and slay them. It is an affront to the Wild, and I shall not allow it to stand."

The four of them—Herne, Max, Elena, and Bloodtooth—stood talking in the junkyard. The seven monster dogs, relaxed for the moment, sat close by, watching. Elena had returned to her fully human self, and her mind was once again her own. She was shaken by what Bloodtooth had turned her into and forced her to do, but she was holding up well enough.

Herne knew Bloodtooth was referring to the animal control officers shooting the feral dogs rather than capturing them and taking them to a shelter. The creatures of the Wild hated guns and viewed them as an unfair advantage.

"I understand," Herne said, "but I can't allow you to kill any more humans. The Balance must be maintained. I can, however, guarantee that no more dogs will be shot in this town."

Bloodtooth frowned. "How will you do this?"

Max grinned. "We'll track the shooters down and have a talk with them. We can be very persuasive when we want to be."

"And I'll do a story for my station about the situation," Elena added. "I'll expose the bastards and tell the world what they've done."

"And this will be effective?" Bloodtooth asked.

"The vast majority of humans despise animal cruelty," Herne said. "Especially when it happens to dogs or cats. The publicity will force the town officials to fix the situation. And I'll return to Bridgewater periodically to make sure it stays fixed."

Bloodtooth looked from Herne, to Max, to Elena, then back to Herne, considering. Finally, he nodded.

"Very well. I accept your terms."

Bloodtooth extended his hand. Amber threads of energy emerged from the monster dogs' eyes, nostrils, and mouths. The energy flowed toward Bloodtooth and into his hand, and as he withdrew his power from the dogs, they reverted to normal canine form. When the transformation was complete the dogs—confused and frightened—scattered.

Bloodtooth fixed his yellow eyes on Herne.

"See that you keep your promise, Warder."

Then he turned, his form blurred, and he loped away on all fours. When he was gone, Elena looked at Herne.

"Warder?" she asked.

Herne smiled. "It's a long story."

He told that story over lunch. They ate at a small café not far from Java Nice Day. They kept a fully stocked med kit in the SUV, and Max cleaned his wounds before they reached the place. His preternatural healing abilities did the rest, and by the time they sat down to eat, his wounds had become scars. By late afternoon, they would be healed completely.

Elena took Herne's story in stride. After what she'd experienced the last few days, she was more than prepared to believe him. As Herne had guessed, Elena encountered Bloodtooth during her investigation, after she'd emailed them asking for help. The manwolf had invested some of his power in her, as he had the monster dogs, and after that, she became bound to him and was forced to do his will. He ordered her to lead Herne and Max to the junkyard, and she had done so without hesitation, something she now felt great guilt over.

"I can't believe he could control me so easily," she said.

"The Wild is a primeval force," Herne said. "It's not easily resisted, even when someone is prepared for it."

"Which you weren't," Max said.

Both Herne and Elena had ordered chef salads. Max had ordered two hamburgers as rare as the cook was willing to prepare them. He'd already finished his food, while Herne was only half done with his salad. Elena had only picked at hers.

"What gets me is that Bloodtooth is responsible for the death of three people," Elena said, "and yet nothing is going to happen to him because of it. He just gets to leave without experiencing any consequences for his actions."

"Do you think I should have killed him?" Herne said.

She looked at him a moment while considering her answer.

"Yes. No. Maybe. I don't know."

"My job is to maintain the Balance," Herne said. "I only kill when I have to. Otherwise, I risk upsetting the Balance even further."

"The Wild has its own rules and its own laws," Max said, "and they don't always match the ones in the human world."

"As long as no more dogs are killed, Bloodtooth should behave himself," Herne said. "On the other hand, if he doesn't—"

"We'll be back," Max finished.

⫸

They said their goodbyes in the café's parking lot.

Elena hugged Max, and Max sniffed the air as she did so. When they parted, Max gave Herne a look, then he climbed into the SUV's passenger seat, leaving Herne alone with Elena.

"Do you have to leave so soon?" Elena asked him.

"Max checked our email on his phone after we left the junkyard. A new request for help came in while we were dealing with Bloodtooth. People have been disappearing near a lake in Michigan, and we need to check it out."

She nodded. "I understand. Well, I'll do what I promised and get working on my expose on the animal control officers. But if you ever need help on case, don't hesitate to call me."

Herne thought he detected a glint of yellow in her eyes, and when she smiled, her teeth seemed a bit sharper than they should be. He understood the look Max had given him a moment ago. He'd sensed the change in Elena was permanent. Herne realized that he hadn't seen Bloodtooth remove the power he'd granted Elena. An oversight on his part, or perhaps a gift in repayment for the trouble he'd caused? It was hard to say. The motivations of Wild creatures weren't always easy to determine.

"I'll do that," he said.

It was his turn to receive a hug, and when they broke apart, she gave him a last smile, then headed for her Prius. He watched as she got inside, turned on the engine, backed out of her space, and pulled onto the road. A moment later she was lost to sight. He stood there a moment longer, then he got in the SUV.

"You miss her already," Max said. It wasn't a question.

Herne turned on the engine and began to back out of the space.

"Time to get back to work," he said.

A minute later, they were on the road and headed for whatever would come next.

APPENDIX TWO
SAMPLE PITCHES

What follows are actual pitches I wrote and sent to tie-in editors.

SUPERNATURAL NOVEL PITCHES

The editor ultimately chose *Children of Anubis* from this group.

Son of Darkness. A monster messiah—the Son of Eve, Mother of all Monsters—appears on Earth and begins to organize monsters. The messiah argues that the advent of the Darkness has shown monsters that they need to band together in order to be strong. Their weakness has always been that they operate separately, but together they will be unstoppable. The messiah takes over a town as his home base and begins transforming the citizens as well as drawing monsters to the town to join his forces. The messiah has a plan to deal with Hunters. He captures some and turns them into monsters who will kill Hunters at his command. Sam and Dean become aware of the messiah when some of his Hunter-killers attack them. During the struggle against the messiah, their mother is turned into a Hunter-killer, and the boys have to find a way to save her as well as stop the messiah and his army of monsters.

Reaper War. In the absence of Death, reapers continue to perform their duties, but they have no leader and no direction. A rogue reaper arises who wants to take over as the new Death, inciting conflict among the reapers as a whole. This conflict has major repercussions on Earth when the balance between life and death becomes disrupted. The rogue reaper has control of all kinds of death-related monsters: ghosts, revenants, specters, poltergeists, etc. Sam and Dean—along with the British Men of Letters—have to deal with the worldwide fallout of the Reaper War, as well as find a way to stop it.

Shadowside. On a dark alternate Earth, everything is reversed. Castiel is evil and rules with his fellow angels as his dark servants, while a good version of Crowley and his demons struggle against them. Evil

Castiel has conquered this Earth, and he desires to extend his empire to other worlds. Evil versions of Sam and Dean are Evil Castiel's servants, and Evil Castiel causes them to switch places with their good counterparts from our world. Evil Castiel wants Evil Sam and Dean to learn what they can about the strengths and weaknesses of this new Earth, while he questions Good Sam and Dean to gain information about the world he wishes to conquer. Evil Sam and Dean wreak havoc in our world, and their mother and Good Castiel have to deal with them. In the shadow world, Sam and Dean are rescued by Good Crowley and work with him to overthrow Evil Castiel and save the shadow world. Unfortunately, they have to contend with evil versions of both their mother *and* father, the latter of whom never died in this world. Evil John and Mary Winchester are Evil Castiel's strongest servants, and there's no guarantee Good Sam and Dean will be able to defeat these twisted versions of their parents.

The Children of Anubis. In the Indiana town of Bridge Valley, people's bodies begin to disappear shortly after their death. Sam and Dean suspect ghouls are responsible, but when they investigate, they discover a type of monster they've never encountered before—a Jakkal—is responsible. They're surprised to learn that their old friend Garth, who is now a werewolf, is also investigating. Garth and his peaceful pack worship the Norse wolf god Fenris, while the Jakkals worship the Egyptian deity Anubis. Jakkals are much like werewolves, but with some differences. Instead of killing their prey, they are primarily scavengers who feast on the dead. They can sense when someone is about to die, and they remain nearby to claim the corpse. They can shift form at will, but when they are in the presence of a dying person, they shift form automatically. Elders among the Jakkals also possess the power to reanimate the dead with their bite. The reanimated corpse obeys the Jakkal's commands for six hours at which point it collapses into dust.

Werewolves and Jakkals are related. Egyptian jackals are, in fact, a species of wolf. But Werewolves view Jakkals as contemptible carrion-eating dogs, and Jakkals see Werewolves as animalistic savages. Jakkals view eating the dead as a way of ushering them into the afterlife and consider their feeding a sacred activity. Over the millennia, the two species have been engaged in a blood feud, and normally they do their best to stay out of each other's way. But now a young member of Garth's pack has fallen in love with a Jakkal, and both packs are determined to prevent the union, even if it leads to all-out war between them.

To make matters worse, one of the pack elders is in possession of the mummified body of Anubis and she wants to bring the ancient god to life to destroy the Jakkals. Unfortunately, once reanimated, Anubis doesn't discriminate: he kills everyone.

Sam and Dean have to stop Anubis and prevent a war between the Werewolves and Jakkals—a war that could result in the death of every man, woman, and child in Bridge Valley. And they want to keep their buddy Garth alive. He might be annoying *and* a Werewolf, but he's family.

Deep in the Darkness. The Oregon town of Twelve Pines is located near Lake Comfort, a popular spot for fishing, boating, camping, and hiking. Over the decades, there have been numerous sightings of strange creatures in the water or prowling on the banks, and there have been several unexplained murders as well. All of this has combined to give Lake Comfort a reputation as a paranormal hotspot, and catering to ghost hunters and monster seekers has become something of a cottage industry for the town.

The crew of a cable reality show called *The Hidden World* are filming a segment at Lake Comfort when they experience a monster sighting. As they record it, they become gripped by homicidal impulses and try to kill each other. Only one crew member—the host—survives. The footage of the attack goes viral, and Sam and Dean travel to Twelve Pines to investigate. A Native American Hunter also comes to town to investigate. Eventually, the three Hunters and the surviving TV host work together to solve the mystery as the monster sightings and senseless killings increase. Everyone is having strange dreams as well, dreams that focus on Lake Comfort and which are a mix of the relatively recent past (the last few centuries) and the primordial past. They are dreams of death and violence, and Sam and Dean can sense a malevolent presence behind them.

Eventually, the Winchesters discover that an ancient creature that possessed humans and caused them to kill each other was banished to the bottom of Lake Comfort by a Native American shaman centuries ago. The creature was wounded, and it's spent the intervening years healing and rebuilding its strength. It absorbs life force from the victims killed by those it possesses. It's a large creature, and its tentacle-like appendages have been mistaken for lake monsters all these years. The creature is almost fully healed now, and it is preparing to leave the lake and resume its feasting on the human race—unless Sam, Dean, and their new friends can stop it. Complicating matters: all the amateur monster hunters who've descended on Lake Comfort and who are in danger of becoming the lake creature's next meal.

APPENDIX THREE
TIE-IN PROPOSAL

This is the proposal I sent Del Rey when I had the opportunity to audition to write a *Sleepy Hollow* tie-in novel. This type of proposal is a cross between a pitch and an outline.

Sleepy Hollow: Dark Legacy
Tim Waggoner

In the fall of 1780, the spy John Andre was captured in Tarrytown by militiamen, thwarting Benedict Arnold's plan to turn over the fort of West Point—along with General Washington—to the British. (This is also the spot where, in Washington Irving's original story, Ichabod Crane first encounters the Headless Horseman.) Tarrytown is located next to Sleepy Hollow in the real world, but the capture of John Andre could be moved to the series' version of Sleepy Hollow for the purposes of this story. Or perhaps the three militiamen who captured Andre could have been born and raised in Sleepy Hollow.

The capture of Andre exposed Benedict Arnold as a traitor. On his deathbed in London in 1801, Arnold was visited by a mysterious robed figure who was a servant of Moloch. The figure gave Arnold a silver coin, one of the thirty pieces of silver that were paid to Judas to betray Christ. The coin restored Arnold to youth and health, and bestowed mystic powers on him. Now beholden to Moloch, Arnold chose to serve the demon in order to preserve his life, and he's been working for Moloch ever since.

Arnold possesses the ability to make people betray anything—friends, family, country, ideals. He can also make people's senses betray them, causing them to see and hear whatever he wishes. His powers—and his extended life—remain as long as he holds the Judas Coin.

At Moloch's direction, Arnold comes to Sleepy Hollow to turn Ichabod and Abbie to the side of evil. Failing that, he is to destroy them. Arnold is thrilled to finally have a chance to get revenge on the town of Sleepy Hollow for its role in his downfall. He's less thrilled to be going after Ichabod, however. Ichabod saved his life during the Battles of Saratoga in 1777, which—unknown to history—possessed a supernatural element. (This incident will be shown in the novel through various flashback scenes from Ichabod's point of view.)

As Arnold goes about his work, Sleepy Hollow begins to change, slowly at first, then with increasing speed. People begin betraying one another, leading to fighting and murder. Some people begin seeing the town as a nightmarish landscape populated by horrible creatures. Eventually, everyone in Sleepy Hollow, including Ichabod and Abbie, believes they are living in a darkly distorted version of their town. Arnold turns Jenny and Captain Irving against Ichabod and Abbie. He eventually turns them against each other.

Ichabod and Abbie come close to killing each other, but they manage to break free of Arnold's spell. Realizing they cannot defeat Arnold on their own, they decide they must find a way to resurrect Ro'kenhronteys, the Dream Demon of Justice also called the Sandman. Since Ro'kenhronteys' purpose is to punish anyone that has betrayed or turned their backs on someone's plight, they believe the demon will make a perfect weapon to use against Arnold.

Ichabod and Abbie manage to free Jenny and Captain Irving from Arnold's spell, and they join the battle against Arnold and the townsfolk he's turned to his cause.

With the help of the Native American Shaman/car salesman Seamus Duncan, Ichabod and Abbie enter the dream realm in spirit form to search for Ro'kenhronteys. Jenny and Captain Irving protect Ichabod and Abbie's unconscious bodies as they search. As Seamus explained to them, they must find the remains of Ro'kenhronteys and offer it "sustenance" to restore it. He gives them a dreamcatcher to contain the demon once it's reborn. After navigating the perils of the Dream Realm, Ichabod and Abbie find the shattered remnants of Ro'kenronteys. Ichabod realizes that since he turned his back on his country when he decided to fight on America's side in the Revolution, he qualifies as the sort of soul the demon punishes. He offers himself to the demon despite Abbie's protests, and Ro'kenhronteys reassembles itself and attacks Ichabod. Ichabod must come to terms with his lingering guilt over leaving his family, friends, and former country behind to side with America in order to resist the demon's attack. At that moment, it's vulnerable, and Abbie captures it in the dreamcatcher.

Arnold, informed by one of his people what Ichabod and Abbie are doing, gathers a force together and heads off to stop them. Jenny and Captain Irving fight to hold them off while Ichabod and Abbie complete their mission.

Ichabod and Abbie return to consciousness, and the real-world version of the dreamcatcher now contains Ro'kenhronteys' spirit. Ichabod and Abbie confront Arnold in the streets of Sleepy Hollow. The town has become more nightmarish than ever, and it's difficult for Ichabod and Abbie to tell illusion from reality. They manage to reach Arnold and unleash Ro'kenhronteys' spirit. The demon forces Arnold to confront his legacy of betrayal, giving Ichabod and Abbie the opportunity to take the Judas Coin from him. Once the coin is out of Arnold's possession, the town returns to normal and everyone under his control is freed. He also begins to rapidly age. Just as Ichabod once saved Arnold's life in the past, he attempts to save him again. As Arnold struggles with the demon, Ichabod encourages the man to face up to what he's done and free his soul from guilt, but Arnold cannot, and he dies.

Ro'kenhronteys regards Ichabod and Abbie, but rather than attacking them, it simply holds out his hand, palm up. Ichabod places the Judas Coin in the demon's hand, and it disappears.

Ichabod is sad that Arnold couldn't come to terms with what he did, but his own spirit is lightened for having faced his own feelings of having betrayed his family and friends in England. No one knows why Ro'kenhronteys took the Judas Coin. Ichabod hopes it's because the coin belonged to the ultimate betrayer, and the demon wished to destroy it. He hopes it won't be given to someone else to use. Abbie reminds him that even if that coin never reappears, there are twenty-nine more out there—a thought which does not comfort either of them.

APPENDIX FOUR
TIE-IN OUTLINE

This is the outline I developed based on the *Children of Anubis* pitch. It's the outline that both the editor at Titan Books and the studio approved, and the one I used when drafting the novel.

Supernatural: The Children of Anubis
Tim Waggoner

HISTORIAN'S NOTE: This novel is set after the Season 12 episode "The One You've Been Waiting For."

Clay Fuller, who recently was arrested for selling heroin in Bridge Valley, Indiana, is running for his life through thick woods. He's being pursued by a pack of werewolves, and they almost get him a couple times, but he manages to escape. He breaks out of the woods near a country road, but the werewolves bring him down before he can find help. While they're tearing out his heart, Amos Bass arrives in his pickup. He gets out with his handgun and begins shooting at the werewolves. The bullets have no effect on them, but they flee anyway, taking Clay's heart with them to devour later.

At the same time, Nathan and Muriel Mansour—pack Elders for the Jakkals—show their grandson Greg how to conduct the monthly rite that keeps their mummified god Anubis in his state of eternal hibernation. Greg messes up, and Anubis awakens briefly and is violent, but Nathan and Muriel manage to calm down the god and get him back to sleep.

Sam and Dean Winchester are finishing an investigation in Foxhollow, Arkansas. They've come to exorcise a ghost from an old house, only to discover that the spirit has become the house. The entire house is a supernatural entity that attempts to kill them, and in the end, they must burn the house to destroy it and lay the spirit that possesses it to rest.

Afterward, the brothers stop at a roadside diner to eat, and as they do, Sam checks several paranormal news websites on his phone. He comes across an item about the bizarre murder in Bridge Valley, and it sounds like some kind of supernatural creature is at work, most likely a werewolf. They decide to head to Indiana to check out the situation—after they shower the smell of smoke off them and get a decent night's sleep.

Sam and Dean arrive in Bridge Valley and, as usual, pose as FBI agents as they begin investigating. The first thing they do is speak to Sheriff Alan Crowder to learn about the bizarre murder, but they find the Sheriff to be uncooperative and almost hostile. He tells them Clay Fuller was a known heroin dealer, and his death was likely the result of some falling out between Clay and his suppliers or customers. As for what Amos Bass claimed to have seen … well, Amos is a few bricks shy of a load.

The brothers leave the Sheriff's Department unsatisfied. It's possible that the Sheriff simply doesn't like working with federal agents, but they have the sense that he's hiding something. They decide to speak with a local reporter next. Who else in a small town would be plugged into what's really happening? They head for the office of the Bridge Valley *Independent*.

Greg and his mother Marta go into town to shop for groceries. In the store, he encounters a girl named Morgan, who's holding her baby brother, Joshua. There are instant sparks between them, and although they can sense what the other is, their differences only serve to heighten their attraction. Morgan isn't entirely sure what Greg is. He's like a werewolf, but not exactly. Greg starts to explain what Jakkals are when his mother comes up to them. She isn't happy to see him speaking with a werewolf. A second later, Morgan's mother arrives, and she's extremely unhappy to see her daughter with a Jakkal. The mothers engage in a staring match, and for a moment it looks as if they might change and begin fighting right there in the store, but in the end, they turn away and take their children with them. Neither the Jakkals nor the werewolves were aware of the other's Pack, and this is huge problem, as neither can tolerate the presence of the other.

The *Independent*'s main—and only—reporter is Melody Diaz. They're surprised to discover that Melody is already speaking with someone, and that someone is former hunter-turned-werewolf Garth Fitzgerald IV. Garth is posing as a true-crime writer who's interested in collaborating with Melody on a book about the strange murder of Clay Fuller, along with the disappearances among the town's less-than-savory citizens which have been occurring at regular intervals for the last several years, which may or may not be related. Garth—still posing as a writer—asks the "FBI agents" if they might consent to an off-the-record interview. Melody is excited, but Sam and Dean say they can't comment on an ongoing investigation, and they leave.

While they wait down the block for Garth, Dean thinks about the first time Sam and he encountered a werewolf in 1992.

Dean is thirteen and Sam is nine, and Bobby Singer is taking care of them at a motel in a town near Seattle while their father John is in Vancouver, hunting a warlock who supposedly has a mystic artifact that can track demons. John hopes to use the artifact to locate the Yellow-Eyed Demon that killed his wife Mary. When Bobby gets wind of what appears to be a werewolf attack in the area, he goes to investigate, instructing the boys to remain at the hotel no matter what. Dean is sick of always being left behind, and he decides to follow Bobby, and he convinces Sam to go with him.

Dean's mind returns to the present day. Garth has no trouble finding the brothers: he knows both of their scents and can track them easily. He hops in the Impala and they drive to a local bar called The Whistle Stop to talk. Melody follows Garth and the boys after they leave her office, and she's surprised to find the three driving off together. Suspicious, she returns to her office, intending to call the Sheriff.

As Marta and Morgan drive home, she calls her husband Alan—who is both Sheriff and the were-wolves' Pack leader—to inform him that there are Jakkals in town. When she disconnects, Morgan asks her what Jakkals are, and Marta gives her an extremely jaundiced view of them as disgusting carrion eaters. Morgan doesn't ask her mother what her father will do about the Jakkals. She doesn't want to think of anyone getting hurt, especially Greg. Marta warns her daughter to stay away from Greg and to put the boy out of her mind.

Alan decides something needs to be done about the Jakkals, and he decides to go in search of their lair and confront their leaders. But before he can do anything, Melody calls to tell him about seeing the two "FBI agents" speaking with her supposed co-writer. She asks what he knows about the agents. When Alan learns she's working on a book about the murder and disappearances—and that she's working with men who might well be hunters—he goes to her office, transforms into werewolf form, and kills her. He then calls his son Stuart and orders him to come clean up the mess.

Greg and his mother return to the abandoned amusement park where their pack currently lives. Jakkals move periodically and they prefer to live in deserted ruins: dead places, in other words. She calls the Pack together and informs them that there are werewolves in town. Everyone is surprised. Greg and his father Walter scouted the town before they moved here, and they saw no sign of werewolves in the area. Greg's mother and father think the Pack should move immediately, but Greg's grandfather disagrees. This is a good place for them, and they have the power of Anubis at their side. They should refuse to be driven away by a Pack of mindless predators. Leaving would also demonstrate a shameful lack of faith in their god. If the werewolves are foolish enough to attack, Anubis shall be brought to full life and he will destroy them. The others aren't happy about staying, but they give in to the Elder's wishes. Greg worries about what will happen to Morgan. His grandmother takes him aside and, as Elder, gently but firmly tells him to never speak to the werewolf girl again.

At The Whistle Stop, the brothers learn that things have been going well for Garth since the last time they saw him. His pack is strong, healthy, and still dedicated to following the peaceful ways of their branch of the Maw of Fenris religion. (They only eat animal hearts; they don't kill humans.) Garth has returned to hunting after a fashion. He investigates murders that sound as if they might have been committed by werewolves. If they are, he tracks down the werewolf and tries to get him or her to agree to follow the peaceful ways of Fenris and join his Pack. If they refuse, he kills them to protect innocent humans. Like the brothers, he learned of Clay's murder and the report of monsters with "teeth and claws" sighted next to his corpse and he came to investigate. Garth suggests the three of them work together—"Just like old times!" Dean is uncomfortable working with his friend because he is technically a monster and could lose control at any time. But in the end, both he and Sam agree to join forces with Garth.

The three hunters go to the town morgue to examine Clay's body, but they discover it's missing. The coroner has no explanation for how this could've happened, but the brothers and Garth strongly suspect that someone got rid of the body so they couldn't see it. As their next step, they find Amos Bass and have him show them where he saw the body and the creatures around it. While there, he tells them the story of what he saw that night, and Garth walks around the area, taking in the scents. Amos leaves and Garth tells the brothers that he's caught the scent of several werewolves. He can track the werewolves' scent trails to see where they lead. Sam and Dean think this is a good idea, and they follow Garth into the woods.

Alan, along with Stuart, tracks the Jakkals to the abandoned amusement park. Alan and Stuart observe them for a bit to get a sense of how many of them there are. When the two werewolves finally decide to approach the Jakkals, Stuart springs one of the Jakkals' traps. As Alan struggles to free his son, the Jakkals approach. Alan and Walter start to fight, but Marta presses a silver blade to Stuart's throat. Silver had no effect on Jakkals, so they are able to wield it without difficulty. Alan backs down, but he warns the Jakkals that they have forty-eight hours to leave town or his entire pack will return to destroy them. Alan also warns Greg to stay the hell away from his daughter. Stuart finally gets free of the trap and the two of them leave. Alan is furious and decides the pack should attack before the forty-eight-hour deadline, when the Jakkals aren't expecting it.

The Jakkals are equally furious, as well as afraid. Their species prefers to avoid direct conflict whenever possible. Nathan and Muriel, as the pack Elders, argue that they should stay. If it becomes necessary, they will animate Anubis to protect them. Greg is worried that the situation is going to lead to unnecessary deaths. He's especially worried about Morgan. She contacts him through social media. He's not supposed to have any kind of online presence in order not to endanger the Pack, but he's kept it secret from his family. Maybe if Morgan and he put their heads together, they can figure out a way to defuse the situation before it becomes any worse. They arrange a place to meet later. Despite the reasons for their meeting, Greg and Morgan are excited to see each other again.

As Sam, Dean, and Garth make their way through the woods, Dean's mind returns to the memory of the brothers' first encounter with a werewolf. Last night's murder occurred in a hospital parking lot. An emergency room nurse was leaving work when the werewolf attacked him. Since werewolves are territorial, Bobby plans to stake out the hospital's parking lot in hope that the werewolf will return to attack someone else there. Dean and Sam arrive on bicycles that they've "borrowed" and hide where they can watch Bobby. Hours go by, and it looks like nothing is going to happen, but when an ER doctor heads for her car, the werewolf appears. Bobby confronts the werewolf before she can attack, giving the doctor a chance to flee. As he fights the werewolf, hospital security officers arrive and start shooting. Although the werewolf isn't harmed by their bullets, they drive her off. Unfortunately, Bobby is struck in the shoulder by one of the rounds. He manages to get in his truck and escape, while the brothers watch in horror. They hop on their bikes and head back to the hotel as fast as they can ride.

Bobby is already at the hotel when they get there. He's treated and bandaged his wound, and he's angry at the boys for leaving. Dean apologizes, and Bobby says he figures the werewolf is out for revenge against people at the hospital who wronged her somehow: a nurse and doctor who treated her badly or maybe failed a loved one of hers. There's only one more night remaining in the cycle of the full moon, and Bobby expects the werewolf to make another try for the doctor. Despite his wound, he plans to go back to the hospital tomorrow night and finish what he started. He's so badly hurt, though, that he looks like he needs a hospital himself, and the boys are worried that he won't be up to fighting the werewolf and will only succeed in getting himself killed. So they concoct a plan.

Back in the present, Sam, Dean, and Garth track the werewolves to the Crowders' property. Sam and Dean want to attack, but Garth wants to talk to the Crowders alone. He wants to determine whether they're hunting on purpose or if one or more of them are compelled to, and if he can sway them to live more peacefully, maybe even join his Pack. Sam and Dean are skeptical, but they agree to let Garth go, but only if he sings out if he needs their help. Garth has a silver blade that he can wield while wearing leather gloves, and he has silver bullets in his handgun. Even shielded contact with the metal causes him some discomfort, but he can deal with it. Garth approaches the house.

Greg and Morgan meet in the town park—a neutral space—to talk. They try to come up with a way that their two Packs can co-exist peacefully, and during their conversation, they give in to their attraction and kiss. Greg's two sisters—Teri and Jean -- followed him, and they break up their conversation. They attack Morgan and she receives a minor wound before Greg can stop his sisters. Morgan wolfs out and is ready to battle to the death, but Greg urges her to leave, and she does, reluctantly.

Garth speaks with the werewolf Pack and learns that they also belong to The Maw of Fenris, but instead of avoiding hunting humans altogether, they only hunt one human a month in what they call the Run. Alan, as Sheriff, finds them someone "bad" to hunt, and that person is turned loose on the Crowders' property and then chased down and killed. The Pack then shares their victim's heart. All the Crowders except Morgan and her baby brother have participated in Runs.

Meanwhile, Sam and Dean are captured by Paul and Diane, Morgan's grandparents and taken to the house.

Alan talks to all three of them. He tries to get Garth to see things their way, but Garth wants nothing to do with killing humans. He attacks Alan, but Alan knocks him out. He decides to use the Winchesters for a Run, Dean first, Sam second.

Sam is turned loose and the hunt begins.

Morgan arrives home, and when she finds out what's happening, she frees Garth and Dean, and together they go out to save Sam. As they go, she begs them not to hurt any of her family. She follows shortly afterward.

Garth, Dean, and Sam manage to escape the werewolves—after wounding a couple—when Alan sees his wounded daughter and forgets about them. He smells Jakkal on her, and in his fury decides it's time for their pack to destroy the Jakkals. He'll deal with the Hunters later.

Garth explains to Sam and Dean what Jakkals are. Jakkals are much like werewolves, but with some differences. Instead of killing their prey, they are primarily scavengers who feast on the dead. They can sense when someone is about to die, and they remain nearby to claim the corpse. They can shift form at will, but when they are in the presence of a dying person, they shift form automatically. Elders among the Jakkals also possess the power to reanimate the dead with their bite. The reanimated corpse obeys the Jakkal's commands for six hours at which point it collapses into dust. Jakkals are also experts at building traps and long ago helped designed traps for pyramids.

Werewolves and Jakkals are related. Egyptian jackals are, in fact, a species of wolf. But werewolves view Jakkals as contemptible carrion-eating dogs, and Jakkals see werewolves as animalistic savages. Jakkals worship Anubis, but not in a morbid way. They view eating the hearts of the dead as a way of ushering them into the afterlife and consider their feeding as a sacred activity. Over the millennia, the two species have been engaged in an on-again, off-again blood feud, and normally they do their best to stay out of each other's way.

Garth isn't the biggest fan of Jakkals, but they're peaceful enough, don't take lives, and keep to themselves for the most part. He urges the brothers to help him protect his "cousins." Sam and Dean agree. First, they have to figure out where the Jakkals' lair is.

Dean remembers the last part of the brothers' first encounter with a werewolf. They slip Bobby some sleeping pills along with pain medicine, and he passes out. The boys take Bobby's weapons—a silver blade and a gun with silver bullets—and ride their bikes back to the hospital. Police officers patrol the lot, and the boys go into the Emergency Room to see if the doctor is working tonight. They see her and decide to hang out and keep an eye on the doctor, pretending they're waiting on a relative who's being treated.

They hear gunfire from the parking lot, and the werewolf bursts through the Emergency Room's glass door. She's come for the doctor. A security guard tries to stop her, but the werewolf kills him. Sam is terrified, so Dean—equally terrified but trying to hide it—gives him the gun and goes after the werewolf, armed with a silver blade. Sam steps in front of the doctor to protect her as Dean attacks the werewolf. But Dean is knocked aside and the werewolf turns and goes toward the doctor. Sam fires, but while he wounds the werewolf, none of the shots strike the creature's heart. Just as the werewolf is going to kill Sam and the doctor, Dean manages to stab it from behind. The werewolf transforms back into human form as it dies, and the doctor recognizes her as the mother of an injured child she was unable to save.

Dean and Sam get out of there before the police start asking them questions. As they ride back to the hotel, Dean is shaken from the experience, but he sees Sam is too. He's also ashamed. He knew Sam probably wouldn't hit the werewolf's heart, but he figured Sam would distract her so she could be attacked from behind. To make Sam feel better, Dean acts like he's pumped up from the fight, and he praises Sam's part in killing the werewolf. This is the first time Dean says werewolves are bad-ass, and his faux enthusiasm makes Sam smile. Dean decides to help Sam practice his shooting, despite their father believing Sam's not old enough. Dean never wants his brother to feel helpless again, and he vows never to use Sam like that again. From now on, he plans to be honest and upfront with his brother.

Back in the present, Nathan believes it's only a matter of time until the werewolves attack, so he and Muriel go to the town morgue to reanimate dead bodies to create soldiers to help them fight.

Sam, Dean, and Garth are researching the town's history on the Internet and learn about the abandoned amusement park. They head for the park. Garth tells them that Jakkals are vulnerable to copper, as the metal was used to make an adze, one of the tools Egyptian priests employed in the mummification process. They make garrotes from copper wire, wrap copper wire around knives and melt it to the blades, and even buy some copper pipe to use as clubs. They already have plenty of silver knives and silver bullets for the werewolves.

Morgan texts Greg to warn him of the attack. He tells his family and the Elders decide to reanimate Anubis. Nathan sacrifices his own life to complete the resurrection rite. The werewolves attack the Jakkals, but they have to deal with traps and with undead servants armed with silver weapons. Anubis—an eight-foot tall black-furred humanoid wolf-thing covered in scraps of mummy wrappings—rises. But instead of obeying the Jakkals' commands and helping them, Anubis kills anything in sight. If he manages to sink his teeth into a victim, they immediately decay into dust. A swipe from his claws causes a necrotic wound that rapidly worsens. Morgan, carrying her baby brother, has come to the amusement park despite her father's wishes and tries to reach Greg. The two come together and are horrified by the fighting but feel powerless to stop it.

The werewolves and Jakkals team up against Anubis, but they prove ineffective against the god. Copper doesn't harm him, nor does silver. Conventional weapons certainly don't affect him. He kills the Jakkals' undead servants, along with most of the werewolves and Jakkals. No matter what Garth and the Winchesters do, they can't stop Anubis. It's all they can do to survive. When the battle is over, Anubis leaves the park and heads for town.

Greg tells them that Anubis wasn't supposed to go wild like that, and Sam theorizes that the god has spent too much time between life and death, destroying his mind and leaving him nothing but a savage monster.

During the battle, Sam noticed Anubis was repelled by Morgan. He started toward her, but then veered off. Sam realizes it wasn't her, but rather the baby, a symbol of life, that repelled Anubis. Sam, Dean, Garth, Greg, Morgan, her baby brother, and her father Alan—who is badly wounded but still alive—all head to town. Anubis is rampaging in the streets and killing people. Despite everything Alan has done, he's still Pack leader, the town Sheriff, and most importantly, Morgan's father, and he sacrifices himself to save her. Dean, remembering how he almost got Sam killed during their first werewolf encounter, is reluctant to use the baby as a weapon. In the end, he decides they have no choice and he'll do whatever it takes to protect the baby.

Morgan uses the baby to corral Anubis and then the brothers—with Garth and Greg's help—manage to tear out Anubis' heart. Anubis is weakened but not destroyed by this. The brothers burn Anubis' heart, and that does the trick. Anubis dies, his body turning to desert sand.

Anubis is dead, and both the werewolf and Jakkal Packs are destroyed.

Only Greg, Morgan, and her baby brother still live. Garth offers to take them to live with his Pack, and they agree. Garth says goodbye to the brothers. They tell Garth how proud they are of him and how much of a leader he's become. He's come a long away from being an annoying dentist-turned-Hunter.

Sam wonders if Greg and Morgan will fit in with Garth's Pack, and Dean reminds him that family is more than blood. The brothers then head off toward their next adventure.

APPENDIX FIVE
SAMPLE CHAPTERS

I haven't been asked to provide sample chapters for a tie-in project very often. Usually, your credentials as a published novelist are already established before you're considered for a tie-in gig, and the editors want to see pitches and then an outline. But it does happen, as was the case when I was auditioning to write *Executioner* novels for Gold Eagle. I'd read a ton of Gold Eagle's action-adventure novels over the years, and I enjoyed them, so I thought I'd give it a try. I contacted editor Feroze Mohamed, and he asked me to write two sample chapters for an *Executioner* novel. For those unfamiliar with the series, Mack Bolan is an ex-cop and ex-soldier known as the Executioner who fights organized crime and international terrorists as a one-man army, sometimes in America, sometimes in locations around the world. Feroze thought my chapters lacked the energy needed to write Bolan's adventures, and I didn't get the gig. Feroze later hired me to write a pair of *Room 59* spy novels, but as I've said elsewhere in the book, the series was canceled before my books could come out.

Death Games
Tim Waggoner

CHAPTER ONE

On a pleasant autumn Saturday at precisely 12:37 pm, Death came to Grigsby, Ohio.

Ironhorse Park was located on the south side of town, a ten-acre stretch of land surrounded by upper-class suburban neighborhoods where dentists, lawyers, architects and their families lived the good life. The park was home to baseball diamonds and soccer fields, oak trees and swing sets, even a meandering creek that ran through the middle of it all. The grass was always neatly trimmed and parking spaces were plentiful. Good thing, too, for this Saturday afternoon every soccer field was in use as the Grigsby Soccer Association's five to ten-year-old divisions battled it out in the season-ending tournament. All the parking spaces were filled, and more than few mini-vans had been pulled onto the grass by parents who refused to park on the street and walk all the way back just to watch their little Johnny or Susie kick a white ball up and down the field.

But there was one person who didn't mind walking. He strode across the parking lot, his open black trench-coat billowing in the late autumn breeze. He was in his early twenties, with short brown hair moist from styling gel. He wore a Slipknot T-shirt under his coat, faded jeans, and worn tennis shoes. The young man's face was devoid of expression, but his gaze was clear and sharp, and his eyes gleamed with anticipation. He carried a pump-action shotgun in his right hand, and his coat pockets bulged with extra shells. More than he'd need probably, but it paid to be prepared. As he set foot on grass still damp from last night's rain, his lips stretched into a cold smile.

Showtime.

The first person to notice the gunman was Gayle Simmons. She was a radiology tech and a single mother, and though she always came to her daughter's soccer games, she got bored quickly and spent most of the time sitting in her canvas chair yakking on her cell phone. Today she'd gotten her daughter to the park just as her game was about to begin, and so she'd been stuck setting up her seat down by the goal, as other parents had already claimed the better spaces alongside the field. This meant that Gayle was the closet person to the parking lot, and the closest to the gunman as he made his initial approach.

She was talking to her supervisor—who also happened to be her lover—when she caught a black flash of movement out of the corner of her eye. Without pausing in her conversation, she turned to see a man in a trench-coat raise his right arm and point something that looked like a long metal tube at her. At first, what she was looking at didn't register because it was so far removed from her everyday reality. But somewhere in the back of her mind, an alarm went off and adrenaline flooded her system. But it was too little, too late. The gunman squeezed the trigger, the shotgun roared, and Gayle Simmons no longer had a face.

Gayle's blood sprayed nearby spectators, along with shreds of meat and shattered bits of phone. Her body slammed into an overweight mother sitting next to her, and the woman screamed as the impact knocked her onto the ground. The gunman ejected the spent cartridge, aimed, fired, and silenced the screaming woman forever.

A moment of quiet followed as children stopped playing and adults stopped watching them. All heads turned toward the gunman and then panic flashed through the crowd like wildfire. Parents leaped out of their seats and ran onto the soccer field to get their children, some of who were already running in the opposite direction. Many children stood frozen, though, staring at the man in the black coat who had just killed two women—two mommies—before their uncomprehending eyes.

The gunman began firing at will. He aimed for adults, but not because he was reluctant to kill children. Meat was meat as far as he was concerned—young, old, what was the difference? He fired upon adults out of simple pragmatism: they were larger, slower targets. The gunman continued walking forward, firing and pausing to reload as necessary. He tried to keep track of his kills as he went, but with all the people running, screaming, and sobbing around him, he lost count. It wasn't important, though.

The entire country would eventually know his final tally, and that meant his friends would too. That was what truly mattered.

A couple of men came at him, obviously intending to play brave husband and daddy and take him out. But this wasn't the movies, and all their attempts at heroism got them an early and very messy death.

He had just finished putting down the last would-be hero when he heard a man shout.

"Freeze, you sonofabitch!"

The voice came from the gunman's right, and from its commanding tone, the man wasn't merely another hero wannabee. He was probably an off-duty cop come to watch his kid play soccer, just another devoted parent who happened to be at the right place at the right time. The gunman grinned. A cop meant extra points.

The gunman whirled and fired off a blast from his shotgun. In the same instant he caught a brief image of a man holding a pistol—a 9 mm most likely—just before a sledgehammer blow slammed into his chest. The impact spun him sideways and knocked him off his feet. He fell to the grass and landed hard on right side. He hadn't heard the cop fire his weapon, but he knew that's what had happened.

The gunman rolled over onto his back and lifted his head to look down at his chest. There was a hole in his T-shirt directly over his heart. His chest hurt like hell, and he was having trouble catching his breath, but he saw no blood and assumed his Kevlar vest had stopped the bullet. He had to admit it had been a damn good shot, though. His realized his right hand was empty, and he knew that he must've dropped his shotgun as he fell. He turned his head to look for the weapon as he started to rise.

"Don't move, or I swear to Christ I'll blow your goddamned head off!"

The gunman turned toward the cop. He got a better look this time and saw the man was in his forties, balding, with a bushy black mustache and a burgeoning pot belly. He was dressed in a yellow polo shirt beneath a blue windbreaker. The left shoulder of the coat was a ragged, bloody ruin, and the gunman was gratified to see that he'd at least wounded the cop. But wounded or not, the man still had hold of his 9 mm and the barrel was trained on the spot directly between the gunman's eyes.

He looked around and saw clumps of people gathered around the prone bodies of his victims. Some attempted first aid, while others simply stood and cried, unable to believe their loved ones were gone.

The gunman smiled. Not bad for a day's work.

Ignoring the cop's warning, he propped himself up on his elbows until he was in a half-sitting position. The cop kept his pistol trained on him the entire time, and though the man had to be hurting from his shoulder wound, his aim never wavered.

The gunman stared into the cop's eyes for a moment before speaking.

"This is just the beginning."

Then the gunman nodded once, and a split second later the top of his head exploded. As he slumped to ground, the cop could only stand and stare at the corpse in confusion, for the final shot hadn't been fired from his weapon.

CHAPTER TWO

At the same moment the trench-coated gunman's heart beat its last, Mack Bolan was driving west on Interstate 80 in central Pennsylvania, trailing a black Jaguar. The overcast sky and heavy rain rendered visibility poor, but that made little difference to Bolan. Though the Ford Acura rental he drove was hardly built for speed, all he had to do was keep the Jag in sight, and Bolan had done so for close to a hundred miles. So far, the Jag's driver had been scrupulous in following the speed limit. The man obviously didn't want to draw the attention of any state troopers, but Bolan knew the driver's caution had nothing to do with the large highway signs posted alongside the road detailing the various fines for speeding.

Ninety minutes ago, the two men in the Jag had paid a visit to an eye, ear, nose and throat doctor whose office was located in the well-to-do Philadelphia neighborhood of Chestnut Hill. There'd been nothing remarkable about either of the men. Both were Caucasian, in their thirties, trim instead of beefy. But just because they weren't muscle-bound didn't mean they weren't dangerous. They carried themselves like pros, scoping out the area with practiced eyes as they headed for the entrance to the ENT's office. Both wore leather jackets—one black, one brown—and the coats were roomy enough to conceal shoulder holsters. Bolan had no doubt the men were armed, and he wouldn't have been surprised if they had more hardware in the Jag.

They two had gone in empty-handed, but when they came out ten minutes later one of them carried a brown briefcase. Bolan had been parked at the curb watching the office, and when the two men got back into their Jaguar and pulled out, the Executioner followed. He'd been tailing them ever since.

If the intel Hal Brognola had passed on to him was correct—and it almost always was—the briefcase contained a half dozen vials of a genetically engineered superflu virus that would make the global pandemic of 1918 look like a case of the sniffles.

The ENT's wife worked in a medical research lab at the University of Pennsylvania, where she'd either created or stolen the samples—it wasn't clear which—and then passed them on to her husband. The husband had in turn made some discreet inquiries of drug companies via the Internet hoping to find a buyer for his deadly wares. A pharmaceutical company could make a fortune by studying the virus, developing a vaccine for it, then releasing it into the general population. The fact that thousands, perhaps millions might die in the process would simply be a few broken eggs on the way to making one very tasty omelet.

The doctor had received multiple offers, but the high bidder was an outfit calling itself Pharm-Tech Industries, based out of upstate New York. The cyber-warriors at Stony Man HQ constantly monitored the Net for the slightest hint of terrorist activity, and Pharm-Tech was on their watch list. The company was a front, but for whom was as yet unknown. A corporation that wished to remain anonymous? Terrorists? A private buyer? Hence the reason for Bolan's road trip on a rainy Saturday afternoon. It was his job to follow the errand boys back to their boss, discover the buyer's identity, and find out what he, she or they wanted with a genetically engineered virus. And if the Executioner left a few bodies along the way, that was just par for the course. After all, he knew how to break eggs, too. In fact, he was an expert at it.

Instincts honed on a thousand different battlefields warned Bolan that something wasn't right. He glanced at the Acura's rearview mirror and saw flashing lights behind him. A state trooper's vehicle, he guessed, approaching fast.

Thoughts raced through Bolan's mind as he shifted from surveillance to combat mode. Neither he nor the delivery boys in the Jag were exceeding the speed limit, and there was no way local law enforcement could've gotten wind of the deadly cargo the Jag carried. Outside of Stony Man, Bolan doubted that a half dozen people—the President included—were aware that a genetically engineered superflu virus was being transported across the great state of Pennsylvania.

Bolan looked in the rearview again. There was no vehicle fleeing from the statey, so that left only one possibility. The trooper was responding to some emergency that had nothing to do with Bolan and the virus. He just hoped the men in the Jag really were pros, because if they were jumpy, they might overreact at the sight of a patrol cruiser coming up fast on their ass with lights blazing. And if that happened—

Bolan never got to finish his thought. The patrol car had almost drawn even with him now, and that was too close for comfort for the delivery boys. The driver of the black Jag tromped on the gas and the high-performance sports car surged forward, rear fishtailing on rain-slick asphalt. For an instant Bolan thought the driver was going to lose control and go skidding off the road. The man managed to keep all four tires on blacktop, but unfortunately, he overcorrected in the process, and the Jag slid into the left lane—directly into the path of the speeding police cruiser.

It's a simple principle of physics that two objects cannot occupy the same space at the same time, and Bolan was about to get a first-hand demonstration.

The trooper tried to avoid hitting the Jag, but it was too late. The cruiser struck the left side of the Jag's back bumper and both cars started to swerve. Bolan swore and took his foot off the gas. He knew better than to slam on the brakes in rain this heavy. The Acura dropped back as the cruiser's rear spun around to the right, and the Jag's front end swung left. It looked as if both cars were going to collide, but despite his earlier jumpiness, the driver of the Jag proved he had some skill behind the steering wheel. He momentarily let off the gas, swung the Jag's nose back toward the front, then stomped on the pedal again. Once more the Jag fishtailed as it leaped forward, but it cleared the spinning cruiser and roared off down the interstate.

Bolan had been conducting his private war on evil for more years than he liked to count. And during all that time he'd held tight to one inviolate principle: civilian casualties were unacceptable. He'd failed to prevent them far too often, but he was only human. He hadn't forgotten the names and faces of those honored dead who had fallen along the way, though, and he never would.

But as much as he didn't want to see any harm come to a cop who'd been simply trying to his job, he couldn't afford to let the black Jag and its lethal cargo get away. He pressed down on the Accura's accelerator and yanked the steering wheel to the right so that he could pass by the spinning patrol car. Still, just because he couldn't stick around didn't mean that he couldn't give the statey a quick hand.

As Bolan's Acura drew near the out-of-control police vehicle, he edged left and with split-second timing tapped the car's right front fender with his bumper. The nudge helped turn the cruiser forward again, but the maneuver proved too much for the trooper to handle, and he swerved toward the grassy strip of land that served as the interstate's median. Bolan continued driving and watched in his rearview mirror as the patrol vehicle slid to a halt in a shower of mud and flying sod. Satisfied the trooper was unharmed and relieved that the man would no longer by part of the pursuit, Bolan focused his attention on catching up to the Jag. The car hadn't gotten very far ahead of Bolan in the few moments it had taken him to give the statey a love tap. The red glow of the Jaguar's taillights was still plainly visible, although receding fast. Bolan would have to haul ass if he were to have any hope of catching them.

Time was of the essence now, for the trooper was undoubtedly already radioing in to headquarters and reporting that a black Jaguar had run him off the road. Before long the interstate would be full of police all looking to serve up some payback for their fellow officer. Bolan needed to intercept the Jag before that happened.

The rain was still coming down hard and heavy, so much so that the Acura's wipers could barely keep the windshield clear. But in one way that worked to Bolan's advantage. The errand boys in the Jag would be looking for the flashing lights of state troopers—not a Ford Acura that was hard to spot with visibility so poor. Especially if he made it even harder for them to see him. He flicked off his headlights and the road ahead of him went dark. The interstate was a straight stretch here, and there was no one between him and the Jag. All he had to do was keep his eyes on their taillights, keep the gas pedal pressed to the floor, and try not to hydroplane himself into oblivion.

The Acura's engine whined loudly and the car shuddered as if it were in danger of shaking itself apart any moment, but Bolan didn't slow down. The thought of what might happen if whoever took delivery of that flu virus decided to use it spurred him on. He'd catch the Jag or end up crushed in a coffin of twisted metal, but he wasn't going to back off.

Luckily for Bolan, the Jag began to slow down a bit. Most likely the driver had either witnessed the statey ditching his vehicle in the median, or perhaps he'd simply noted the absence of flashing lights in his rearview mirror. Either way, the Jaguar was still moving at a good clip. The delivery boys had to know other officers would soon be looking for them, but it seemed they'd calmed down enough to decide not to risk driving all-out in this weather if they didn't have to. That gave the Executioner the chance he needed.

The Jag was driving in the left lane, and as Bolan came up on the vehicle's tail, he switched to the right. The incident with the state trooper had convinced him that the errand boys were too erratic for him to simply follow anymore. Bolan intended to stop them and retrieve the briefcase full of death before it could cause any harm. Hal wouldn't be happy, and the people in Washington he reported to would be even less thrilled, but that didn't matter to Bolan. He was a soldier, not a politician. He did his duty as he saw it, consequences be damned.

With his headlights still off, Bolan pulled even with the Jag. He thumbed the button to lower the driver's side window, then drew his Beretta 93R from its shoulder rig. A quick glance in his rearview mirror showed the road behind him was clear, at least for as far as he could see. No need to worry about anyone else becoming involved in what was about to happen.

As soon as the window was two-thirds of the way down—cold rain pelting him in the face like bullets of ice—Bolan aimed the Beretta at the Jag's passenger window and fired a three-shot burst. Safety glass exploded inward as the 9 mm Parabellum rounds penetrated the Jag's interior. The vehicle swerved violently to the left and its driver's side tires went off the road and caught hold of the grassy median. That was more than the driver—assuming he was still alive—could compensate for, and the Jag whipped around, flipped into the air, and came crashing down on its top.

Bolan hit the Acura's brake, sending the car skidding, but he managed to keep the vehicle under control with only one hand on the steering wheel, and brought the car safely to a stop on the shoulder. Still holding onto the Beretta, he threw open the driver's door, grabbed a metal object shaped something like a soup can from the canvas bag on the passenger seat, and then plunged out into the storm. He ran to where the overturned Jag had slid to a halt, tires still spinning, wipers slapping back and forth. Bolan was soaked to the skin by the time he reached the car, and he saw that the driver—the errand boy in the black leather jacket—had already managed to crawl halfway out of the shattered driver's side window. The man's face was covered with blood, either from one of the Parabellum rounds, as a result of the crash, or both. The specifics didn't matter to Bolan. All that mattered was that the damage had been done.

There was no sign of the man who'd been riding shotgun, but Bolan wasn't foolish enough to think that meant the man was no longer a threat. A kill was only a kill once it was confirmed. Until then, a smart soldier assumed all unfriendlies were still alive and dangerous.

Bolan drew a bead on the driver with his Beretta.

"Give it up! The race is over, and you lost!" Bolan had to shout to be heard over the wind and rain.

"Fuck … you." The man's voice was weak, and Bolan had to read his lips to make out what he was saying. The errand boy waggled his right hand then, and Bolan saw that he held a glass vial sealed with a rubber stopper.

The man called the Executioner knew he was looking at a killer far deadlier than he could ever be. The fluid inside the vial was clear, but Bolan didn't delude himself into thinking that meant it was harmless. The most effective killers always came silent, swift, and unseen.

"Stay back or I'll … break it." Bloody froth bubbled past the wounded man's lips, and Bolan knew he was near death.

Bolan had no idea whether breaking the vial would release the superflu virus, but even if it did, the rain should keep it from becoming airborne. But Bolan hadn't survived as long as he had by taking chances. He lowered the Beretta and brought the thermite grenade up to his mouth. He bit down on the pull ring and yanked the grenade away. He spit out the metal ring, crouched down, let go of the release lever, and quickly tossed the incendiary weapon past the dying man and into the Jag's interior. As he did so, he caught a glimpse of the other man inside, still buckled into his seat, blood-stained body limp. If the man wasn't already dead, he soon would be.

"You sonofabitch!" the driver said, loud enough to be heard this time.

Bolan straightened and started running back toward the Acura. He thought he heard the sound of the glass vial breaking, but he couldn't be sure. He felt a wave of heat roll over his back as the thermite bomb ignited, but he was far enough away that he wasn't burned. He stopped and turned back around to watch.

The crumpled remains of the Jaguar were engulfed in white-hot flames. Rain hissed as it was instantly vaporized by the 4000-degree heat. The fire would only last for 30-45 seconds, but during that time it would burn hot enough to reduce the car to molten slag—assuming the gas tank didn't blow first. Regardless, the samples of superflu virus would be completely destroyed. And as for the two men inside the car, as far as Bolan was concerned, when you played with fire, you got burned.

The Executioner holstered his Beretta, then turned and began running toward the Acura as the Jag's gas tank exploded with a sound like the thunder of final judgment. His work here was done.

JUST ADD WRITER